All Things Made New

All Things Made New

A Theology of Man's Union with Christ

by

LEWIS B. SMEDES

WILLIAM B. EERDMANS PUBLISHING COMPANY
GRAND RAPIDS, MICHIGAN

To
Catherine
Charles
John

Preface

How can a person who lived nearly two thousand years ago radically change a human life here and now? How can Jesus of Nazareth *radically* affect us, as persons, to the depths of our being? How can He reach out over the great span of time that divides us from Him and change us so profoundly that we can become "new creatures" in Him?

Does the Jesus of the past become, in fact, the Jesus of the present? The Apostle Paul says that He does. And this is the difference between His influence and that of any other influential person. He touches us here and now, not merely by the ripples of the historical currents He once set in motion, but by entering into union with us personally. Union with Christ—this is the sum and substance of the Christian person's status, the definition of his relationship to Jesus, the large reality in which all the nuances of his new being are embraced.

Paul, whose message is our primary source for the doctrine of union with Christ, talks about our being "in Christ" (II Cor. 5:17). He also says that Christ is "in us" (Eph. 3:17; Gal. 2:20), which would seem to be something different. Then he says that we experienced the history-shaking events of the cross and resurrection along *with Him*: he says that we died with Christ, were buried with Christ, and were raised with Christ (Rom. 6:1-4; Eph. 2:5, 6). He drops this shocking language by the way, as it were, and inserts it into a bewildering variety of contexts, shifting the actual terminology about so that we are finally left wondering whether anyone can grasp it all. But the phrase "union with Christ" does well to capture all the Pauline vocabulary, at least as a general heading.

I have written this book out of the conviction that union with Jesus Christ is at once the center and circumference of authentic human existence, and from a sense that the theology behind the doctrine of union with Christ overshadows much of the larger

7

ecumenical dialogue. Christian faith has no genuine reality and the
Church no unique mission in the world if men cannot share the
life and destiny of Jesus Christ. Amid all the issues that have
separated the great Christian traditions, the question of how men
are united with Christ has long been and still is the issue that lies
closest to the heart of the Church. Further, there has probably
never been a time as promising as our own for the possibility of
understanding the different perspectives through which the doctrine of union with Christ has been seen. I hope, therefore, that
this study will find its way into the dialogue. Its subject points to
the core of the Church's mission.

As Calvin said of sacramental grace, Paul's doctrine of our
union with Christ is more easily experienced than explained. And
explanations themselves often need a lot of explaining. I have
tried, sympathetically and patiently, to set out the main lines of
how various people have understood Paul's doctrine, and then I
have turned to St. Paul himself, letting his thought make its own
criticism of these explanations.

The first two chapters are rather long preliminaries to the rest
of the book. Anyone eager to get to the main course may begin
reading at Chapter Three; I hope, however, that he will come back
to the first two chapters later, for they are really the foundation
for the rest. Chapter One is about Jesus Christ, who He was and
what He managed to accomplish. Everyone who has ever tried to
explain what St. Paul meant by the Christian's union with Christ
has had to fit his explanation into the story of why Jesus Christ
came into the world; the more central union with Christ was in the
whole Christian scheme, the more vitally it had to be related to the
doctrine of Christ Himself. So, in the first chapter, I try to show
that, in fact, the important christological traditions carry in their
own perspectives the makings of a doctrine of our union with
Christ. This is why I argue that the first step in understanding
Paul's doctrine of union with Christ is to understand his Christology.

Chapter Two is about the Holy Spirit, and how He is related to
Jesus. Anyone who thinks at all about what Paul tells us of our
union with Christ also thinks about the Spirit. Nothing is clearer
than that Paul thinks *Spirit* when he thinks *union with Christ*. So
I thought it would be useful to conduct a patient, if sometimes
belabored, discussion of Christ and the Spirit. How can we understand anything at all of how the Spirit unites us with Jesus unless
we understand how the Spirit Himself is united with Jesus?

I have not tried to be fashionable; this book is not an effort to make the gospel palatable to the mood of modern man—whoever he may be. What I have written will not be advertised as another "radical reconstruction" of theology for our time. What I have wanted to do is to understand the very elusive and dynamic notion of our union with Christ, to understand it as Paul did and as he wrote about it. My only claim to an original contribution is my attempt to take the mysterious reality of union with Christ off the sidetrack of individual spirituality, and to set it on the main track of God's creative route through history.

I owe a word of thanks to the Calvin Foundation for a grant that made it possible for me to reduce my teaching load for a semester in order to tie the loose ends of this study together. I send it out in the hope that it may serve as one signpost, pointing to God's exciting invitation to union with Jesus Christ.

—Lewis B. Smedes

Grand Rapids, Michigan

Contents

11

Chapter One

A Christology for Union with Christ

A. THE CHRIST "OUT THERE"

The purpose of this chapter is to explore the area of Christology to see if we can arrive at a view of Jesus Christ—His acts and His identity—that will help us understand at least something of what union with Him means and how it is brought about. We shall take a look at ways theologians have found for relating Christology to the experience of union with Christ; but our eventual aim is to come to some understanding of our own. To *be* in union with Christ is vastly more important than to *understand* it, and knowing that it is possible is far more crucial than having a doctrine of how it works. But understanding has its own significance, and doctrine its own importance, even though our doctrines are only images that point in the direction of reality.

Our task here is to relate Paul's understanding of Jesus Christ in the first century with the Jesus Christ who is united to us in the twentieth. We begin with the first part of the relationship: who is Jesus Christ and what did He do? James Stewart has said that when we confess that we are "in Christ, we are wittingly or unwittingly framing a christology."[1] But we ought, at least initially, to let Christology tell us what being "in Christ" means. We probably will never wholly avoid asking the christological question in the way J. K. S. Reid does: "How must we construe the person of Jesus Christ so that he is able to function as the one in whom man can be said to be?"[2] But this way of putting the question could tempt us to force Christology into the mold of our doctrine of union with Christ. In fact, it has often done so. How we

[1]*A Man in Christ* (London, 1935), p. 154.
[2]*Our Life in Christ* (Philadelphia, 1963), p. 53.

13

"construe the person of Jesus Christ" and how we construe our
experience of Him are intertwined. We should not say: This is our
Christology; now let us make the doctrine of union with Christ
conform to it. But neither should we say: This is our doctrine of
union with Christ; now let us make our Christology conform to it.
The person of Christ and Christian experience are of one piece
theologically. We could begin by talking about either one of them.
But we must make a choice, and it is reasonable to begin at the
beginning, with the person and work of Christ.

One chapter of the history of modern theology could be devoted, I think, to its interlacing of Christian experience and
Christology in such fashion as to rule out the possibility of a real
union with Jesus Christ. I can illustrate what I mean, briefly, by
these examples. First is the German scholar Wilhelm Herrmann,
whose influence on Bultmann, among others, was apparently considerable. He wrote a book at the turn of the century called *The
Communion of the Christian with God*. The title betrays the mo-
tive behind the book: it is an antidote to Christian mysticism.
Unsympathetic to the idea of mystical union with Christ, Herrmann
concentrated the weight of significance on the *historical* Jesus. But
why is the Jesus of history important? The answer is simple: the
Jesus of past history is the only Jesus we have. The notion of an
exalted Jesus is unthinkable and, in fact, unusable. But what
significance does the Jesus of history have for our life here and
now? The answer to this is also simple: He has significance only
as we grasp for ourselves the kind of life He lived. He has power
"to set free ourselves, so that we become aware of God."[3] Does
Jesus save us by *His* power? The "saving fact is the personal life of
Jesus *when it is grasped by us as a reality*."[4]

The saving event occurs when I, here and now, decide to live
the truly moral life in communion with God. The factual Jesus of
history belongs to the dead past; He cannot reach out to touch us
here. But the living tradition of His past life compels us to "see"
that communion with God is possible, if we but grasp it.[5] The

[3]W. Herrmann, *The Communion of the Christian with God* (London,
1930), p. 287.

[4]*Ibid.*, p. 80. Herrmann did not suppose that we could reconstruct the
life of Jesus by historical investigation. But he did insist that the real
Jesus *behind* the apostolic preaching of Him was the Jesus that really
mattered to us. For it is His life of communion with God, a life actually
lived in history, that we must re-duplicate in our own lives. Cf. p. 76.

[5]*Ibid.*, p. 200. To know Jesus, then, is to dispense with mysticism
(p. 199).

truly Christian life is the moral life in fellowship with God, the moral force of the universe. A union with Christ is out of the picture; history, the distance between Jesus and us, rules it out.

A second—quite different—modern approach begins with the premise that the mystical union is exactly what Paul teaches and what is essential to Christian experience. And the reality of union with Christ *defines* Christology. But if the union is real, it cannot be a union with Jesus of Nazareth. J. Weiss suggested this train of thought when he said:

> Christ is said to be not merely in one person, but in all the faithful, and at the same time all the faithful are in Christ. This is possible only if the idea of Christ becomes vague, and if his personality is dissolved in a pantheistic manner.[6]

So, here we begin with union with Christ and end *without* the Jesus of history. The individual Jesus of history is not adequate for the reality of mystical union. This mystical reality is so real, so universal, and so intimate, that in order to fit it, Christology must make of Jesus Christ a sort of universal spirit, an airy, ephemeral, and vaporous thing that, like the atmosphere, can be in us all and contain us all in it.

Rudolf Bultmann is my third example. Here are the relevant premises:

(1) As a historicist, Bultmann is sure that no event of past history can radically affect our personal existence in the present.

(2) As one who accepts scientific criteria as normative for understanding *all* reality outside of our personal experience, Bultmann is sure that there is no risen and presently living Christ with whom we can be united.

(3) As a New Testament critic, Bultmann is sure that we are unable to know enough about the Jesus of history for Him to serve as our ethical model.

(4) As an existentialist, Bultmann is sure that the only possibility for having "eternal" life is the possibility of a free decision to live a genuinely personal (or spiritual, or free) existence here and now.

According to the first premise, the possibility of the Jesus Christ of history reaching out now to affect us personally is ruled out. According to the second, the possibility of a genuine union with Jesus Christ is ruled out. According to the third, Herrmann's hope

[6]*Der 1 Korinther Brief* (Göttingen, 1910), p. 303.

that the life of Jesus will inspire or empower us to live the moral
life is ruled out. Hence, everything rests on the fourth premise.
Where does Christology fit in here? It fits in not as a description of
Jesus Christ, but as a message about His cross, the one thing we
are sure about, which challenges us to live the kind of life that the
cross epitomizes. This is a life in which all that matters is personal
freedom, willingness to let go of everything for the sake of genuinely free and so authentic human existence. In short, as Herrmann
ruled out union with Christ for the sake of Jesus, and as the mystic
rules out Jesus for the sake of union, Bultmann rules out both for
the sake of free human decision.[7]

One conviction unites these very distinct approaches: Christian
experience here and now cannot be a union with the concrete,
specific, individual Jesus. There are many prejudices that help to
account for this conviction. But it must be granted that, to any
sober realist of the twentieth century, Paul's realistic language of
union is hard to reconcile with the fact that Jesus of Nazareth is
"out there" in history or "out there" in heaven. And it is not surprising that one who takes union with Christ seriously tends to
dissociate it from the historical Jesus, and that one who takes the
historical Jesus seriously tends to eliminate the possibility of a real
union with Him. For this reason, the first decision we must make is
this: is the Christ who enters into union with us the same individual called Jesus of Nazareth? Let us put the question this way:
Was the Christ who "lived in" Paul the same as the one Paul
preached as crucified?

I accept the thesis that the Christ whom Paul says lives in him is
the same Jesus who was born in Judea and ended His normal life
on a cross outside of Jerusalem.[8] But how can *that* Jesus be the
Christ who not only calls us to union with Himself today, but
graciously takes the initiative Himself?

What follows is a review of three ways that readers of Paul have
taken toward an answer. Each assumes that the Christology behind
our union with Christ must be one that deals with Jesus Christ who
was made incarnate, lived, and died for our salvation. And each
works out a Christology that helps explain our union with Christ.
What distinguishes each from the others is the place where the

[7]Perhaps the quickest way into Bultmann's theology is to read his essay
in Bartsch's *Kerygma and Myth,* I (Naperville, Ill., 2nd ed., 1964) and his
lectures on *Jesus Christ and Mythology* (New York, 1958).

[8]I think that this is Paul's working assumption, and for evidence refer
the reader to Additional Note 1, pp. 252-254.

central significance of Jesus Christ is discovered. Each discovers the heart, the *leitmotif*, of Jesus' redemptive importance in a somewhat different dimension of His person and action than do the others. Each points us in a somewhat different direction in the search for the possibility, necessity, and effects of our union with Jesus Christ of yesterday and today.

The names I have given to these Christologies—Sacramental Christology, Personal Transaction Christology, and Situation Christology—are only a matter of convenience and have no footing in traditional vocabulary. I could have added a fourth, Pneumatic Christology, but have decided to reserve discussion of this for the next chapter. Of course, there is probably no one theologian who fits any of these categories wholly. All we can demonstrate is that some people lean more toward one than toward another.

B. SACRAMENTAL CHRISTOLOGY

According to Sacramental Christology, it is the incarnation of the Son of God around which the action of redemption moves. For when the Word became flesh, human nature was lifted into personal union with God. Whatever happened after Christmas morning was in some sense anticlimactic. The great miracle for the redemption of man and his world happened when man was lifted to the level of personal existence within the person of God's Son.[9] This Christology is sacramental insofar as it sees the union of God and manhood in Christ as the answer to man's need. We are justified in calling this a Sacramental Christology because, in keeping with the universal character of the sacramental, it looks to a finite life lifted by God to the status of a vehicle of transcendent meaning and power as the center of God's act for our salvation.

An astounding variety of Christologies could fit into this very general categorization. The romantic and the idealist see in Jesus Christ the symbol of nature's potential to become the bearer of the transcendent. Goethe said that we all partake of heavenly food when we eat the bread of nature; he was probably quite willing to let the story of Jesus illustrate his ability to taste an invisible grace in all the visible forms around him. The theologies of the sacramental universe common in the last century were sometimes only

---

[9]The background of this sentence is the word *enhypostasis*, a phrase associated with Leontius of Byzantium, which indicates that the human nature of Christ was not *im*personal, but *in*personal. See H. Relton, *A Study in Christology* (London, 1917).

baptized versions of Hegel's philosophy of nature and history, as the emergence of the absolute in finite forms. Paul Tillich's Christology, too, must be reckoned in a broad sense as sacramental; for Tillich sees Jesus as the bearer of ultimate being, in which finite existence can participate. As the Christ He symbolized the potential within finite existence for participation in the (divine) ground of being without becoming identified with it.[10]

The purposes of our study will be better served, however, if we limit ourselves to a Sacramental Christology that is set within classical Christian theology. Such a Christology shares with other Sacramental Christologies a penchant for finding the ultimate solution of the human dilemma in participation in the absolute or divine life. It is distinguished from them, however, in that it locates that possibility actually and exclusively in the unique union of God and man that took place in Jesus of Nazareth.

There is a clause in the Athanasian Creed that offers sympathy to this kind of Christology. It reads that God became flesh, "not by the conversion of God into flesh, but by the taking [assumption] of manhood into God." The assumption of a human nature into personal union with God was so creative an event that it opened up to all of mankind a doorway into the destiny that God had planned for it all the while. A reservoir of supernatural life was made available to all by lifting one human nature to the level of existence in God. This does not mean that Sacramental Christologies suggest that Jesus could just as well have left the earth the day after His birth. Man had sinned and atonement had to be made. Furthermore, the humanity of Christ had to be glorified and transformed so that its reservoir of life could be tapped for the life of other men. Even so, sacramentalists emphasize this *sine qua non* of redemption: the manhood of Jesus was united personally (enhypostatically) in the Person of the Divine Word.

We can get a sense of the grand sweep and hopeful vision that a sacramental theology offers from a single statement by the respected Anglo-Catholic theologian E. Mascall:

> The Incarnation did not only set upon man the seal by which God guarantees man's imperishable importance and dignity; it brought into the world a new thing and inaugurated a new era of human history. The human organism which the Son of God took from his Virgin Mother and in which he died and rose again from

[10]Tillich, *Systematic Theology,* II (London, 1957), 139ff.

the dead was not destroyed by his resurrection and ascension; it was transfigured and glorified and made accessible to men. . . . By the new birth of baptism (a man or woman) becomes a member of the restored human race, whose first member and head is Jesus Christ. . . . His further progress is then not progress within the natural order, but within the supernatural order of grace and redemption, though within the supernatural order the natural order will itself be fulfilled and transfigured. And what is God's will for individual human beings is his will for the human race. . . . For Christian faith, the ultimate term of human evolution is the Total Christ, consisting of Head and members in intimate union, sharing a common supernatural life. . . .[11]

This is a magnificent Christian vision that on the one hand honors the unique status of Jesus Christ and on the other shares the Pauline faith that in Christ "all things" on earth and in heaven shall be reunited. But it must be recognized that the possibility for the realization of the "ultimate term of human evolution" is the elevation of human life into the supernatural life, a possibility provided by the elevation of humanity into the life of God at the incarnation. The union of God and man is the answer to man's most basic need, a need built into man by his distance, his metaphysical separation from God.

Sacramental theologians do not ignore the crucial significance of the historical events of the cross and resurrection. But they do have trouble integrating a theology of eventfulness—the theology of Jesus *doing* something crucially significant for history by dying on the cross and rising from death—with a theology of incarnation and the subsequent extension of the incarnation to the rest of humanity. They are frequently forced to speak of the redemptive work of Christ as being on two levels; and the more influence biblical theology has on them, the more distinct these two levels become. On one level there is union of manhood with God and a pouring out of that manhood's new life into other men in history. On another level there is a decisive intervention into the forces of history by the powerful acts of dying and rising again, acts that achieved a victory over the supernatural forces that had frustrated and made chaotic the moral life of man and threatened to abort the destiny that God had set for human history.

An impressive example of this two-level Christology is found in

[11]*Christian Theology and Natural Science* (London, 1958), pp. 314ff.

the Roman Catholic theologian, Jean Daniélou.[12] In his book, *Christ and Us,* Daniélou presents a theology compounded of sacramental strains that would be a credit to any of the Greek fathers and of historico-redemptive strains that are bred of a discerning involvement in biblical theology. The result is an exciting and comprehensive attempt at synthesis between sacramental and historico-eschatological theologies. Speaking of Christ's *historical* actions, Daniélou writes:

> St. Paul declares that in Jesus Christ the decisive divine act intervened, that it constituted the essential happening of sacred history. In this his theology is in line with the Old Testament, which bore witness to divine acts and heralded an eschatological action of God which was to be the decisive action.

Here we have the one level, the historical, the acts of God in history as saving acts. But,

> On another level Paul shows how this divine action is not only God's action, but that it involves sharing in the life of the Son of God, and therefore that it is in so far as He is the Son of God that Christ brings about in us the sharing of His life. In other words, it is not only a question of communicating the divine life, but of communicating the life of the Son of God.[13]

There are two levels of christological interest, then, and the critic cannot deny that the sacramental theologian makes great efforts to assimilate them both. Yet, the sacramental level is primary.

> The centre of God's design becomes the very Person of Christ the Son of God. It is in him first of all that the work of God is

---

[12]Another splendid example of the two levels—sacramentalist and eschatological—is the theology of the Anglo-Catholic L. S. Thornton. Two of the works that reveal the complexity of his thought are *The Common Life in the Body of Christ* (Westminster, 1946) and *The Dominion of Christ* (Westminster, 1952).

[13]*Christ and Us* (London, 1961), pp. 59, 60. "The man Jesus," writes Dennis O'Callaghan, "has a plenitude of grace at his disposal because of the hypostatic union. . . . This plenitude is willed by God as the source of grace for all men" (*Sacraments, the Gestures of Christ* [New York, 1964], p. 33).

accomplished which joins divine nature to human nature. . . . It is in and through the manhood of Christ that the other purpose of creation is achieved, namely the divinization of man. . . .[14]

The cross and resurrection do achieve something redemptive in their own right. They are required by an additional and, in a sense, accidental, emergency in human life: disobedience and sin. The cross and resurrection were God's response to human disobedience: God provided a perfect priest to expiate human guilt. That side-issue having been resolved, the divinized humanity of Jesus could be poured out into other human lives to give them a share in that gloriously perfected humanity of Jesus.

Always, in Sacramental Christology, the movement is upward; humanity is lifted up, nature is elevated, into the life of God. There is not much need for elaboration on the events of gospel history. What we get, far more likely, from sacramental theologians, is a combination of theology and a description of nature.[15] For sacramental theology is always a combination of biblical and natural theology. If man's needs are answered by a union of the divine and human, it must be shown how nature and supernature can be and are united without insult or injury to each other.

There is also a certain natural necessity to the incarnation. If creation's need is for an insinuation of extra-terrestrial life, that

[14]*Op. cit.*, pp. 61, 62. "The incarnation thus appears as . . . the decisive moment, the supreme efficacious intervention, by which human nature is infallibly guided towards the end for which it was eternally destined in the secret counsels of the Trinity" (*ibid.*, p. 130).

[15]One attractive facet of Sacramental Christology is its integration of the supernatural with the organic development of natural life. In Teilhard de Chardin's majestic harmonization of theology and science, Jesus Christ and the end of the evolutionary process are one. Jesus, through the elevation of humanity into the life of God, is the *omega*, the goal, of creation's developmental alphabet. He does not come at the end of the evolutionary process; He comes to *be* the *telos*, the goal, and hence the end. "If the world is convergent and if Christ occupies its centre, then the Christo-genesis of St. Paul and St. John is nothing else and nothing less than the extension, both awaited and unhoped for, of that neogenesis in which cosmogenesis . . . culminates. Christ invests himself organically with the very majesty of his creation. And it is in no way metaphorical to say that man finds himself capable of experiencing and discovering his God in the whole length, breadth, and depth of the world in movement" (Teilhard de Chardin, *The Phenomenon of Man* [New York, 1959], p. 297). By means of the incarnation, Christianity is able to "save and even to take the place of evolution."

need was in creation from the beginning. And if there were no possibility for nature to reach that goal by itself, some kind of divine action was necessary. One of the greatest of sacramental theologians, Emile Mersch, whose brilliant career as a Jesuit theologian was cut short in a strafing raid during World War II, does not hesitate to say so.

> This deification is obligatory, not simply because God desires its presence in all His works, but also because of the dignity of our human nature; when man voluntarily rejects the supernatural nobility that is offered him he sins against his own nature.[16]

"Against his own nature" could be understood in different ways, but Mersch's meaning is that man was intended by creation to be more than the stuff of which creation is made. And, of course, the "supernatural nobility" is set loose to flow into humanity by one thing—the incarnation. "Nothing else is required; the sole and sufficient reason for its deification is the fact of its assumption by the Word."[17]

The pieces of this picture fit together with astounding simplicity (though not, of course, in God's doing of it; it is from beginning to the end a miracle of grace). Creation moves upward toward a unified and integrated life of man in community. Two things keep it from achieving its goal: its limitations as finite nature and the intrusion of sin, which complicates and intensifies the built-in frustrations. God acts by embracing a specific human nature—that of Jesus—into His very life as the Person of the Son of God. This human nature, after passing through a sacrificial death on the way, is glorified in such a manner that His deified human nature can spread its supernatural life into the rest of humanity.

Sacramental Christology stands and falls with the historical Jesus. But it cannot be called a Christology that finds the center of meaning in historical events; it finds the center in metaphysical elevation of humanity to a new level. There is indeed a new creation, a new being that *is* Christ. But the primary note in the new creation is its being, not its action; therefore it is not a historically defined, but a sacramentally defined Christology.[18]

[16]E. Mersch, *Le Corps Mystique du Christ,* II (Louvain, 1933), 347.
[17]*Ibid.,* p. 220.
[18]See Additional Note 2, pp. 255-257.

C. PERSONAL TRANSACTION CHRISTOLOGY

Eric Mascall once asked whether the "supreme commemoration of our redemption"[19] is Christmas or Good Friday. He adds that to pursue this question rigorously would push us into a false division, for both the incarnation and the cross are indispensable. But in the sacramentalist practice of devotion the incarnation tends to dominate; Christmas is in fact the "supreme commemoration" for Sacramental Christology. Calvinists would not want to choose between these either; but in their practice of devotion Good Friday wins out. Christmas sermons in Calvinist churches tend to be prefaces to Good Friday; it is always evident that the cross casts its shadow over the manger, that Jesus was born in order to die, that God became man in order to *do* something for our salvation.

John Calvin must be set within what we shall call Transaction Christology. When he was preoccupied with his defense of a genuinely effective sacrament, he sounded sacramentalistic; he talked of the life of God being siphoned into the humanity of Christ and from there tapped into ours. But when he spoke of Jesus Christ, he let the *offices*, the *action* of Jesus dominate. It was no accident of theological history that the concept of offices—prophet, priest, and king—was developed most fruitfully by the master of Geneva. The unity of man and God in Christ was a necessary means to the end that Christ be our *Mediator*, and mediation is an action. *Cur Deus Homo?* He became man to obey, to die, to sacrifice, and to atone. The heart of Christology lies in what Jesus did personally to transact with God for our atonement.

Calvin realized as keenly as any sacramentalist that a real union with Christ is the indispensable context of Christian existence. In a sentence that sets the ground rules for all further discussion of Christian reality, he says: "As long as Christ remains outside of us, and we are separated from him, all that he has suffered and done for the salvation of the human race remains useless and of no value to us."[20] The sentence begins and is meant to control Cal-

---

[19]*Christ, the Christian, and the Church* (London, 1946), p. 69.

[20]*Institutes* iii.1.1. Some time ago, in reading the two volumes by Emil Mersch, I failed to find a reference to this or any of many similar statements by Calvin. But Mersch does insist that for Calvinists religion is essentially a "separation from Christ" (*Le Corps Mystique du Christ,* II [Louvain, 1933], 263). Other sacramentalists betray the same blindness to the respect that Reformation theologians had for the mystical union. See Y. M. Congar, *Chretiens Desunis* (Paris, 1937), p. 112; and H. de Lubac, *Catholicisme* (Paris, 1938), p. 45.

vin's entire discussion of the grace of sanctification and justification. But the sentence must be read with care. Calvin does not say
that all that Christ *is* as the divine-human Son of Man will be
useless, but that what Christ *did* would be of no value to us. Union
with Christ is the *sine qua non* of our sharing in what "he has
suffered and *done*." Union with Christ, then, is the basis for our
benefiting from the event—and the event is the obedience of Jesus
Christ.

For Calvin, the roots of man's troubles lie in his disobedience.
The first man was called to be a man by living in obedience. By
nature, as he was created, man was free and able to be all that
God meant him to be; he needed no infusion of the supernatural
to enable him to be his highest and best self. But he had to "prove
that he was willingly under God's command." As it happened, he
"was led away from God's Word [command]" and "revolted from
God's authority." Thus, "disobedience was the beginning of the
Fall." Adam used his divinely given freedom to rebel against its
Author.[21] Pride and ambition and ingratitude followed; but his
disobedience was the first act. More than did Augustine, who saw
pride as the quintessence of sin, Calvin stresses the dynamic and
voluntaristic view of man's dilemma and guilt. Man *did* something wrong; he flaunted his superior, he *acted* in rebellion.

Calvin's language is ethical. He is not interested at all in specu-
lation about whether man's finite nature is inadequate for the
achievement of supernatural virtues. Neither is the solution to be
sought in the elevation of human nature; it must be found in the
submission of its will.[22] Moreover, since God's authority was
violated and transgressed, God Himself had to see to it that obedience was restored. It is not surprising, then, that Calvin's Christology is slanted toward Christ's obedience. The restoration of man
had to be premised on the restoration of obedience. Jesus was the
Mediator; the essence of His success as Mediator lay in His fulfilling all obedience, just as He Himself said: "It becometh, it is
proper for the Son of Man to fulfill all obedience." When Calvin
hears Jesus say: "I have not come to destroy, but to *fulfill the
law*," he discerns the heart of Jesus' mission. Does it not fit the
situation perfectly that Calvin should discuss in copious detail the
significance of the moral law right after he has talked of human sin
and just before he introduces Christology?

[21]*Institutes* ii.1.4.

[22]Consider Calvin's account of his own conversion. God, he said, "re-
duced his heart to docility" (*Preface* to the *Commentary on the Psalms*).

The climax of Calvin's search into the meaning of Jesus Christ for us comes when he introduces the final chapter of his section on Christology with the title *Christ Rightly and Properly Said to Have Merited God's Grace and Salvation For Us*. Christ did something to *earn* grace and salvation. What did He do? He suffered and died, indeed. But these form the epitome of His radical and uncompromising obedience. "*By his obedience,* however, Christ truly acquired and merited grace for us with his Father" (italics mine).[23]

Christ did things for us. He completed a transaction with God the Father. This is how Jesus merited or earned salvation. He earned from God an unlimited treasury of spiritual qualities. He "was made for us both righteousness and sanctification"—one of Calvin's favorite Pauline sentences. His glorification was not only a relief from His humiliation. Nor was it *only* his coronation as Lord of all. It meant that He was given a kind of reservoir of spiritual benefits. In a way that we cannot understand—and that Calvin does not try to explain—Jesus possessed after His ascension the personal qualities of holiness and righteousness in a far greater measure than He did while on earth. The difference is that while on earth He had them for Himself, in heaven He was given them for everyone else. He needed no more for His own sake; He earned them for us. They are the personal, human qualities of Jesus Christ. They are His, not by virtue of His nature but as a reward for His works.[24]

The connection between Calvin's Transaction Christology and his doctrine of man's union with Christ takes on a dimension wholly consistent with everything he says about the meaning of Jesus Christ. The problem that remains at the end of his book on redemption is this: how can the personal characteristics of Jesus, earned through active obedience, be appropriated by sinners? Clearly, a mere assenting belief in the atonement is not enough; it is not enough merely to assent to the factuality of the event. Such a belief would leave persons as they were. Only as those who believe also share in and personally possess the qualities of Jesus can they be affected by the act of atonement on the cross. "*As long*

[23]*Institutes* ii.17.3.

[24]Of course, Calvin is careful to say that the ultimate source of our salvation, of the rewards given to Christ the Mediator, is the same as that which brought Christ to earth as Mediator in the first place; it is the gracious election of Christ by God, and our election in Him. See *Institutes* ii.17.1.

*as Christ remains outside of us, and we are separated from him,
all that he has suffered and done for the salvation of the human
race remains useless and of no value to us."*

The end of union is a personal share in the human qualities
that Jesus was given by God for His obedience on earth. Calvin's
doctrine of union fits perfectly into his Christology. His Christology tends to require that God be fully present in Christ primarily
so that the humanity of Christ can perform the work perfectly.[25]
So, it is particularly the humanity of Christ that is significant both
in Christology and our union with Christ. Calvin was indignant with
anyone who insisted on a union with Christ's divine nature. We
must be united with His humanity, for it was in His humanity that
he fulfilled obedience on our behalf, and in His humanity that He
"contained" the benefits of His obedience.

Calvin's Christology makes it clear that nothing less than a
personal union will do for us. We must have "Himself" as well as
"His benefits" for the simple reason that the benefits are in, over,
under, and around Himself; indeed they *are* Himself, the moral
ingredients of His person. And this provides an insight into the
intensely sacramental—or mystical—language that Calvin uses
about union with Christ. When he speaks of getting the very
substance of the life of Christ, we must understand that for him
the *moral qualities* of righteousness and holiness *are* the substance
of personal life. For a man's authentic self is expressed in action,
in moral and religious relationships. The following sentences reveal the context in which he speaks of getting the substance of
Christ's life:

> What was the purpose of this subjection of Christ to the law but
> to acquire righteousness for us, undertaking to pay what we could
> not pay? Hence, that imputation of righteousness without works
> which Paul discusses (Rom. 4). For the righteousness found in
> Christ alone is reckoned as ours. Surely the only reason why

[25]That Calvin was not wholly successful in stating the case for the deity
of Christ seems clear. That "God was in Christ" aiding the human Jesus
to complete the awful transaction hardly fits the biblical picture of the
travail of God in *giving* His Son. Of course, Calvin would not have
wanted to say that God was only alongside, urging and helping, without
being really involved in the passion of Jesus. But when he states the
"reason" for the necessity of Jesus' being fully God, he leaves this unfortunate impression.

Christ's flesh is called "our food" (John 6:55) is that we find in him the substance of life.[26]

Here we are forewarned that for Calvin substance is not a metaphysical matter, but a moral one. *Righteousness* is the substance of human life. To be a man is to be obedient. And to be obedient is to be righteous. Only by means of a Christology of personal atonement can one conceive of true manhood in principle restored. Only by means of a union with Christ is true manhood, which is to say, obedience and gratitude, in fact regained.[27]

In many ways Karl Barth's Christology is similar to Calvin's. For both, the significance of Jesus Christ is centered on what He *did* for us. And what He did for us was to transact a personal exchange on our behalf with God. But there are some differences.

It would be obviously incorrect to suggest that Barth is not interested in the Who and What of Jesus Christ; but it is clear that the Who and What are defined by the How—the action of Jesus Christ. Jesus Christ is historical; He is *in* and *of* history. His importance to *us*, however, lies in the actual fact that He *is* history. "The existence of the man Jesus is this history. It is nothing more."[28] But to say this is only to inject a puzzle into the conversation. We have to backtrack to get Barth's point in focus. He wants us to know that Jesus is a real man, and that being a real man is a matter of what man *does*. Man is, by definition, action. But more than this, man is *real* man only in a certain *kind* of action. The kind of action that makes a man genuinely human is *action in partnership with God*. Simply speaking, the real man is the one who responds to God in obedience and gratitude.

Now when Barth says that Jesus is the true man, and even more when he says that Jesus is the true history of man, he is saying

[26]*Institutes* ii.17.6. In the light of this, as we shall see, Calvin's strikingly sacramental language must be taken with considerable reservation: ". . . the flesh of Christ is like a rich and inexhaustible fountain that pours into us the life springing forth from the Godhead into itself" (iv.17.9).

[27]Calvin does speak of a "mystical union," though sparingly. Barth and some other students of Calvin regret that he used the expression at all. Barth says: "We should never do this unless we state precisely what we have in view when we speak of 'mysticism'—and it would have to be a mysticism *sui generis* in this context" (*Church Dogmatics*, IV/3/2, p. 539). One has to agree with Barth. The loose, fuzzy, and usually unhelpful phrase "mystical union" has become common currency without much functional value. Calvin used it to indicate that the union was beyond our *rational* comprehension.

[28]*Church Dogmatics*, III/2, p. 160.

something of great christological interest. He is not merely saying that Jesus had a human nature that included everything common to humanity; when we say this, we are really defining Jesus' humanity in terms of what we already know about ourselves, and so do not learn anything *new* about ourselves from Jesus' humanity. Barth is saying that Christ is the true man because He is the solitary instance in the life of the human race of a man acting consistently in gratitude and obedience with God; He is the perfect covenant partner. Therefore, if we want to know what man is, we must look to what *Jesus did*. And if we want to be true men, we must derive our humanity from Him.[29]

But Jesus is not only *a* true man, not even *the* true man. He is human history—once again theologically speaking. The real history of man is man in partnership with God, and *this* history takes place, truly and concretely, only in one man's history. Jesus is that history in concrete fact. The miracle behind it all is this: God became man and *as man* He Himself moves with dynamic consistency in partnership with God's purpose for the service of man. This is where human history was fulfilled and made real. Here is where we must find the significance of Jesus Christ.[30]

God Himself becomes man and thus acts in obedience as man for man. This brings us to the personal transaction in Barth's Christology. God "shows Himself the One He is by the obedience He renders as man."[31] He became obedient unto death. This is the epitome of the history of man. Christ is judged; He fulfills and becomes man's history by being crucified. What He endured was meant to be, but never could be, endured by all men. But since He—the man Jesus—was judged, all men can say: He does what my manhood meant me to do and could not.

Christ's dying, obediently and willingly, is the transaction. For

[29]Jesus is His true self "as He does the work of God, and in so doing is one with God. . . . It is in this way, in the doing of the work of God . . . that He is Himself. . ." (*ibid.*, p. 65). "Jesus is man as God willed and created Him. What constitutes true human nature in us depends on what it is in Him. . . . What man is, is determined by God's immediate presence and action in this man [Christ], by His eternal election and the mighty work of His life and death and resurrection corresponding to this election. . . . We derive wholly from Jesus, not merely our potential and actual relation to God, but even our human nature as such" (*ibid.*, p. 50).

[30]"Jesus exists only in this history, i.e., in this history of the covenant and salvation and revelation inaugurated by God in and with the act of the creator. Jesus is, as this history takes place" (*ibid.*, p. 160).

[31]*Ibid.*, IV/1, p. 208.

"His dying implied, and to that extent was, our own dying."[32] If our real history was to be lived, we had to die, to have our alienated and rebellious selves put away, so that we could be real men in partnership with God. "Man who has become an enemy must be totally wiped out of existence and brought to nothing."[33]

The resurrection is the positive side of Christ's death. "According to the resurrection the death of Jesus Christ as the negative act of God took place with a positive intention. It had as its aim the turning of man to Himself, his positive self, his putting on of a new life, his freeing for the future."[34] The resurrection is the turning point, but its significance is seen only when it is appreciated as an aspect of the transaction at Calvary. The cross and the resurrection together mean that God judged man and affirmed him, that the old man of disobedience actually died and the new man of partnership came alive. All this happened in the history that is Jesus.

But, as far as we are concerned, it did not remain a solitary and isolated event of past time. "It was history in His time to become as such eternal history—the history of God with the men of all times, and therefore taking place here and now as it did then."[35] A great change took place for all mankind and all human history. "The world, every man, exists in this change."[36] It cannot be emphasized too much that, theologically speaking, Jesus-history is the history of everyman. Now men can only be summoned to be what they have in God's sight and God's will become—partners with God. Man's new history was achieved, his real being was attained, when God in humiliation, incarnate as Jesus Christ, was judged in our place and arose for our new reality.

Barth's Christology of personal transaction has clear implications —which he draws out consistently—for the doctrine of union with Christ. A hint of this connection lies in the heading under which he discusses union with Christ—"vocation, man's calling." Man is called to be a "concretely active being."[37] To be united with Christ means to be doing something, just as for Jesus to be Christ meant to be doing something. Man as man is defined as action. Jesus as the Christ is defined as action. Man as man in union

[32]*Ibid.*, p. 325.
[33]*Ibid.*, p. 326.
[34]*Ibid.*, p. 310.
[35]*Ibid.*, p. 313.
[36]*Ibid.*, p. 309.
[37]*Ibid.*, III/2, p. 545.

with Christ is defined as action. And the action is Christ's kind of
action: obedience to God in the service of man.

Barth breaks with almost all traditional notions of how one
shares in the reality of Jesus Christ. He is unlike the sacramentalist,
who says we are infused with the divine life of Christ. He rejects
the optimistic moralist, who sees the history of Jesus as one that
has to be and can be imitated by us. He distinguishes himself from
the existentialist, who says that the only real event of salvation is
the decision a man makes here and now to be a free man. For
Barth the significant event for all men happened when Jesus died
and rose again. And therefore His history is the truth about us,
whether we believe it or not. But we are called now to *live* the
truth.

The differences between the Christologies of Barth and Calvin,
and their implications for the doctrine of union with Christ, are
now beginning to come to light. For Calvin the problem was how
the personal *benefits* earned by Christ could be insinuated into us.
For him union with Christ begins at the point where the virtue, the
strength, or the human life of Christ is transferred to the life of
believers. For Barth, the problem is how the *action* of Jesus
(which, in God's view, was the action of all men) could become
the action of the rest of us in actual practice. For Barth union with
Christ is the goal to which men are called and the privilege to
which they are invited because it is the reality that has already
come about in Christ Himself. It is not strange for Calvin to talk
of a *mystical* union; whereas the phrase is totally foreign to Barth.
And the reason for this difference is rooted in Christology.

D. SITUATION CHRISTOLOGY

The third Christology we have to consider is what I call Situation Christology. The difference between this and the Christology
of Personal Transaction is mostly one of emphasis. Both Situation
and Transaction Christologies stress the effective *action* of Jesus
Christ; in distinction from the Sacramentalist, these Christologies
find the central significance of Jesus in what He *did*. Both are
Christologies of event. But there is a difference. Christologies of
Personal Transaction see the chief participants in the event of the
cross and resurrection as God the Father and Jesus Christ the Son;
the cross was a transaction between them that accomplished atonement for people of all times. Situation Christologies, on the other

hand, see the chief actors in the drama of redemption as Jesus
Christ and the "principalities and powers," or Satan. Transaction
Christologies emphasize that Christ radically changed the personal
relationship between God and man. Situation Christologies stress
that Christ radically changed the historical situation in which men
live.

Before examining Paul's Situation Christology, it is well to take
a brief look at the word "situation" in this context. Today we are
very aware of the interdependence between a person's character
and environment. The individual is both the creator and the product of his situation. Environment undergirds him, supports him,
and in a sense creates him; it also confines, limits, and possibly
destroys him. The balance between the limitations and the crea-
tivity, the confinement and the possibilities, of an environment
depends upon its character—as well as on the mysterious differences within individuals. In our day we have come to see how
destructive of personal freedom and growth the situation of men
can be.

The time is long past that a moral individual could drive into the
inner city, get out of his new Buick, pat a little child on the head,
and tell him that if he tried hard he could become almost anything
he wanted to be. The little child may be locked in by his social
and political situation. Let us say that his home is broken. He lives
in a cold water flat, crowded by two other families of people and
several families of rats. His mother supplements her ADC allot-
ment with part-time work at a neighborhood bar. The block is
infested with alcoholics and dope addicts; the most innocent spec-
tator sport is the floating crap game. The back yard is a stinking
garbage heap. And there is no way out. If what the moralizer says
is to be true, and not a demonic lie, the child's situation has to
be changed. The social structure that presses the child down must
be transformed. And this is the task that, so far, has been beyond
the will or power of the richest and most powerful society in
history.

To extend the picture one step further, we must say that the
situation is a political one. Behind the situation are "powers and
principalities" that must be conquered. Slum landlords must be
shaken from their affluent indifference. Political leaders must be
compelled to overcome their destructive inertia, self-interest, and
defeatism. Behind the child of the slum stand such political matters
as the tax structure, the political machine, the system. In short,
behind the physical and moral situation of the individual lurk a

political situation and personal powers. If something is to be done for the child, something must be done about the situation.

Situation Christology sees the significance of Jesus Christ in terms roughly parallel to the slum situation. The individual who gives hopeless encouragement to the slum child is like the "law" in Paul's vocabulary; the law is "weak because of the flesh." The slum situation is the human situation. The political powers of the city are the "principalities and powers." And Jesus Christ is the one man who was able to and who did conquer the "powers that be" who destructively controlled the slum situation that is mankind. The central meaning of Jesus Christ is succinctly put by Paul when he said, "He put to shame the powers of this world" (Col. 2:15). Jesus radically and permanently changed the human situation by defeating the "political powers" behind it.

But is this Paul's Christology? We would be blind to a great deal that Paul writes about Jesus Christ if we saw only a Situation Christology in his letters. Our question is this: does Situation Christology give us a clue for understanding the context of his doctrine of our union with Christ? The rest of this chapter deals with this question.

To get a clear and consistent outline from Paul is not easy, because he does not work things out systematically. Deissmann's impression of Paul as a mystic is inaccurate,[38] for Paul was a theologian. But he was not a systematic theologian. The cosmic and profound inner significance of Jesus enters the discussion by way of a liturgical hymn here, a stern exhortation there, and an intense argument in another place—often dropped as if in passing.

From Paul's occasional remarks, however, rises the outline of a drama. We get a picture of a strange invasion into hostile territory. The Son of God goes behind enemy lines and enters the arena of life in the corrupt but tenacious regime of His ancient enemy. He comes incognito—in the "form of a servant" (Phil. 2:7). He accepts all the conditions of life there. He is "born of a woman, born under the law" (Gal. 4:4). He is a blood native of the people, elected among others to fulfill the plan of God; "according to the flesh" he is a Hebrew (Rom 1:3). He is tempted to line up with the old regime, but, obedient to His mission "even unto death," He assaults the enemy's position where it really matters—the place of death. Somehow, in a moment and in a way that eludes historical

[38]Cf. A. Deissmann, *Paul, A Study in Social and Religious History* (New York, 1957), p. 107. He says that Paul's was a "mystical-prophetical character, and . . . the theological almost entirely disappears" (p. 79).

description or poetic metaphor, He defeats the enemy just at the moment when He seemed to have been defeated. At the cross, He powerfully mastered the masters of the world. At the resurrection, He appeared on the balcony, as it were, to announce His conquest. It was a strange performance, so strange that it could be called God's foolishness and God's weakness, which outwitted the wisdom and outfought the strength of the world (I Cor. 1:23, 24).

What happened took place *in* history. But, more important perhaps, it took place *for* history. Jesus was in history, but what He did He did *to* history. And even what happened *in* history was more than the kind of event that can be catalogued, classified, described, and compared by historians with other events of history. The events of Jesus Christ were transhistorical in that while they occurred on the fields of human history they also occurred, at the same time, behind the scenes. The two critical scenes are the crucifixion and the resurrection. But what happened in those events can never be captured by watching a man die and walk out of his grave alive—astounding as the sight would have been had any seen it. The encounter that changed the human situation for all time took place between the two great powers just outside the arena of tangible and recordable events. It happened "out there" in the arena of cosmic politics. The decisive event was able to alter the human situation fundamentally precisely *because* it took place *behind the scenes* of the human situation.

When Jesus came away from His encounter with death, He came away from an engagement with the powers that for ages had been pulling from behind the curtain the strings of the human, earthly scene. He came away as victor. At the cross and resurrection, God "disarmed the principalities and powers and made a public example of them, triumphing over them in Christ" (Col. 2:15). The reason that the cross is the "power of salvation" for individuals lies in what occurred outside the realm of personal experience. Whatever new hope and new possibilities individuals may discover in association with Jesus, the prior fact is the event of conquest beyond their experience. Our personal salvation rests in what God

> accomplished in Christ when he raised him from the dead and made him sit at his right hand in the heavenly places, far above all rule and authority and power and dominion, and above every name that is named, not only in this age but also in that which is to come; and he has put all things under his feet, and has made him head over all things for the church . . . (Eph. 1:20-22).

This may be the language of liturgy. It is surely rhapsodic. But the intent is not apocalyptic symbolism; Paul means it as fact. A cosmic *coup d'etat* was the one thing necessary to reroute history back to the mainline of the Creator's original purpose. And the one thing necessary has happened.

There is a "god of this world" (II Cor. 4:4) who, even after his defeat, tries to hypnotize people into a state of delusion about the real state of affairs. He is the devil who, strangely, can still destroy men with this delusion (I Cor. 5:5). He is the "prince of the power of the air," who still manages to dominate the lives of those who fail to enter the new situation created by his defeat (Eph. 2:2). Beginning with the "first Adam" and his act of disobedience, the age of men has been dominated by superhuman powers beyond every individual's undoing. Paul considers their real existence and their actual defeat to be a matter close to the heart of Christ's significance for us. Negatively, the debacle of Satan is the first meaning of Jesus Christ.

The repercussions of Satan's defeat are felt like shock waves over the whole course of history and the entire universe. For the positive side of the picture is that the "god of this age" has been turned out of the palace and replaced by Jesus who is made the "lord over all things in heaven and on earth." Jesus Christ is Lord. This is the heart of the gospel. We cannot afford to hesitate about the objective status of the new situation resulting from Christ's triumph. As Cullmann says, it is "the present Lordship of Christ, inaugurated by his resurrection and exaltation to the right hand of God, that is the centre of the faith of primitive Christianity."[39] It is the premise on which the whole structure of Paul's redemptive theology rests. Unless Christ is Lord, there is no change, no possibility of change, no hope for change in the weakness and guilt that frustrate human progress.

Tempting as it is to focus concern only on the vistas opened up by Christ to individuals in their moral or religious needs, we must focus attention specifically on the radical change of course in the objective order—the political order, if you will—that controls and dominates the human situation. With Satan overcome and Christ as the present Lord, the old regime was turned out of power and a new era was begun; a new ebb and flow of history started when Christ arose. The time of promise was fulfilled. Now the day of salvation had come—not merely made possible for some future

[39]*The Earliest Christian Confessions* (London, 1949), p. 58.

time, but actually here (II Cor. 6:2). The world had come to an
end—the old world of the former regime; the "end of the ages"
had arrived (I Cor. 10:11). "The old has passed away, behold
the new has come," said Paul (II Cor. 5:17), referring not to the
individual experience of people but to the turn of events in objective history. As Geerhardus Vos said, some time before the phrase
"realized eschatology" was coined, "There has been created a
totally new environment, or, more accurately stated, a totally new
world. . . . The whole surrounding world has assumed a new
aspect and complexion."[40] And therefore the Christian has been
"transferred into a new world, a world which differs *toto genera* in
all its character, its whole environment . . . from the present
world."[41]

The change of administration may not be obvious at the grass-
roots level; but the change is final and real. The prevailing "god"
of this age has given place to Jesus the Lord. Those who are on
the Lord's side have been transferred from one regime to another
—from the kingdom of darkness into the kingdom of light (I
Thess. 2:12; Col. 1:13). But the very finality of the victory, the
universality of its effects, and the radical character of the change
in history that results from it create a whole tangle of problems.
The more one accents the *situation*—rather than personal opportunity—in Christology, the more profound and unsettling the
problems become. Let us look at some of them.

* * * * *

One of the prominent words in Paul's Situation Christology is
aeon, often translated as "age," sometimes as "world." For Christians, the evil age has come to an end. On the other hand, the age
in which Christians live—*Anno Domini*, the year of our Lord—is
the "present evil age" (Gal. 1:4). There is a decided ambivalence
between the passing of one age and the beginning of a new age;[42]

---

[40]*Pauline Eschatology* (Grand Rapids, 1935), p. 47.

[41]*Ibid.*, p. 150.

[42]Sometimes the word *aeon* refers to God's own eternal life in contrast
to what we would call the temporal world. But since the biblical writers
were not taken up with the sheer eternity of God as over against the
temporality of man, they did not find it embarrassing to use the word *aeon*
for a long stretch of time. The word, then, acquired a sense somewhat the
opposite of its original intent (see Sasse, in Kittel, *Theological Dictionary
of the New Testament*, I, 202). But when Paul uses the word, he insinuates
another sense into it. He is not concerned with the length of the age, nor
with the fact that it is temporal rather than eternal. He is concerned with
its character and its implications for the present and future of human life.

we seem to live in one, with the powers of the old still present as a strong subversive influence. When Paul says that the end of the age has come for Christians he does not mean end in a simple chronological sense. The age is finished as the *force of the future*; it is not finished as a reality and threat in the present time.

Has the situation really changed since Jesus came on the scene? Has the history of men actually undergone an abrupt and radical transformation? Has the end of the ages arrived, and is the present time the time when Christ is actually Lord of "all things"? Were the demonic powers who dominated the time prior to Christ really and utterly defeated when Christ came? Are the "old things" actually passed away? This is, in various forms, the question we now face.

We are dealing with the meaning of Jesus Christ—the significance of His coming as far as a real change in the human situation is concerned. The question is forced on us by two very clear realities: (1) Paul himself calls Christians constantly to look ahead to the future when the great change is going to take place; and (2) the brute facts of history shout loud and clear that nothing seems to have radically changed at all.

Paul urged Christians to expect Christ's coming at any time, adding the promise that the coming would mean the real end to evil and the real beginning of life. The fact that Christians had to look forward to the future for fulfillment of their hopes never seemed to cast a shadow on the announcement that Christ had already transferred them into the kingdom of light. And the proclamation of Christ's victory in the past never seemed to give Paul ground for saying that everything God has in mind for history had already come. The situation has already radically changed, but we also look forward to a radical change.

At first sight, this would seem to be a highly paradoxical situation that Paul took in stride. Probably the key word here is *parousia*, meaning "coming" or "appearance." By itself it does not imply a future coming.[43] But there is no doubt that when Paul speaks of it his eyes are on tomorrow, not on yesterday. We are waiting for the "glorious appearance"—the *parousia*—of our Lord (Tit. 2:13). What is the relationship between waiting for the end and looking back to the end?

[43] A. Oepke says that the word *parousia* never has an explicitly future reference; in Paul it refers to Christ's coming without saying anything about *when* (Kittel, *Theological Dictionary of the New Testament*, V [Grand Rapids, 1969], p. 868).

The *parousia* signals the climax of history, the end of the waiting period. In brief, the *parousia* does in one way what the resurrection did in another way.

> For as in Adam all die, so also in Christ shall all be made alive.
> But each in his own order: Christ, the first fruits, then at his
> parousia those who belong to Christ. Then comes the end, when
> he delivers the kingdom to God the Father after destroying every
> rule and every authority (I Cor. 15:22-24).

The *parousia* marks the end of the age. But it does not happen
until the powers behind the age are destroyed. Obviously, then,
they must not have been annihilated at the resurrection, but only
dethroned. The powers survived to fight another day. But on the
basis of their defeat, their ultimate destruction is a sure thing.
Meanwhile, Christ is now in fact Lord while His enemies pose a
real, but, *as is known only to faith,* eventually futile threat.[44]

The tension between Paul's kerygma of the accomplished victory of Christ at Easter and the hope of the coming victory of
Christ at the *parousia* must give any of his readers pause. An easy
way out is to suppose that at first Paul thought of Christ's coming
as imminent, and therefore thought in terms of a future victory that
was as good as won. Then, as time betrayed these expectations, he

---

[44]Actually, Paul seems sure that the *parousia* is so close that he himself
would live to see it. "We who are alive, who are left at the coming of the
Lord," he writes, "shall not precede those who have fallen asleep" (I Thess.
4:15). Some people had died since the resurrection, and their place in the
Kingdom was a problem for their friends. Paul assures them that people
like himself who will be alive at the *parousia* have no advantage over the
ones who had died in Christ. In another place he says, "We shall not all
sleep"; that is, perhaps Paul and others shall not need to rise from the
dead to meet Christ (I Cor. 15:51). How seriously we need to take these
statements is debatable, for in other instances, such as II Corinthians 5:1
and II Timothy 4:6 ("the time of my departure has come"), he seems to
intuit his own death. Just how Paul thought about the length of time before
the *parousia* is hard to calculate. But, regardless of the calendar, it was
always "at hand." Its assured reality was the one fact in the universe that
called, promised, and judged men's lives.

Still, it must be said that Paul does not talk like one who expected that
there would be a twentieth century after Christ. "Salvation is nearer to us
now than when we first believed," he writes (Rom. 13:11). "I mean,
brethren, the appointed time has grown very short; from now on, let those
who have wives live as though they had none" (I Cor. 7:29). True, he
qualified this intense sense of imminence by reminding the Thessalonians of
certain events that had to happen prior to the *parousia*—for example, the
parousia of the antichrist (II Thess. 2:3). But this was by way of quelling
irresponsible impulses to desert the world prematurely.

came to emphasize the theme of Christ's real, though hidden, victory at the past moment of the resurrection. On this explanation Thessalonians and Corinthians represent the period of Paul's *futurist* kerygma; Ephesians and Colossians, later letters, represent the period of his kerygma of the *parousia* already achieved at Easter. The difficulty with this theory is that the early letters are spotted with references to the present lordship of Christ and the later letters with references to the future (see Eph. 4:30 and Col. 3:4). That Paul's emphasis shifts is undeniable, it seems to me. And it may well be that the delay in Christ's *parousia* led to his stress on the basically triumphal note in Christ's *first* visit. But the problem cannot be resolved satisfactorily by saying that Paul's basic point of view changed.

The fact is that Paul gives no sign of being embarrassed by his double focus. His hope for the future, indeed, is based not on a doubt about the efficiency of Christ's work in the past, but on the conviction that Jesus is indeed Lord and has been so since His elevation to the right hand of God. The reason Paul was so sure about the *parousia* for the future was his conviction that the "appointed time" (II Cor. 6:2), the day of salvation, was already here. Christ is coming—we know—*because* He was victorious over the powers of the past. The reciprocal feeding of both convictions is clear. The change of situation that took place in history and for history at Easter behind the scenes is the basis of hope for change in the future. It does not make the eschatological future irrelevant any more than the hope of the future makes the proclamation of the great event of Easter suspect.[45] But while Paul senses no need of accenting one focus at the cost of the other, his own stress on both leaves us with the problem of relating them. The problem comes down to this: in view of the triumphant revolution in the world situation that took place at the resurrection and in view of the fact that the triumph is still waited for (after two millennia), what is the meaning of the *present time?* We are not asking for a philosophy of history; we are asking for a christological interpretation of the present existence of Christian people.

Had the time been very brief, one might be able to explain it by analogy to contemporary political life. The time between Easter and the *parousia* would be parallel to the time between the

[45]Two recent Dutch works stress this point most effectively. I refer to Berkouwer's *De Wederkomst van Christus,* I (Kampen, 1961), 122ff. and H. Ridderbos's monumental volume *Paulus* (Kampen, 1966), p. 544.

inauguration of a new president and the implementation of his program, the "first hundred days" of a new administration. But if we
take this comparison seriously, we are surely forced to conclude
that Paul's expectations of the finally effective working out of
Christ's victory in the cities and villages of the earth has been
betrayed by the two millennia of ambiguous and frustrating history since the inauguration. Two thousand years seems too long to
fit any "first hundred days" analogy.[46]

The two millennia since Easter confront Situation Christology
with its most disturbing question. If the resurrection took place
not only in but also for history, and if a radical change in situation
was effected by Christ's defeat of the "powers," why do we see so
little of it in actual history? Barth phrases the problem this way:
"How could it be that this event, so laden with incomparable force,
should not yet have by a long way the corresponding total, universal, and definite effect, but that time and world-occurrence in
time should seem to go forward and should still seem to do so even
yet, as if nothing had happened, as if the last and first hour had not
struck, as if Christ were not risen?"[47] Brunner cuts through the
question by saying that we should not look for the effects of the
victory of Christ within our history.

> The cross of Christ is not the absolute turning point simply as an
> historical event. . . . The course of history has been altered, it is
> true, and it is different from what it would have been if this had
> not taken place. But who would assert that the decisive factor in
> this course of history has been Christ? It is quite possible to defend
> the thesis that, historically speaking, Christianity has been a
> fiasco.[48]

A fiasco, indeed! But if we are not to look for the effects of
Christ's victory in history, where then are we to look for them? In

[46]Harvey Cox sidesteps this problem with an old but still ingenious
biblical theology. Looking for a theology to justify Christian acceptance of
revolutionary social change, he finds it in the biblical gospel of the coming
of the Kingdom. He finds a fascinating syntactical parallel between the
biblical proclamation of the *eschaton* and the advent of rapid social change.
This use of the biblical doctrine of the Kingdom—or new creation—is
analogical only; it only illustrates how people ought to look at life during
revolutionary times. Hence, it avoids the problem by throwing the reality
of the new creation out of the picture. See *The Secular City* (New York,
1966).
[47]*Op. cit.*, IV/3, p. 317.
[48]*The Mediator* (London, 1934), p. 504.

what sense was the human situation changed, if not in the sense of
this world's history?[49] Brunner's attitude is parallel to that of the
millennialist. The millennialist tends to have a two-*foci* outlook on the coming of Christ, with little concern for the question
of the time and space in between the *foci*. He looks backward to
the miraculous intervention of Christ's first coming. He then turns
ahead as though the only thing that now matters is the second
coming, when time really begins again. The time between is a long
intermezzo; God's history is sidetracked; it is only a waiting period.
Millennialism must be credited with keeping its perspective on
history. But its deficiency is that it has its eyes only on *future*
history. The evangelical millennialist believes in a Situation Christology, but with the situation being changed only at the future
parousia. For the present, only individuals are changed.

Escape from the tension is provided from the opposite direction
through the idea of "realized eschatology." C. H. Dodd offers this
option. Paul's illusion that Jesus was going to return soon was
blown away by the turn of the years; but the disillusionment only
led him to see the greater depth of meaning in Christ's cross and
resurrection. A less profound man would have been stymied in his
attempts to reconcile the passing of time with the promised return.
Paul, however, began to see that the "end" of things meant much
more than the conclusion of human history. As a naïve Hebrew,
Paul thought in terms of lines of time that began at a point and
ended at a point; but he learned to think more like a Greek—like
Plato, to be specific. Thus, he came to see beginning and end not
in terms of time, but of the fulfillment of design. "The beginning
is not an event in time; the end is not an event in time. The beginning is God's purpose, the end is the fulfillment of His purpose."[50]
So Paul found it, in this frame of mind, fairly easy to adjust his

[49]Rudolf Bultmann makes a pre-theological assumption that no modern man can honestly believe that such a cosmic affair as Paul makes
of Christology is possible. There is no room in our scientifically defined
world structure for the demons that Jesus defeated; there are no "principalities and powers." But there is the human situation. There is
the universal human experience of subjection to a life of anxiety which
results from a deep commitment to things that lie before us, tangible,
visible, and *apparently* controllable. But the fact of experience is that the
human spirit is controlled, not in control, that it is in bondage, not free.
The change in situation did not occur "back there" or "out there," apart
from individual involvement; it occurs only as men decide here and now to
be free.

[50]C. H. Dodd, *History and the Gospel* (London, 1938), p. 171.

thinking to a new dimension of meaning in the cross and resurrection of Christ. They are far from being the "last things" on the agenda of ordinary history; they are nowhere near the "end" on the calendar of time. But they are "end" as far as God's accomplishment of His purpose is concerned. At the resurrection, the final things, the eschatological design of God, was realized.

The question is, however, whether Paul viewed the realization of the whole eschatological intention of God as having been achieved at the death and resurrection of Christ. Did Paul really undergo so remarkable a conversion in the midst of his career as to shift his entire understanding of the course of God's program in the world?[51] Did he really stop hoping for a final and decisive fulfillment of God's purpose in the future? Was his eschatology completely concentrated on the death and resurrection of Christ? If so, our hardest problem is solved. We can say with Dodd that being "in Christ" is a spiritual experience of participation in the power of the risen Christ. Those "in Christ" are in the "new creation" even while, in an ordinary sense, they are in the old creation and the old age. For Christians living in faith the old age is "passed away" in the sense that God's purpose has been fulfilled and they are gradually entering more deeply into that purpose. The trouble is, however, that Paul cannot be shorn of his futurist outlook.[52]

Paul does not force us to choose between a millennialistic futurism and the exclusive present of realized eschatology. The new creation is both future and present. But if this is true, we are left with profound questions. Did Jesus actually win a universally effective victory at the cross? Did He defeat the powers of darkness? Are we actually living in the era of Christ's very real lordship? What is the present situation of history and what is the

[51]*New Testament Studies* (Manchester, 1952), p. 122. Dodd recognizes a hint of the old eschatological pattern coming through in the later Paul, for instance in Romans 2, where Paul is speaking of a coming judgment. Dodd comments: ". . . Paul here has in view the traditional Day of Judgment. . . . This is in accord with the eschatology which primitive Christianity inherited from Judaism, and his Jewish hearers would recognize it at once" (*The Epistle of Paul to the Romans* [London, 1932], p. 33). But this, says Dodd, is only a slight concession to the Hebrew. Actually, in Paul's thought at this time (Romans), the judgment to come was only an extension of the judgment that was realized in Christ (*ibid.*).

[52]N. Q. Hamilton criticizes Dodd's view from a similar standpoint. *The Holy Spirit and Eschatology in Paul* (Edinburgh, 1957), pp. 53ff.

present situation for the Christian community? What is the meaning of the present time for Christian people?

For Paul, tomorrow is the day of salvation because today is the time of salvation. Paul does not look ahead because today is empty of meaning. Tomorrow is full of hope because today's *reality* assures him that tomorrow's reality means the "new creation" in which Christ is all in all.

In short, the present reality is the reality of union with Christ. And union with Christ is the experience of people who are introduced into the new age, with Christ as Lord. The remainder of this book attempts to grope inside the mysteries that the idea of union with Christ contains. Groping is the best we can do, but perhaps we will be able to lay our hands on at least some of the outlines of this enormous reality.

Chapter Two

Christ and the Spirit

Paul's good news was that a specific individual, Jesus of Nazareth, did something to open a new route for human history and to change the human situation. Both the actor and the action are crucial to Paul. He who did something for us was a concrete person in all the "out thereness" of His unique individuality. He was born at a point in the distant past, lived His life in the provincial limits of Galilee and Judea, was hanged on a cross, was brought to life again, but went into a realm of existence removed from us by a gulf even wider than the gulf between our present and His past. This is the man with whom the apostle says we are united in an association more intimate and basic than any association we can have with our contemporaries in our world.

Paul was the apostle of that Jesus Christ in the new age He introduced by His death and resurrection. Paul's message was Christ crucified. The object of his preaching was to summon men to a decision about Jesus. The content of the tradition that was passed down through the history of the Church was Jesus Christ and His works. The new creation was established "in Christ." But Paul was the apostle of Christ in the new age of the Spirit.

Christ is the content of preaching, but the Spirit makes the preaching work. Christ establishes the new creation, but the Spirit dominates it within history. Christ calls men into union with Himself, but the Spirit creates an entrance into men's lives. Christ is the cornerstone of the Church, but the Spirit is its mortar. The head of the body is Christ, but it is the Spirit who keeps the body alive.

The Spirit is the living contact between the victorious Jesus and all who are united with Him. There is a Spirit of Jesus Christ. Between Him and us there is no gulf in time or space. But if this Spirit does bring us into so intimate an association with Jesus

43

Christ that Paul can speak of Christ being in us, we must assume
that He is Himself on an even more intimate basis with Christ. For
it is He who "brings" Christ over the gulf in time and space.

A few notes from Paul may serve to underscore what has just
been said. After His resurrection, says Paul, Jesus Christ, the
Second Adam, "became a life-giving Spirit" (I Cor. 15:45).
Whatever weight is given to the verb "became," it is clear that it
comes close to identifying the risen Jesus with the divine Spirit. In
a verse that has proved troublesome to interpreters, Paul says,
"The Lord is the Spirit" (II Cor. 3:17); had he said, "The Lord
sends the Spirit" or "The Spirit is divine," he would have made
things simpler. But we have to deal with what he actually says.
Another problem is the interweaving of Spirit and Christ in Romans 8. In the span of a few sentences Paul has "Spirit in us" and
"Christ in us" as well as "Spirit of God" and "Spirit of Christ."
So, brushing aside all nuances of context and grammar, we can
say this much without further examination: Spirit and Christ are
inseparable. *How* they are united is another matter.

The question of this chapter is this: what is the relationship between the Spirit and the Christ? If this question seems abstract, we
should add that it is a core issue of Christian reality and existence.
We will follow the same method here as in several other chapters,
taking a look first at two different ways of answering the question
in the past; then looking at some key sentences in Paul's letters;
and, finally, drawing some conclusions.

A. TWO THEOLOGIES OF THE SPIRIT AND CHRIST

1. The Spirit as the Evaporated Christ

About the turn of the century, the comparative study of religions
seemed to open the door to an exciting new possibility for understanding Paul's mystical theology. The chief concern here was for
Paul's doctrine of union with Christ, which to some scholars never
was really coordinated with the rest of the gospel of Jesus. When
scholars discovered certain oriental religious tracts that contained
mystical writings from a period roughly the same as Paul's, they
thought they had found the key to Paul's own mystical religion.[1]

---

[1]One set of tracts, called the Hermetic writings, probably came from the
early years of the Christian period as revelations from one Hermes
Trismegistos, an Egyptian god of revelation. One of the tracts in particular,

Now oriental mysticism could not tolerate dependence on specific and real historical events or attachment to concrete historical personalities. The one thing needed was to escape the specific and the concrete things of history and to be immersed into the divine life. The new birth of an individual was secured by absorption into the universal divine spirit. According to students of comparative religion, Paul borrowed from oriental mysticism and gave the divine spirit the names and character of Jesus but abandoned for the most part allegiance to the historical Jesus as a requisite for an experience of union with the Spirit. In this interpretation of Paul's theology, then, Christ was evaporated.

Scholars who followed this line seemed sure that Paul's doctrine of our union with Christ was conceivable only as a radical turning away from the concrete individual, Jesus. Mysticism and history were incompatible as foundations of religion. The trend continued, though less radically, with impetus from Wilhelm Bousset, whose book, *Kyrios Christos* (Göttingen, 1926), examined the shift in Christian thought from Christ *Jesus* to Christ the *Lord*. Bousset maintained that it was Paul's concept of Christ as Lord that opened the way to a substitution of an ephemeral and universal Spirit for Jesus.

The young Gentile Church had to meet keen competition from the cultic centers of Hellenistic religions. The competition focused on *experience*. In the Greek cults, the devotees could boast of exhilarating "trips" outside themselves that transformed their very beings—at least while the trip lasted. Each center of worship had its own lord or *kyrios*; he was not a specific or real historical person, but a localized form of the universal spirit. When the novice had arrived at a deep enough level of understanding, he was initiated into the experience of the divine lord; he was swept

called *Poimandres*, seems to provide a beautiful parallel with Paul's mystical doctrine. R. Reitzenstein, who did much to edit, interpret, and publicize the Hermetic literature, had, of course, to ignore the historical and eschatological theology of Paul to give the impression that mysticism was the only thing that finally dominated the apostle's mind. For the literature, see R. Reitzenstein, *Die hellenistischen Mysterienreligionen nach Ihre, Grundgedanken und Wirkungen* (Leipzig, 3rd ed., 1927), and *Poimandres* (Leipzig, 1904). See also Deissner, *Paulus und die Mystik seiner Zeit* (1920). For criticism of the thesis, see A. Schweitzer, *The Mysticism of Paul the Apostle* (New York, 1955), pp. 26ff.; J. Gresham Machen, *The Origin of Paul's Religion* (Grand Rapids, 1947), esp. the final chapter; H. Ridderbos, *Paulus en Jesus* (Kampen, 1952), pp. 83ff.; A. Wikenhauser, *Pauline Mysticism* (New York, 1960), pp. 163ff.

up ecstatically into the spirit and became one with the *kyrios*. It was tough competition for the Church; how can a Presbyterian preaching service compete with an LSD session?

The Christians, it is contended, took up the challenge. They claimed to have wonderful experiences in the spirit too. Without meaning to downgrade devotion to Jesus of Nazareth, they did emphasize the claim that real worship was attained when a person gained entrée into the life of the Spirit. They too had their lord. But their Christian attachment to Jesus and their ecstatic experience of the Spirit stayed at loose ends, if not at odds with each other.

This is, Bousset says, where Paul's creative genius came in. He could recognize a valid religious experience, and he set out to baptize it into the service of the gospel. First of all, he said, this "lord" is none other than Jesus; our Jesus is the real "lord." So thereafter Jesus became the Lord Jesus, and the Greek *kyrios* was assimilated into the Christian religion. But this only began the adulteration of Christian attachment to the Jesus of Nazareth. Secondly, Paul said, the Spirit whom you experience is the Spirit of Jesus the Lord. The thought was finally crystallized when he made the identification complete: "The Lord is the Spirit" (II Cor. 3:17).

But for this, the proclamation of Jesus as the specific, concrete individual who called men into the rigors of discipleship had to be dispensed with. Paul's achievement was to take Christ out of the cabined quarters of historical episodes and set Him in the broad expanse of the universal spirit. That he did this while ascribing moral character to the Spirit, as though the Spirit had the moral influence of Jesus' own personality, was Paul's enduring contribution to religion. "This remarkable mingling of abstraction and personality, the connection of a religious principle with a person who had walked on earth and had here suffered death, is a phenomenon of peculiar power and originality."[2] This may be true; but the fact remains that Bousset's Paul transformed the risen Jesus into Spirit. Christ was evaporated. The locus of all this is

[2]W. Bousset, *Kyrios Christos,* p. 113. The whole matter of the relationship between the New Testament use of the title *kyrios* and the Greek use is terribly complex. The Greeks had no single function for the title, but a variety of functions. And so does the Bible, for that matter. But when Paul said "Lord Jesus," he meant to ascribe lordship to the specific person called Jesus of Nazareth. See Foerster, in Kittel, *Theological Dictionary of the New Testament,* III (Grand Rapids, 1965), 1039ff., for a study of both Hellenistic and biblical uses of the term.

Paul's theology; one need not assume that Bousset thought it actually happened to Jesus.

Adolf Deissmann had another way of treating the same matter. Deissmann, I think, supposed that the evaporation of Christ into Spirit took place, not merely in Paul's thought, but in reality. Paul, he said, came to his doctrine by way of his encounter with the risen Jesus on the Damascus road; he did not borrow it from the Greeks. Here, in his own experience, he came to know that the exalted Lord was the Lord always at hand, present and ready to enter into vital union with the person ready to receive Him.

The combination of the lordship of Christ above with the mystical experience of Him below is possible because Christ has become Spirit. "The living Christ," says Deissmann, "is the Pneuma. As Pneuma, as Spirit, the living Christ is not far off, above clouds and stars, but near, present on our poor earth where He dwells and rules in His own."[3] Paul never managed a clear explanation of *how* Christ became Spirit. He was not a theologian. But when he did think about it, he "probably thought of some light, ethereal form of existence, such as he attributed to God. But there is no binding definition."[4] Christ has become a "reality and power of the present, an 'energy', whose life-giving powers are daily expressing themselves. . . ."[5] Instead of a mere historical personage, Jesus has become a "reality and power of the present."[6] Here again we have the classic dilemma. How can Paul's doctrine of mystical union with Christ be related to the gospel of the historical Jesus? According to the thesis under consideration, it cannot really be related: "mystical communion with the Spirit-Christ transforms all that we call the 'historical Christ' . . . into a present reality."[7] An ordinary person, plying his trade, suffering his daily frustrations, groping for some meaning and perspective in his dull existence, is given the chance to experience transcendent power through living contact with the Spirit who carries in His breath the moral influence of Jesus of Nazareth. Jesus is gone. Now we have the Spirit. The secret is a mysterious metamorphosis; Christ has been evaporated.[8]

[3]*Paul, A Study in Social and Religious History* (New York, 1957), p. 138.
[4]*Ibid.*, p. 142.
[5]*Ibid.*, p. 136.
[6]*Ibid.*
[7]*Ibid.*, p. 143.
[8]For further discussion of Spirit Christologies, see Additional Note 3, pp. 258-259.

2. The Spirit as the Creative Agent of Christ

John Calvin's thought is an example of a way of thinking about the Lord and the Spirit[9] that maintains the specific identity of Jesus at all cost. He offers a useful example because one of his major premises is that the ascended Lord Jesus is none other than Jesus of Nazareth, glorified, but localized and limited as is proper to a human being. It is this human Christ who is, by means of the Spirit, present here and now in the believer.

When Jesus ascended He left the earth and went to another place.[10] He is separated from us by whatever kind of gulf that divides our kind of reality from His mode of being at "the right hand of God." Jesus is there and not here. He did not, Calvin claims, become ubiquitous. He certainly was not transformed into an ephemeral spirit.[11] Yet "all that He suffered and accomplished for us" must become ours if we are to be helped by Him at all. He saved us by what He *did*. But what He offers us from "out there" is Himself; the benefits of His actions are now inseparable from His person. His benefits are not located in some heavenly reservoir alongside of Jesus; they *are* Himself.

The Spirit is the living bond between Him and us. He takes what is Christ and brings it "down" to us.[12] The Spirit is always pictured in dynamic terms. He is not like a pipeline through which some material called life is poured to us at the other end. He is always a living, dynamic creator of life; He brings us to our spiritual senses, opens our eyes to the reality of Christ, nourishes our faith, disciplines us, and above all, engrafts us into the living Christ. The dynamic, functional way in which Calvin thinks of the Spirit is apparent in his discussion of the Trinity. Even though he takes up the subject independently from the history of redemption and distinct from his discussion of the work of the Spirit in the human experience of salvation, he speaks of the Spirit mostly in terms of what the Spirit *does*. That Calvin thought of the Spirit as a distinct

[9]B. B. Warfield called Calvin the "theologian of the Holy Spirit" (*Calvin and Augustine* [Philadelphia, 1956], pp. 485f.). Brunner said that the doctrine of union with Christ is the "center of all calvinistic thinking" (*Vom Werk des Heiligen Geist* [Tübingen, 1935], p. 38). One work on the subject of Calvin's doctrine of the Spirit that should be mentioned here is a study by Werner Krusche, *Das Wirken des Heiligen Geistes nach Calvin* (Göttingen, 1957). It is thorough and has a splendid bibliography.

[10]See *Commentary on Acts* 3:21; *Institutes* iv.17.26.

[11]See *Institutes* iv.17.32.

[12]*Institutes* iii.1.1-3.

subsistence within the Trinity is clear enough.[13] But a modern reader must remember that Calvin did not hold a modern, psychologically defined notion of a person. We moderns cannot think of a person without thinking of an individual center of consciousness; and so the traditional statement of the Trinity always takes us to the edge of tritheism. Calvin thought of the three subsistences as personal, but not as persons in the modern sense.

Calvin assigns to the Spirit the power and efficacy of all divine action: ". . . to the Father is attributed the beginning of activity and the fountain and wellspring of all things; to the Son, wisdom, counsel, and the ordered disposition of all things; but to the Spirit is assigned the power and efficacy of that activity."[14] All of God's works are the Spirit's works in the sense that it is the Spirit who makes the divine decisions effective on earth. The Spirit never carries on a private enterprise. He is the power that brings to a fruitful end the work of God. The Spirit *is* God at work, sustaining life, developing God's creation, keeping the history of men from lapsing into demonic nihilism. There is no doubt that Calvin's thought is wholly in line with the Church's doctrine of the Trinity. Still, the Spirit is not defined as a person in the modern sense. He is God in effective and imminent action in the affairs of man and history. What is interesting is that, without notable zeal for precise definitions in the matter, Calvin tends to look at the Spirit's relationship to the glorified Savior in essentially the same way as he does the Spirit's relation to God the Creator.[15]

A clear picture of Calvin's view is hard to come by. Sometimes,

[13]*Institutes* i.13.17. But the words he uses to show that the Spirit is a distinct entity are interesting: "Christ implies the distinction of the Holy Spirit from the Father when he says that the Holy Spirit proceeds from the Father. He implies the distinction of the Holy Spirit from himself as he calls the Spirit 'another,' as when he announces that he will send another Comforter. . . ." That the Spirit "proceeds" from the Father would show His dependence, but not necessarily His distinction as a person. And that the Spirit is "another Comforter" from Jesus does not yet prove His distinctness from the eternal Son.

[14]*Institutes* i.13.18.

[15]In the inner life of the Trinity, the Spirit seems especially involved with the unity of the three subsistences. Calvin calls Him the *communis* between Christ and the Father (*Institutes* i.13.23) and also the *conjunctus* between the eternal Word and the Father (iii.1.2). The entire subject is very complex. A way must be found to avoid the heresy of modalism, which subverts a genuine Trinity, while at the same time avoiding the tritheism that modern definitions of "person" tend to suggest. Calvin's problems in finding this *via media* are amply discussed by Krusche, *op. cit.*

he seems to view the Spirit as the effective power of Christ as Mediator. Writing about why the Spirit is called the Spirit of Christ, he says,

> He is called the Spirit of Christ, not only because the eternal word of God is united with the name Spirit as the Father, but also with respect to his character as Mediator. For if he had not been provided with this power, His coming would have been of no value to us (*Institutes* iii.1.2).

If Christ's work as Mediator is to be effective *for us*, He must have "this power." The power referred to is the ability to unite Himself to us in spite of His human limitations, and this is ascribed specifically to the Spirit.

But since the Spirit can hardly be thought of as merely another way of making ubiquitous Christ's humanity—a notion Calvin adamantly rejected—there was a tendency to identify Him vaguely with Christ's divinity. While Christ "is removed from us in bodily presence, he fills all things by the power of his Spirit. Wherever the *right hand of God,* which embraces heaven and earth, is displayed, Christ is spiritually present by his boundless power."[16] Christ is present by means of His Spirit; but the Spirit now seems to be the same as the right hand of *God.* To this Calvin adds: "As his body was raised up above all heavens, so his power and energy were diffused and spread beyond all the bounds of heaven and earth."[17] How are we to take "power" and "energy" here? Is this Calvin's way of saying that the presence of the Spirit is actually Christ's presence in effective action, as the Spirit was the Father's "virtue and efficacy"?

Calvin is sure that union with Christ is a union with His whole self, especially His humanity. Equally evident is the fact that Calvin interprets the Spirit as the bearer of Christ. But when he faces the possibility of an essential identity of Christ with the Spirit, he stops short. In his comment on Paul's dramatic identification of the Lord and the Spirit (II Cor. 3:17), Calvin says that Paul

---

[16]*Commentary on Ephesians* 4:10. The same overlapping between the divinity and the Spirit of Christ is found in the Heidelberg Catechism. Question 47 asks whether Christ, since the ascension, is not after all with us to the end of the world. The answer is that "with respect to His human nature, He is no more on earth; but with respect to His Godhead, majesty, grace, and Spirit, He is at no time absent from us." Are "Godhead, majesty, grace" different from Spirit?

[17]*Institutes* ii.16.14.

"simply points out His (that is, the Spirit's) office." That is, the Spirit is identified with the risen Mediator in *function*, but not in being.

We have not formulated a logically precise statement in all this. Perhaps, however, a summary of what has been said will be helpful. The Spirit is in Calvin a distinct subsistence within the godhead. In spite of his stress on the function of the Spirit as the effective power of God, Calvin gives no hint of avoiding a genuine doctrine of the Trinity. Jesus Christ is the mediator, limited and confined in His humanity. Yet, He is united to us here on earth. That is, Christ is present, and it is in Spirit that He is present. Herein lies the problem. Is the Spirit the same as Christ's ever present divinity? Is He the effective power of Christ, a power to effect things on earth even while He is personally absent? Or is the Spirit the administrative assistant to Jesus Christ, distinct from Christ personally, yet subordinated wholly to Him in function?

Most likely, Calvin meant the last option to be his real thought on the matter. But, always, he wants us to understand that the Christ with whom we are united is not an ersatz Christ. He is present. But He is spiritually present and spiritually at work. He is accounted for by the Spirit. Beyond this Calvin does not go. What we are sure of is that he does not allow the crucified Savior to be evaporated as Spirit. The implication is that he wants to interpret the Spirit, *functionally,* in terms of the total mediatorial work of Jesus Christ.

We must proceed, I think, in this direction. But we should first consider at some length the material in Paul's writings to see if it can take us any further.[18]

[18]The Anglo-Catholic theologian L. S. Thornton develops his doctrine of the Spirit in a way surprisingly similar to Calvin's. He calls the Holy Spirit the alter ego of Christ (*The Common Life in the Body of Christ* [Westminster, 1946], p. 347). This is meant to say that the Spirit retains His identity as Third Person; Thornton makes the Trinity out to be more of a social relationship between three distinct entities than does Calvin. But in terms of *function,* according to Thornton, the Spirit is at least indistinguishable from, while not identical with, Christ. Thornton tries his hand at assigning distinctions of function: The Lord is the content of the new life, while the Spirit is the *creative source* of that life (*The Incarnate Lord* [Westminster, 1929], p. 178). This is a fairly good distinction, though it does not tell us *how* Jesus Christ is actually the content of the life. In another place, Thornton calls the Spirit the "quickening cause" and Christ the "effect of the quickening" (*ibid.*, p. 324). This distinction is possible only if one has a rather specific understanding of what Christ's presence in us is. Thornton tends to think of this in terms of a substance-like presence

B. JESUS AND THE SPIRIT

Jesus was never without the Spirit. He was not born without the Spirit; He never spoke, or thought, or acted without the Spirit. This much is clear from the evangelists. But it is just as clear that He was not identified as the Spirit; He is one person, the Spirit is another.

By a creative act, the Spirit prepared the way for Christ's human existence. Christ was conceived by the Holy Spirit (Matt. 1:20). The Spirit qualified Him and presided at His inauguration into His public career (Mark 1:10). The Spirit led Him into the wilderness, where He was tempted to defect to the enemy (Mark 1:12) and where He made it decisively clear that the issue between Him and the "powers" was nonnegotiable. It was through the power of the Spirit that He demonstrated the character of His kingdom by miraculous signs (Matt. 12:28). It was through the Spirit that He gave His followers the mandate to represent Him as firsthand witnesses of His resurrection (Acts 1:2). In sum, it was the Spirit who endorsed, qualified, and energized Him to bring in the Kingdom of God (Acts 10:38).

Always, however, the Spirit was an auxiliary. The Savior is the acting subject. He is the concrete man, acting as a personally responsible agent. What Jesus could have done without the Spirit, simply as the Incarnate One, is a pointless question. What freedom He had to resist and frustrate the Spirit is something we cannot tell; that it was *in* freedom that He cooperated with the Spirit is, however, undeniable. That He never did anything without the Spirit is clear. Like the men who held up Moses' arms while he prayed, the Spirit is always present with Jesus, not as a substitute but as an assistant. That Jesus needed the Spirit is a wonderful attestation to His genuine humanity.

Now and then Jesus seems to stress the difference between Himself and the Spirit. Anyone, He says, who speaks against Himself can be forgiven. But anyone who blasphemes the Holy Spirit has set himself outside the area of forgiveness (Luke 12:10; Mark 3:28ff.). Anyone who willfully persists in ascribing the works of

---

of Christ's divine life. In this sense, the Spirit on behalf of the person of Jesus Christ infuses something of Christ's life-stuff into our spiritual depths. Understandably, Thornton attributes the work of "infusion" to the Spirit, and thus somewhat more clearly than Calvin can, keeps the Spirit ontologically distinct from Jesus Christ.

Jesus Christ to the powers of the enemy of Jesus Christ has eliminated himself from the Kingdom of God. He is "in danger of eternal damnation" (Mark 3:29), which suggests that there is always the possibility of change. At any rate, Jesus points to the Spirit as the source of His power, distinct from Himself.

At the close of His ministry, the words of Jesus—especially as recalled by John—shift their emphasis. Jesus is leaving, but only in one sense. In another sense He is staying. The marvelous intertwining of "leaving" and "staying" in the closing chapters of John anticipate the outlook of Paul. Jesus is going away to prepare another place; but He is going to come back again later (John 14:1-3). So on the one hand He says, just a little while "and you will see me no more" (John 16:16), and on the other hand, "I will pray to the Father, and he will give you another Counselor, to be with you forever" (John 14:16). Jesus is leaving and the Spirit is replacing Him. Still, He says, "I will not leave you comfortless: *I* will come to you" (John 14:18). When He comes, the world will not see Him, for the world has eyes only for appearance and does not see things as they really are. But He will come, not only at the end, but at the beginning. His coming and the Spirit's coming are indistinguishable.

When Jesus promises the Spirit and His own presence, He must be saying the same thing that Matthew reports: "Behold, I am with you even to the end of the age" (Matt. 28:20). And His presence must be seen in the light of this optimistic word: "Be of good cheer, I have overcome the world" (John 16:33). Jesus knew, even before the final encounter, that the tides of human history had made the decisive shift. Before the actual event, He spoke as though He were already the Risen One. And all His allusions to the coming of the Spirit have His victory over the world as their premise and foundation.

C. PAUL'S POINT OF VIEW

We have already discussed two broad options of interpretation. Was Jesus strangely transformed into a diffuse Spirit? Did Paul, in his theology, forget about Jesus "according to the flesh" and concentrate on the Spirit? Is the word "Spirit" merely a personal metaphor that points to the ongoing influence of a Jesus who is dead and gone? Or is the Spirit clearly distinct from the Christ, acting as a separate person who illumines our minds as to the true identity of Jesus; is the Spirit a kind of administrative assistant to

Jesus Christ, working out in the hinterlands while Jesus Christ is aloof in glory? Or is there perhaps another meaning that can be found, one that will do justice to the identity of the Spirit and Christ and still keep the one identity from swallowing the other?

To answer these questions we shall have to examine more closely some of the crucial sentences in Paul.

1. "The Lord is the Spirit" (II Cor. 3:17)

Paul makes this comment in passing, as though his meaning would be perfectly clear. His words are indeed dramatic, but hardly clear. They are especially dramatic to the reader who comes to Paul with his head full of dogmatic definitions, looking for corroboration by canonical proof texts. After all, the Lord is Jesus Christ. The Spirit is the third person of the Holy Trinity. The whole point of trinitarian doctrine is to say that while essentially one, the Spirit, Father, and Son are distinct persons. Now, the Incarnate Son Jesus—whom Paul calls Lord—is said *to be* the Spirit. What are we to make of this development in Paul's thought?

a. The Context

The broad context of Paul's astonishing statement is his indignant defense of the genuineness of his apostolate: his calling, he asserts, is far superior to that of the pseudo-apostles of the subversive Judaizing cult in the Corinthian church. Though at times he seems a little too sensitive about his personal effectiveness, he is not justifying himself; the question is not hinged to his person. His remarks about his own behavior enter in only because he must concede in humility that his personal presence does not match the awesome authority he has as apostle. The real question is one of the legitimacy and superiority of his office. And thereby he introduces a still larger and more important theme.

His office, he contends, is superior to that even of Moses, because he lives and works within a superior era of covenant history. His whole argument hangs on the reality of a *history* of redemption. There is an old covenant and a new covenant, and the latter is incomparably superior to the former. It has a vastly superior glory. It is as different from the old as life is from death, as freedom is from bondage, confidence from fear, or hope from despair. The new has come into the world and has brought the people of God into a new era of history. Paul's apostolate belongs to the later age of covenant history, and for *that* reason it is a superior apostolate.

The new covenant is Christ Jesus. This must be said here by way of anticipating the problem of verse 17. Ingenuously, Paul has had one message for the Corinthians: ". . . what we preach is not ourselves, but Jesus Christ as Lord, with ourselves as your servants for Jesus' sake" (4:5). Jesus is Lord! As Lord He gives the new covenant its meaning, its life, its destiny, its power. The words are important because they pinpoint the identity of the Lord (*kyrios*) as the historical person named Jesus. Paul is convinced that Jesus by His death introduced a new life possibility for all men: ". . . one has died for all; therefore all have died. And he died for all, that those who live might no longer live for themselves but for him who for their sake died and was raised" (5:14, 15).

Paul's stress on the specific Jesus as the Lord of the new covenant and, more explicitly, on Jesus' death and resurrection as the pivotal event of the new covenant, is, of course, related to his message about the new day. "Behold, now is the acceptable time; behold, now is the day of salvation" (6:2). With the eschatological burden of these words, Paul is emphasizing that a new day has dawned, a new age of grace and freedom, and a new time of responsibility. Christ is the dominant person, the founder, the head, the character-giving leader of the new time and the new community formed in it. The new age, in fact, is new creation. The old has passed away. Anyone who is "in Christ" is part of the new reality (II Cor. 5:17).

The single most important factor of this broader context is the fact that Paul is concerned with the history of salvation. And the meaning of the change in this history is centered in Jesus of Nazareth, who has become the Lord of a new creation. This must be remembered as we now consider the more immediate context.

Paul makes the claim "The Lord is the Spirit" in a chapter devoted to the superiority of the new covenant to the old. The new covenant is the "dispensation of the Spirit" (3:8). The acts of the Spirit give character to the new era. So, in this brief look at the immediate context of verse 17, we shall try to distinguish the excellence of the new covenant in the terms that Paul lays down: the new covenant as the time of the Spirit.

The contrast between the new and the old covenant is a contrast between the Spirit and the "written code." The Spirit gives life. The "written code" kills. The contrast is absolute. This, by the way, underscores, again, the superiority of Paul's apostolate—it is authenticated by the life-giving Spirit (3:6). There are other contrasts, but this one is the most crucial.

What Paul means by the "written code" is not hard to see. He means the sentences of the law written on tablets, the law given at Sinai. But it is this law *in its function* within the Judaic community that Paul is talking about. The law is the shadow cast over the entire old covenant. It is the constitution around which human life was organized in the old dispensation. It is the standard by which human life is measured and judged. It is the means by which a proper status with and in the Israelite community is attained. And for this reason, the dispensation under the law was a "dispensation of death, carved in letters of stone" (3:7). For no man can be *helped* by this means.

In the new covenant, God creates and sustains His community not by an external code, but by the dynamic presence of Himself as Spirit. The new covenant has arrived, Paul insists, and the confirmation of his own service within it is the experience of the Spirit in the community of the covenant. The people in this very community are examples of what the prophets envisioned as happening to people. They are attestations, written "not with ink, but with the Spirit of the living God, not on tablets of stone but on tablets of human hearts" (3:3). The Spirit is the effective agent of God in the new order of life. The new order is so dominated by the action of the Spirit that it can be called the "order of the Spirit." What the law could not do in the old covenant, the Spirit accomplished in the new.

The black-and-white contrast between the Spirit and the law is accounted for by seeing each as the prevailing and dominating power in the life of the two communities. The law dominated the old covenant as the immanent, constitutional authority giving the community its moral character. Moreover, it epitomized the hopes and the claims that the community had as the people of God. The Spirit plays the same general role in the new community. He dominates life, gives it its moral tone, and provides it with both its hope and its claim as the community of God. But unlike the law, He is adequate to this function. He is not powerless to transform the community inwardly. He is the life-giving Spirit. In short, Spirit and law are contrasted not simply as person and letter but as the dominating forces of moral renewal and moral sterility in the two communities.

Now, however, it must again be recalled that Jesus Christ is the head of the new order. It was Christ, after all, who did in the likeness of sinful flesh what the law could not do (Rom. 8:3). And Paul himself had called Christ Jesus the "life-giving Spirit." Here, too, he refers to the people as "a letter *from Christ*" that was written by the Spirit (II Cor. 3:3). There is no contradiction, no tension here. While everywhere in II Corinthians Paul asserts the preeminence of Christ, he insists here that the immanent action of God within the community of the new covenant is the action of His Spirit. As the prophets said, in the new covenant God's Spirit prevails. But now it is clear that that Spirit is the Spirit of Christ.[19]

It seems to me that this rather tortuous examination of the context of Paul's statement has established the following propositions:

(1) Paul's line of thought is historical: the present era is superior to the old.

(2) Jesus Christ is the head of the new era; the new age was created by His death and resurrection and is the age of His lordship.

(3) The Spirit is the prevailing and character-giving power of the new era; it is the Spirit who writes the law on men's hearts and brings dead men to life.

(4) These objective facts about the new covenant form the basis for the superiority of Paul's apostolate: he is a minister of this new covenant.

These propositions give us warrant for at least some general conclusion about the relationship between the Lord and the Spirit.

b. The Meaning of the Statement "The Lord is the Spirit"

(1) Who is "the Lord" in the sentence? Interpreters have sometimes thought Him to be the Jehovah of Exodus 34. The stress would then be that the Spirit of the new covenant is really the Spirit of Jehovah and that there is no contradiction between the Old Testament and the New. But Paul's whole argument is not to show the identity but the contrast between the covenants. He wants to say that Israel has been brought to a stage which is new in history, a stage calling for a new decision, a moment when they are now confronted specifically with the claims of Jesus, the surprising Messiah. The only real help that we find in reading "the Lord" as Jehovah is that it avoids confrontation with the difficult statement identifying Jesus with the Spirit.

But the Lord is Jesus. This is the core of Paul's message here and everywhere. The Lord in verse 17 is the concrete individual

---

[19]For a further development of the context see Additional Note 4, pp. 260-261.

Jesus who died and rose again and is now Lord of "all things."
This identifiable and concrete person is the Spirit.

(2) Who is "the Spirit"? A plausible answer is that Spirit refers
to the content of the Old Testament. Paul would then be saying
that, once the veil is removed from its eyes, Israel would recognize
that Christ is the hidden content of the law. Paul would be con-
tending for a spiritual or christological intent of the Old Testament
over against the literal, legalistic intent.[20] But Paul has not been
trying to show the basic unity of the two covenants; he has been
stressing their differences. He is not merely saying that the Jews
have misunderstood the old covenant; he is saying that the old
covenant is in fact inferior to the new. What he is stressing is the
new event, the new age, and the new manner of life in the Spirit
that arrived at Christ's death and resurrection. And he scorns the
Judaizer for hanging on to the old when it has been outmoded by
Christ.

If we approach Paul's statement with an abstract definition of
the Trinity in mind, we shall have trouble with the copulative "is."
We can hardly assume that the Spirit, on one hand, is a person
distinct from the Son and then suppose that Paul is being literal
in identifying Him with the Lord. We should have to conclude
that Paul has a kind of teamwork in mind, the Lord and the Spirit
striving together to the same end.

The answer to the question of who the Spirit is must be in keeping with the movement of redemptive history. A new phase has
come into the history of God with His people. It is the phase of
the Spirit. Paul is telling the Corinthians that the Spirit in whom
they have life and freedom is Christ's means of reaching out to
them. While the Lord is "out there"—however that may be conceived in our spatial imagery—He is also here, present in action
within the Christian community. The Spirit creates our opportunity
to experience the Christ and His work. We need not be touchy
about the Trinity. Paul is not talking abstract theology; he is
characterizing the life of the new covenant as being the life dominated by the Spirit who is none other than Christ in His continuing
actions on earth.

This fits the entire picture. Christ is Lord. He dominates the

---

[20]This view has notable supporters: among others, John Calvin, *Com-
mentary on II Corinthians* 3:17; C. H. Dodd, *History and the Gospel*
(London, 1938), p. 56; and F. W. Grosheide, *Commentary on the First
Epistle to the Corinthians* (Grand Rapids, 1953), pp. 150ff.

new era even as He began it. But the work of reconciliation and sanctification goes on in the new age. It is still His work. But the Spirit does it, as it were. The Spirit at work is the Lord at work. The Spirit is the Christ imminent. And for this reason, the Spirit—as we shall see next—is the down payment on the life that is to come, when Christ—not the Spirit as such—shall be all and in all.

History, plus experience. A new day has come—the day of the new covenant. A new experience has been given—the writing of the law within the heart. The new day is the day of the Spirit's presence. The new experience is the experience of new power through the Spirit. But the new day and the new experience are also, decisively, the day and experience of the Lord Jesus Christ. The experience of the Spirit is the experience with the Lord. In the new age, the Lord is the Spirit.

2. The Spirit of Resurrection

Since the work of God takes place in history, it has turning points. Decisive events signal the course and method of God's reconciling action. History is one thing after another, with certain things making more difference than other things do, and with one thing making all the difference in the world—the resurrection of Jesus Christ. For the resurrection turned history around and became the new magnetic pole in the human situation. But what is sometimes forgotten or, at least, underestimated is that it was also the turning point in the life of Jesus Christ. The crucial before and after is marked off for the Savior by what happened in Joseph's garden when no one on earth was looking.

What happened to Jesus is intimately associated with the Spirit. The Spirit seems to be woven into the fabric of all the acts of God in history. So at the resurrection. We will content ourselves with two Pauline passages that indicate how completely Christ and the Spirit are collaborators. The first is Romans 1:4: ". . . and designated Son of God in power according to the Spirit of holiness by his resurrection from the dead, Jesus Christ our Lord. . . ."

Before saying this about the resurrection, Paul reminds us of the status of Jesus up to that point. He was a man, a Jew, "descended from David according to the flesh" (Rom. 1:3). This is the situation before the turning point of Easter. Paul is not telling us that before the resurrection Jesus was a mere man. He is locating Jesus in the history of redemption. This was the time before the time of power; it was the time of weakness, the time of concealment, the time of striving before the time of crowning.

By the resurrection Jesus was designated "Son of God in power." His status and role changed. The word "power" suggests the meaning of the change. Paul is not telling us that Jesus became the Son of God after His resurrection; the whole gospel of the entire life and work of Christ was the "gospel concerning His (God's) Son" (Rom. 1:3). But the Son of God incarnate entered a new phase of His own history. Now, He was designated the Son of God *in power*. Now the robe of weakness is shed and the time of concealment is past. The new age has broken through and the new epoch of human life begun. Now, Jesus Christ is Son of God not in weakness, but in open power. This is to say that Jesus Christ is Lord (1:4).

Why does Paul say that Jesus was designated as Lord *"according to the Spirit of holiness"*? The phrase seems to form a parallel with the preceding sentence. As He was Son of David according to the flesh, so He is Lord (Son of God-in-power) according to the Spirit. His new post-resurrection status is tied in with a new relationship to the Spirit. Jesus was constantly companioned by the Spirit during His earthly life. But after the resurrection, the relationship is something other than that of a partnership. The Spirit is indispensable to Christ's effective lordship, to *being* Son of God-in-power. Christ could not become nor effectively act as Lord without the Spirit.

The phrase is hard to translate. The New English Bible tries it this way: He was designated Son of God in power "on the level of the spirit—the Holy Spirit." The translators are reading Paul as saying that on the level of the flesh, He was merely the Son of David; on the level of Spirit, He is Lord.

As flesh, which is to say, in weakness, subject to death and judgment, the Son of God was designated the Son of David. As Spirit, the Son of God was designated Lord over death and of judgment. In both situations—flesh and Spirit—the Son of God was man. But in one situation He was under the law and judgment. In the other situation He (the man Jesus) became Lord of freedom and grace. The Spirit makes the crucial difference.

But Paul faces us with a still more remarkable tie-in between the Spirit and the resurrection turning point in Jesus' history. He says: "The last Adam became a life-giving Spirit" (I Cor. 15:45). The sentence can never be understood by itself, apart from the history of salvation and its decisive turning point. In the light of everything else we know, we must assume that the last Adam *became* something at and after the resurrection.

Here Paul draws a line between Adam and Christ. Adam stands for the origin and kind of psychic body we now have. He is a created being, perishable, weak, physical. Paul does not say that Adam became this kind of being *after* the fall: indeed, the allusion is to creation. God breathed life into Adam and he became, therewith, a psychic, living creature. But Adam does in fact also stand for the fallen and condemned race. He is the prototype, the theological origin of man's death-destined life. He, as the phrase now goes, is the "corporate personality" of the old race of men. As psychic and physical, Adam represents ordinary life; as fallen, doomed life. But he has been replaced. There is a new Adam and, with Him, a new race. There is a new Adam, and, with Him, a new life.

The Second Adam is the prototype of a new kind of life, a life begun at His resurrection. But the parallel stops here. For the Second Adam does not simply become a creature with a higher kind of life. He is not simply spiritual in contrast to Adam's psychic life. He is a life-giving Spirit. He becomes a life-giving Spirit at the resurrection. This gives Him not only a new status, but a new power.

The power that Paul attributes to the risen Lord is the power everywhere ascribed to the Spirit. In the Old Testament, the Spirit is He who broods over creation and brings forth life from chaos. God withdraws His spirit and living flesh fades as grass (Psa. 104:29). He sends out His Spirit and the dry bones come alive (Ezek. 37). It is the Spirit, says Jesus, who gives life (John 6:63). The letter kills, but the Spirit gives life (II Cor. 3:6). Now, says Paul, Jesus Christ, at the turning point of God's saving action, assumed these life-giving activities of the Spirit. He *became* the life-giving Spirit.

The sentence could perhaps be read this way: "The risen Jesus is the source of the resurrection life." So, as far as His power is concerned, He is what the Spirit has always been. He, in action, becomes the Spirit. The new epoch is the time of Jesus Christ. But it is equally the time of the Spirit. And as far as our life in Christ is concerned, there is no difference. The Spirit is now the personal power of Jesus Christ extended. Christ now is able, because of the Spirit, to extend His reach, the power of His lordship, without limit. The Spirit is now, in the functional sense, Christ in the personal extension of His creative power.[21]

[21]N. Q. Hamilton makes a very valuable contribution to this subject. See his *The Holy Spirit and Eschatology in Paul* (Edinburgh, 1957).

3. Life in the Spirit and in Christ

The reality of union with Jesus Christ is as broad and deep as
life. It is not limited to fragments of experience. It defines the
whole of life. It is a present fact and a future goal; it is a reality
and a vision; it is accomplished here and now and it is held out as
the climax of our future. But whether fact or goal, it is a reality
that reaches into every nook and cranny of life.

The phrase "in Christ" is a hint of how wide and deep the
concept is, of how completely a man is involved in union with
Christ. But what is fascinating here is that the same totality of
involvement is expressed in terms of the Spirit. We are not only
"in Christ" but are "in the Spirit."

Probably the most striking passage is Romans 8:9-10: "But you
are not in the flesh, you are in the Spirit, if the Spirit of God really
dwells in you. . . . But if Christ is in you, although your bodies are
dead because of sin, your spirits are alive because of righteousness." Several things bid for attention in this passage. First, Paul
makes no distinction between having the Spirit in us and having
Christ in us. They are one and the same. Second, Paul does make
a distinction between being "in the Spirit" and having the Spirit
in us; evidently, having the Spirit within is a necessary corollary
of one's being "in the Spirit." Being "in the Spirit" suggests one's
involvement in an objective situation; having the Spirit in him
suggests a change in the condition of one's own life. Thirdly, Paul
makes no distinction between the Spirit of Christ and the Spirit of
God. And therefore he makes no distinction between the Spirit
of God as a reality within and Christ as a reality within.

Notice this series of parallels between Christ and Spirit:

> We are sealed in Christ (Eph. 1:13).
> We are sealed in the Spirit (Eph. 4:30).
>
> We are consecrated in Christ Jesus (I Cor. 1:2).
> We are consecrated in the Holy Spirit (Rom. 15:16).
>
> We are righteous in Christ (Phil. 3:8, 9).
> We are righteous in the Holy Spirit (Rom. 14:17).
> We are righteous in both (I Cor. 6:11).
>
> We have life through Christ (Eph. 2:1; Col. 3:4).
> We have life through the Holy Spirit (Rom. 8:11).
>
> We have hope grounded in Christ (I Cor. 15:19).
> We have hope grounded in the power of the Spirit (Rom. 5:5;
>   Gal. 6:8).

Christ is the alternative to the law of sin and death (Rom. 10:4).
The Spirit is the alternative to the law of sin and death (Rom.
8:2).

The following suggest a more dynamic picture; they press us for
action:

We are commanded to stand fast in the Lord (Phil. 4:1).
We are told to stand fast in the one Spirit (Phil. 1:27).

We are told to rejoice in the Lord (Phil. 4:4).
We are told to have joy in the Holy Spirit (Rom. 14:17).

We are told to live in Christ (Col. 2:6).
We are told to walk in the Spirit (Eph. 4:3). (See also Gal.
5:25.)

Paul speaks the truth in Christ (Rom. 9:1; II Cor. 2:17).
Paul speaks the truth in the Spirit (I Cor. 12:3).

We are called into the fellowship of Christ (I Cor. 1:9).
We are blessed with the fellowship of the Holy Spirit (II Cor.
13:14).

Can we draw any conclusions from Paul's interchange of Spirit
and Christ through all these passages? We are saying something,
of course, simply by noticing that Paul does not make a distinction
between our life in the Spirit and our life in Christ. And if while
we say this we recall the statements that "The Lord is the Spirit"
and that Christ "has become a life-giving Spirit," we have further
evidence that in terms of Christian experience there is no difference. Further, recalling that this sort of interweaving of Spirit and
Christ into Christian reality is a post-resurrection phenomenon,
that it is a different sort of picture than one gets from the synoptics,
we may also say that the Spirit-Christ identity marks a *phase* of
the *history* of reconciliation.

Of course, scholars have not agreed on all the implications of
this identity. Deissmann, naturally enough, takes it as evidence
that Christ has been changed in Paul's theology into a kind of airy
stuff, like the breath that is outside of us and inside of us at the
same time. Albert Schweitzer thinks that Deissmann read Paul
very wrongheadedly, but he does agree on this: "Being in the
spirit is only a form or manifestation of being-in-Christ. Both are
descriptions of one and the same state."[22] Ingo Hermann goes so

[22]*The Mysticism of Paul the Apostle* (New York, 1955), p. 167.

far as to say that all of the passages in St. Paul which refer to the
Spirit must be read as meaning Jesus Christ.[23] Wikenhauser has
reservations. Closer examination, he says, shows that "Paul always uses the phrase 'in Christ' when he is speaking of salvation
as such, while he reserves the phrase 'in the Spirit' for the conduct
of the faithful as contrasted with the life of the natural man . . . or
when he is dealing with the effects of the Spirit on the interior life
of the believer."[24] I take it that Wikenhauser means something
like this: when Paul says that we are "in Christ" he means that
we are in the saved status, in the new situation, of which Christ is
the representative personality; when Paul says that we are "in the
Spirit" he means that the life power of Christ has entered us or
ought to enter us to conform our practical living to the new
objective situation in Christ. This is, I think, a plausible distinction.

But it does not hold. To be sure, Paul likes to speak of the
Spirit as the power that enters our lives, and he surely credits the
whole life of the Christian to the Spirit. But he does the same with
Christ. We rejoice in Christ, we speak in Christ, we pray in Christ,
and we walk in Christ—just as we do these things in the Spirit.
Moreover—we must go further into this later—the phrase "in the
Spirit" refers to the new objective situation just as much as does
the phrase "in Christ." In Romans 8, for instance, life in the Spirit
stands for the objective norm or dominant pattern that controls life
in the new age as the law (of sin and death) was the objective
pattern that controlled it in the former age.

For the sake of balance, however, we must note passages in
which a difference between the Spirit and Christ is surely implied.
The clearest one, perhaps, is I Corinthians 12:3: "Therefore I
want you to understand that no one speaking by the Spirit of God
ever says 'Jesus be cursed!' and no one can say 'Jesus is Lord'
except by the Holy Spirit." One would never conclude anything
from this sentence suggesting an identity of the Spirit and Christ.
Here the Holy Spirit seems a distinct third party, a witness who
alone can convince a person that Jesus is really the Lord. Christ
is still He who died and rose again (Rom. 8:34). Paul desires to
be with Christ: he never expresses a desire for a different relationship to the Spirit after death (Phil. 1:22). Christ, not the Spirit,
is King and Lord (Rom. 14:9). Christ, not the Spirit, will return
as judge (I Cor. 4:5). Paul does not identify Christ and the Spirit

[23]*Kyrios and Pneuma* (München, 1961), p. 140.
[24]*Pauline Mysticism* (New York, 1960), p. 54.

in a sense that alters his belief that the Jesus who is Lord is the Jesus who died and rose again in this world. Their identity is always in reference to Christ's presence in the world after His glorification and in reference to the Church's experience of Him. At the present time, in the new age, we are "in Christ" *and* "in the Spirit"; and these are not two places, but one place.

4. *The Spirit as a Foretaste of Tomorrow*

For Paul, however, the reality of life is never severed into the simple categories of past, present, and future. Christ changes his ways of thinking about the times. For Christ has brought the real future into the real present. The real future is the future that God has hidden for us in Christ. The real future is the goal that history is destined to achieve now that Christ is Lord. The real future is God's future, defined by the decisive action that God took to change the human situation. This is why Paul can assert that the future is already, in some way, ours; tomorrow is now. The explanation is twofold: Jesus Christ is Lord today and the Spirit is present among us. And these two facts are parts of one reality.

We have already talked about how, on the one hand, Christ has decisively changed the human situation and brought into being a new creation while, on the other hand, the new creation is a promise to be made effective sometime in the future. We saw that while the old regime has been thrown out of the palace, the old evil age is still very much "the present evil age." While we have already, even now, been translated out of the kingdom of darkness, we are still looking into the future for the advent of the kingdom of light. Christ is Lord here and now; but we stand on earth hoping for His coming as Lord of glory. We have died and risen with Christ (Rom. 6:1-4), and even now are blessed in Christ "with every spiritual blessing in the heavenly places" (Eph. 1:3); but meanwhile the bodies of our friends are rotting and our own lives are defined by their termination.

Paul's solution to the dilemma is the actuality of the Spirit. The Spirit is the dimension in which the elusive future is already present. He is the pledge and the first payment of the inheritance that is still outstanding. He is the reality of tomorrow that has become present today. Most biblical scholars agree that for Paul the Spirit of Christ is the eschatological reality. Geerhardus Vos wrote that for Paul the Spirit is "that which characterizes the mode of existence and life in the world to come and consequently of that anticipated form in which the world to come is even now realized in heaven."[25] I would only add "and on earth." There is hardly a scholar to be found who does not both agree with this and, what is more, find in it a clue to Paul's doctrine of the Holy Spirit. N. Q. Hamilton, for example, says, "Just as in the synoptics the future Kingdom breaks into the present in the action of Jesus, so in Paul the future age has broken into the present in the action of the Spirit."[26]

Paul draws two fairly distinct pictures of the actions and role of the Spirit. One is directed to persons rather subjectively. The other is directed to the human situation rather objectively. One shows that the Spirit is at work within us; the other shows that the Spirit is at work as the dominant force in the new order. We shall note the more subjective aspect first. No one is part of the new order but he who has the Spirit of Christ within him (Rom. 8:11). The indwelling Spirit is the augur of things to come. Paul has various metaphors to say this. For instance, the Spirit is the "first fruits" of the redemption that we still hope for (Rom. 8:23). The term "first fruits" is an allusion to the part of the flock or crops brought as an offering to Jehovah in the Old Testament cult. The first fruits are different from the rest of the flock only in that they are first; they are materially the same as the rest. Just as the first-born is of the same family as the later-born, the first fruits are of a piece with the remainder.[27] We have the first fruits of the coming Kingdom when we have the Spirit within us, working on and in our human spirits. This could be read as meaning that the first fruits are an *effect* of the Spirit. The New English Bible, however, translates this way: "We, to whom the Spirit is given *as* first-fruits. . . ." This

[25]*Pauline Eschatology* (Grand Rapids, 1961), p. 59.

[26]*Op. cit.*, p. 23. Cf. H. Ridderbos: "His statements about the Spirit show that for Paul the *after* of salvation history does not evaporate into a timeless transhistorical, but rather that the pneumatic element is subordinated to his proclamation of Christ as the exalted and coming Lord" (*Paulus* [Kampen, 1966], p. 90). Also, Bultmann: "Everything indicates that by the term 'Spirit' he [Paul] means the eschatological existence into which the believer is placed by having appropriated the salvation deed that occurred in Christ" (*Theology of the New Testament*, I [New York, 1951], p. 355). And I. Hermann: The Spirit "is the bridge between the present time and the future age" (*op. cit.*, p. 33).

[27]See Delling, in Kittel, *Theological Dictionary of the New Testament*, I, pp. 485f. The "first fruits" is religiously more significant and therefore "set apart"; but in *kind* it is of a piece with the rest. The "first-born" is more important as to authority and status, but is nonetheless, in kind, a brother. So the idea of "first" has both notions, oneness of kind, but superiority in status.

is more in line with other sentences in Paul, as for instance when he says that the Spirit Himself is a guarantee of the future life (II Cor. 5:5).

The passage in Romans 8 is interesting because of what Paul says about our "groaning" for full redemption. We groan, of course, in anticipation. The cry is irrepressible: How long? The reality around us and in us is pockmarked with frustration, futility, and failure. But we do have a taste, whetted by the Spirit. The promise is known. A foretaste is given. But we live in the tensions of having the new, yet having the old large as life within and around and over us. We want the full reality, not because we have had nothing, but because we have had a taste of what is coming.

Paul also calls the Spirit a guarantee (Eph. 1:14). The Greek word is *arrabon,* and it can be translated as "down payment" or "first installment." It is a pledge on the payment in full. An *arrabon* is never a thing by itself; it is an engagement of the person who has it to something even bigger yet to come.[28] Once again, those who believe are "sealed with the promised Holy Spirit"—in Christ. The seal assures us of the reality and certainty of the promised inheritance. It could be like a mark of identification put on products to indicate their genuineness: "none genuine without this seal." It can also be a badge that invests a person with authority and power. The basis for our guarantee is not the fine print of a legal document, but the dynamic of a correlation between Christ's Spirit and our faith.

What is remarkable, however, is that Paul uses some of these same metaphors about Jesus Christ. He says, for example, that Christ is the "first fruits" by virtue of His own resurrection (I Cor. 15:20). He is, as risen Lord, of a piece with what we are to be. A similar instance is his reference to Jesus as the "beginning, the first-born from the dead, that in everything he might be preeminent" (Col. 1:18). This sentence is very revealing. Christ is the end, but He is also the beginning—not simply in the sense of the first in a series, but in the sense of the creative power and source of what follows. Being the first-born, He is, like the first fruits, different only in being set apart for a special purpose: He is cut of the same cloth as the rest. But He is the first-born *so that* He might be preeminent.

Now when we put all these statements together and keep in

[28]Behm, in Kittel, *Theological Dictionary of the New Testament,* I, p. 475.

mind our whole context, we must conclude that the Spirit as the "first fruits" and the "down payment" is not to be isolated or even separated from Christ. We are joint heirs with Christ (Rom. 8:17). We look forward to sharing the glory of Jesus Christ (II Thess. 2:14). We expect to be like Christ; our mortal bodies are going to be made like His immortal body (Phil. 3:21 and I Cor. 15:49). What Paul wants in his Christian life is to "know him [Christ] and the power of his resurrection" (Phil. 3:10). In short, everything that the believer hopes for is located in Christ and everything he desires to be is what Jesus is. Both Christ and the Spirit are the present reality on earth of the future reality which is to come.

The Spirit, then, is the down payment and first fruits of the life and existence that is embodied in Christ. He brings into reality within our lives nothing other than the reality of Christ. This is illustrated in a dramatic way by what Paul says in II Corinthians 3:18. Recall that in the verse just before this one, he identified the Lord as none other than the Spirit. Having said that the Lord is the Spirit, he goes on to indicate the force of this for our expectations in life. "And we all, with unveiled face [that is, with our eyes open to the fact that Christ is the Lord] beholding the glory of the Lord, are being changed into his likeness from one degree of glory to another." The present reality is the gradual transformation into the character of the resplendent Christ, a transformation already begun. The future reality is the full transformation of our entire existence into the character of Christ. But what Paul then says, to account for it, is telling from our point of view: "for this comes from the Lord who is the Spirit."

The upshot of this brief glance into the eschatological facet of the Spirit's presence is that the Spirit represents Jesus Christ, wholly and completely. The invasion of the future into the present is the invasion of Jesus the Lord into the present. The Spirit is the ascended Jesus in His earthly action. "Christ is the *pars* directed toward the *totum*, and the Spirit is he who leads from the *pars* to the *totum*. The Spirit is the movement from Christ to the consummation, from the first fruits to the full harvest."[29]

There is another, more objective side to the eschatological role of the Spirit.[30] The difference between the objective and subjective is not hard and clear, of course; but there is some distinction. In

---

[29]H. Berkhof, *The Doctrine of the Holy Spirit* (Richmond, 1964), p. 105.
[30]See H. Ridderbos, *Paulus*, especially pp. 234ff.

one sense the Spirit is the Christ indwelling us, empowering us, praying through us, and pushing us into conformity with Christ. In another sense the Spirit is also the prevailing norm or rule within the new order in Christ; of course, He is a special kind of norm, very different from written rules. We find this more objective side in Romans 8.

This chapter is really about the two orders of life; it is quite eschatological. It is about two orders of reality, the two aeons. Jesus Christ is Lord of the new age. Satan, not mentioned by name, is lord of the old. But within the two orders, we have the Spirit contrasted with both "the flesh" and the "law of sin and death." Later, in the third chapter, we will take a longer look at the meaning of these phrases. Here all I want to point out is that what begins (in verse 1) as a general description of the free status of people "in Christ" goes on to become a complex discussion of life "in the Spirit."

The Spirit represents the present power and dominance within the new order. The new order is obviously not divided from the old order by the calendar: the old order is still here, along with the new; they exist side by side. But Christ is Lord of the present time over "all things" even though He is not "all in all." And His lordship is executed and effected by the Spirit. This is why those "in Christ" are ruled by, live according to, and have their minds set on the Spirit (verse 5).

Christians are people who live in a new situation, where a new pattern of life prevails. The prevailing pattern is the "law of the Spirit of life in Christ Jesus" (verse 2). Those who submit to that "law" are those who are "in the Spirit" (verse 9). Spirit and flesh are both shorthand for the whole situation which each dominates. Being in the Spirit means being in the new situation, created by Christ and dominated by His Spirit. Within the new order, the Spirit represents, indeed *is,* Christ.

All that we have said about Paul's key statements on Christ and the Spirit can be summarized in a paragraph. Jesus is the head of a new epoch in the world; He is the eschatological Adam. He is also the life of the new epoch; for He is become the Spirit. His presence among us and over us is the entrée of the future "new earth" into our present time; but He is present as the Spirit. There is no touch of the Spirit that is not the touch of the Master's hand. There is no act of the Spirit that is not also the action of Christ. This is no place to talk about the Spirit being submerged into the being of Christ. But it can be said that in the *history* of God's actions for man's redemption, Jesus Christ is in the here and now because the Spirit is here now.

D. CONCLUSION: THE SPIRIT AS JESUS CHRIST AT WORK IN OUR HISTORY

Paul does not give us a systematic essay on the relationship between the historical Jesus and the Spirit of Christ. I have, here and there, emphasized that the Jesus Christ of Paul's gospel is the Jesus who comes as a specific and identifiable individual in history and who as that same individual is the Lord of "all things" and will come again. Paul's gospel is always the good news of reconciliation through *that* Jesus. I have also argued that, as time went on, Paul's message regarding the meaning of Jesus Christ centered increasingly on the decisive change which Christ made in the human situation by His death and resurrection. Jesus Christ is not merely in history; He changed the historical situation. This means that Jesus is centrally and radically important *to us*, not merely because He rescues individuals from a bad situation and changes them morally while they abide for a while in that situation, in human history, but because He first and most basically turns that situation into something different from what it was before. Of course, this occurs on a plane that is beyond history. He does it by overcoming, behind the scenes, the landlords of history who were leading it to ruin. Putting this in Paul's language, Jesus is not only the Savior of men, He is the Lord of "all things."

Since Jesus Christ arose and ascended, we are in a new situation, living under a new authority, called to subject ourselves to the discipline of the new order and invited to the joy of men set free from slavery. History moves on, with Christ in control. Jesus Christ is not only *of* history, and He not only changed the course of history: *He is the subject of history.* Christ is at work, in the world, in the Church, in men. He calls men to His side and summons them to take hold in the Christian enterprise. He awakens them to His lordship and makes them partners in His action. He demands that men within His sphere of authority shape up the pattern of their personal lives accordingly. He offers Himself as leader, as Lord, as Head, and yet as partner. His lordship is not limited to those who know and bow to it. There are many who live in the delusion that history is still without Christ. But His lordship is nonetheless over all and He works toward the time when it will be in all. Meanwhile, He calls men into union with Himself.

This forms the background of Paul's teaching about the Spirit and Christ. What he says about the Spirit is not in the setting of a doctrinal discourse about persons of the Trinity. What he says about the Spirit is rather in the setting of the movement of Christ's saving actions; it is in the setting of a new situation in history and a new phase in God's work. What we have seen in some of Paul's statements reveals how his response to the Spirit is connected to that crucial point in history which is the death and resurrection of Christ.

Paul's way of relating the Spirit to Christ is not really different from the way the Old Testament speaks of God and the Spirit. The Old Testament is not a handbook of doctrines any more than are Paul's letters. In the Old Testament, God is the God of creation, of movement, of action: He is on the move, changing the human situation, setting loose currents of historical change that give hope for the future. The Old Testament does not reflect on the inner relationships between God and the Spirit; it declares how God is *at work* for man's salvation. But it is, we are told, the Spirit who moved on the face of the waters (Gen. 1:2). The Word of the Lord created the heavens, but it was done by the breath or spirit (*ruach*) of God's mouth (Psa. 33:6). The life of man hangs by a thread; it can at the instant of God's departure slip into nothingness. But God sustains it by the present power of His Spirit: "When thou sendest forth thy Spirit, they are created; and thou renewest the face of the ground" (Psa. 104:30). "The Spirit of God has made me, and the breath of the Almighty gives me life" (Job 33:4). Let God withdraw, let Him draw back the Spirit, and we collapse: "If he should take back his spirit to himself, and gather to himself his breath, all flesh would perish together, and man would return to dust" (Job 34:14, 15). We do not need to suppose that God the Father has withdrawn and left the work to the Spirit. The Spirit *is* God, God on the move in creation, God present in the world, God at work among the things He made.

But God's Spirit is associated with the work of God in human history from another point of view. The life of man, the human situation too, needs a radical change, for it has been alienated at heart from God and His Spirit. Therefore, the Spirit is God in action aimed at the future, changing the situation and changing men in it. The way to the new covenant is paved by God; but the advent of the new covenant arrives within the Spirit comes to work in a new way. This is the gist of the vision related by Jeremiah when he talks about the law of God written no longer merely on

external tablets, but within the heart of God's people (Jer. 31:33).
A new vitality within men, a new disposition and a new relationship is promised as the Spirit comes in power (Isa. 32:15). The
coming Messiah will be equipped with the Spirit: "Behold my
servant . . . I have put my Spirit upon him. . ." (Isa. 42:1). We
may recall that Jesus, in His day, identified Himself in these same
terms: "The Spirit of the Lord God is upon me, because the Lord
has anointed me to bring good tidings to the afflicted. . ." (Isa.
61:1, 2).

In that day, God shall bring life to men and understanding to
their minds. Israel is dead in sin, a grotesque heap of dry bones.
But God says, "I will cause my spirit to enter you and you shall
live." And again, "I will put my spirit within you, and you shall
live" (Ezek. 37:5, 11). Associated with the life-giving presence of
the Spirit must be the Spirit's power to reveal. This is what Joel
stresses. Young men shall see visions and old men shall dream
dreams. How so? It is because God will pour out His Spirit (Joel
2:28-32). In the new day ahead, the Spirit of God will be at work
again, in a new creative way, bringing about a new order of life
and knowledge. This is how the apostles interpreted the coming
of the Spirit at Pentecost (Acts 2:15, 16).

In all this there is no clear line drawn between God and His
Spirit. God is at work through His Spirit. The Spirit is God on the
move in the history of men, making it His own history of salvation
and His own history of revelation. We are dealing here with the
Old Testament givens, and they indicate that wherever God is
present in the cities and plains of human life on earth, there He is
as Spirit. When David asks in Psalm 139, "Whither shall I flee
from Thy *Spirit*; whither shall I go from *Thy* presence," he indicates the same thing. God is the inescapable; we meet Him everywhere, for He is with us in His Spirit. For the Spirit is God "down
here" where the action is and wherever we are.

There is a remarkable parallel between Paul's treatment of the
Spirit of Christ and the Old Testament language about the Spirit
of God. The Spirit, in the new age promised through Jeremiah
and others, is the Christ at work on earth. The Spirit of God has
become the Spirit of Christ, being no less for that reason the Spirit
of God. As the Spirit of Christ, He opens the eyes of men to the
fact that Jesus is Lord (I Cor. 12:3, 11): He is the Spirit of
revelation. As the Spirit of Christ, He brings life to dead men; and
so is the Spirit who creates life (II Cor. 3:6). He is the Spirit who
forms the believing and obedient community as the body of

Christ and the new Israel (I Cor. 12:12, 13). But all the while, the Spirit is Christ Himself in His own direct involvement in and guidance of the Church. In the new era, the Spirit is to Christ what, in the old covenant, the Spirit is to God. He is the outgoing power of Jesus the Lord.

Do we, in speaking this way, rub away the distinction between Jesus Christ and the Spirit, a distinction that is obvious in the Gospel accounts? Perhaps we do, in a sense. But we must keep before us Paul's message of the Christ. This does not change. The Spirit is not identified with Jesus in a way that blurs the clear and concrete reality of the Lord. As H. Berkhof says, the Spirit is *not* "merely another name for the exalted Christ."[31] Christ remains the Lord. E. Schweizer captures the distinction in this way, which seems to me correct:

> In so far as Christ is thought of in His significance for the Christian community, that is, in His powerful acts on its behalf, He can be identified with the Spirit. In so far as He is Lord in Himself, controlling the exercise of His power, He must be distinguished from the Spirit, as the ego must always be distinguished from the personal power that goes out from it.[32]

In his penetrating study of the relationship between the Lord and the Spirit in Paul's letters, Ingo Hermann concludes that the Spirit is the "christological category of realization."[33] This is an illuminating phrase. It means that when Paul speaks of the Spirit He is talking about the Christ at work realizing in human life the goals of redemption. Hermann speaks about an identity of function between Christ and the Spirit, but means more by this than the word "function" may suggest. He does not mean that the Spirit is merely on the same team, as it were, with Christ. Rather, the Spirit is Christ *in* redemptive functions. The Lord has, in Hermann's

---

[31]H. Berkhof, *op. cit.,* p. 28.

[32]Kittel, *Theologische Wörterbuch zum Neuen Testament,* VI (Stuttgart, 1933), p. 416. William Barclay points to a necessary distinction in Paul's identification of the Lord and the Spirit: "When Paul wrote that, he was not thinking in terms of the doctrine of the Trinity and the persons of the Godhead; he was not thinking theologically at all; he was speaking from experience, and his experience was that to possess the Spirit was nothing less than to possess Jesus Christ" (*The Promise of the Spirit* [Philadelphia, 1960], p. 68). My reservation is only this, that Paul was not merely speaking from personal experience, but from a faith that the Spirit represents Christ in a manner that transcends personal experience as well.

[33]*Op. cit.,* p. 142.

understanding, not changed; but He has a way of bringing His
finished work of atonement into the present time, and that way is
the way of His Spirit.[34]

No one has wrestled more deeply with the doctrine of the Trinity
in modern times than has Karl Barth. While there are semantic
hints of modalism in Barth, he is aggressive in his defense of the
trinitarian doctrine, including the Western statement that the Spirit
proceeds from both the Father and the Son. On the other hand, he
works out his own statement in a way that reminds us of Augustine
and Calvin. He is willing to call the Spirit the *vinculum caritatis*,
the bond of love, that unites the Father and the Son. Doing so, he
is assured that the Spirit we meet in human life is in fullest reality
the divine Spirit. Since the resurrection and ascension of Christ,
however, the Spirit is concretely the Spirit of Christ. And now, He
is the *vinculum caritatis* between the Lord and His disciples. The
Spirit who unites us to Christ is peculiarly and specifically the out-
reach of Christ Himself to us. "It is strange," Barth says, "but true
that fundamentally and in general practice, we cannot say more of
the Holy Spirit and His work than that He is the power in which
Jesus Christ attests Himself, attests Himself effectively, creating
in man response and obedience."[35] This is an extraordinary sentence. The Holy Spirit is "the power" in which Jesus Christ calls
men into union with Himself. Christ calls men, creates them as a
community of believing witnesses to the saving action of God, and
so unites them in Christ's own history. But to say "power" is not
to suggest that the Spirit is impersonal. The power of Christ is the
outgoing of the concrete person whom we know as the Christ.

The Spirit is Christ Himself—in personal action. "The Holy
Spirit," Barth later wrote, is Christ "Himself in the action in which
He reveals and makes Himself known to other men as the One He
is, placing them under His direction, claiming them as His own, as
the witnesses of His holiness. The Holy Spirit is the living Lord
Jesus Christ Himself in the work of the sanctification of His particular people in the world, of His community and all its mem-

[34]Hermann is sure that all of Paul's statements about the Spirit can be
interpreted in this light. "All genuinely theologically pregnant statements
about the Spirit in Paul's letters are christologically informed" (*ibid.*, p.
144). This sounds at first hearing like an exaggerated statement, but it does
follow from the premise. If the Spirit is indeed, in our dispensation, the
christological category of realization, then the Spirit is that always.

[35]*Church Dogmatics*, IV/1, p. 648. Cf. the same terminology in Calvin,
Institutes, III/1/2.

bers."[36] There is no doubt that Barth is on the side of those who say we must be radically consistent in interpreting the Spirit christologically. We may add here the words of C. H. Dodd who, in speaking of the creation of the Christian community, writes:

> It was not enough to say that Christ, being exalted to the right hand of God, has 'poured forth' the Spirit. The presence of the Spirit in the Church is the presence of the Lord. The personality of Christ receives, so to speak, an extension in the life of His body on earth.[37]

Is the Spirit not to be thought of as a person in His own right? He must be thought of as a person, but not in His own right. And for this we honor Him the more. The difficulty we have is with the word "person." We moderns can hardly escape our psychologically formed ways of thinking about persons. To us, a person is in some sense an individual center of consciousness and action. If a human being is not personally centered as a distinct individual, we think of him as less than a person. So if we called the Spirit a person in His own right, we would be inclined to think of Him as an individual, thinking and acting independently, though in close collaboration with Jesus. But this would not be Paul's way of thinking.

The Spirit is experienced and known and honored as a person. He is the most personal being we have ever encountered. But not in His own right. He is a person, but to us He is only known and experienced as Christ. This suggests that we do not serve a helpful purpose in insisting on the Spirit as a person who is distinct and even separate from the person whose name is Jesus Christ. Bavinck, in his great systematics, said: Christ "has Himself become Spirit. Through His passion and death, He has made the Spirit of the Father and Son His own Spirit, the Spirit of Christ. He gives His Spirit as He wills, even as the Spirit takes all that He has to offer from Christ."[38]

---

[36]*Ibid.*, 2, p. 522.

[37]*The Apostolic Preaching* (New York, 2nd ed., 1954), p. 62.

[38]H. Bavinck, *Gereformeerde Dogmatiek*, IV (Kampen 1911), p. 113. See also, Ridderbos, *Paulus*. Ridderbos insists on the history-of-salvation approach to Paul's theology, and sees, rightly I think, the Spirit as the representative power and authority of the present order under Christ the Lord. The concept of the Spirit, he says, is used by Paul in the same sense that the Old Testament employs it: God in action within history, bringing about His redemptive goal. See especially pp. 234ff., but the entire book points in this direction.

The relationship of the Spirit to the exalted Lord may be cautiously crystallized by the following assertions:

(1) The Spirit is Christ in action, fulfilling and realizing His redemptive program on earth.

(2) The Spirit is Christ as He is experienced in and by the Church.

(3) The Spirit is Christ in His earthly function as the reigning Lord of the new creation which is here and now and yet must be realized fully in the future.

(4) The Spirit is the objective but dynamic norm for the life of freedom within the new creation, as the law was the static norm for the life of bondage in the old.

(5) Therefore, as far as life in the new covenant is concerned, the Spirit is Christ in the present time.

It goes without saying that this construction of Paul's thoughts must have considerable bearing on the subject of our union with Christ. We need not think of the Spirit as a kind of separate message bearer from Christ. Nor need we think of the Spirit as a sort of impersonal channel through which some substance-like stuff called the "life" of Christ is infused into us. Nor, surely, need we think of Jesus Christ as having been evaporated into an airy substance called Spirit. When we are united to the Spirit, we are united to the individual who is "out there" and whose name is Jesus. When we are in the Spirit, we are in Christ. And when the Spirit is in us, Christ Himself is within us. Union with Christ is not complete when the Spirit confronts and influences us. But there is no experience of the Spirit, no reality of the Spirit, that is not at the same time by virtue of that experience and reality, the experience and reality of Christ Himself.

When St. Paul insisted that the risen Lord was at work on earth effecting salvation among men, bringing into actuality the new creation, and that He was at work as Spirit, he both united the old and new covenants and distinguished them. The Spirit experience in the new community was the Spirit of God, the same Spirit who was God at work creatively within the old community. Thus, the unity of redemptive history was assured. But the Spirit, since the crucial events of the cross and resurrection, was the Spirit of Christ —not merely an independent emissary, but Christ Himself in action. This meant that the new creation was really new; it was new with the newness of Christ Himself.

When Paul said that the Lord was the Spirit, he was saying that the Spirit was divine. He was saying too, just as emphatically, that the Spirit was a personal, not a natural energy. Thus, the *intention* of the trinity formula was *assumed*. But he was adding this dimension: within the community of Christ's disciples, the Spirit was Christ Himself at work. He wanted us to understand that when we were brought into fellowship with God and with each other by the Spirit, we were in direct contact with the risen Lord.

Chapter Three

Being in Christ

A. "IN CHRIST": THEME AND VARIATIONS

Paul's favorite expression for man's union with Christ is surely the phrase "in Christ." Deissmann counted 164 times that it appears in Paul's comparatively small corpus.[1] The count is disputable, but it is certainly accurate enough to indicate how easy it was for Paul to include the whole of Christian existence in this little phrase. The expression was a habit with Paul.

He creates a symphony of language out of it, however. The variations on the theme are many. He does not, of course, use it in the same depth of significance each time, though each time the deeper significance is at least in the background. What we are eager to find out is the central meaning that this phrase has for Paul's understanding of the Christian life. We want to know what the phrase tells us of what it means, essentially, to be a Christian, or to be in union with Christ.

We shall begin with a review of the types of passages in which the remarkable expression occurs. The divisions we make of the passages are merely suggestive; they are not hard and fast or terribly important. But all told, they do give us an impression of how varied and how large a place the expression "in Christ" takes in Paul's speech.

1. God in Christ

Without much concern for technical exactness, Paul says that "God was in Christ reconciling the world to himself" (II Cor. 5:19). I mention this only to separate this sort of "in" phrase from the kind that interests us here. The presence of God in Jesus

---

[1]*Die Neutestamentlich Formel "In Christo Jesu"* (Marburg, 1892).

78

Christ does, of course, lie at the root of Paul's doctrine of salvation. If God were not immersed in Christ, our being in Christ at all would be inconceivable. For it is God in Christ who enabled the resurrection to take place (Rom. 8:11), God in Christ who at the cross replaced man's assessment of the meaning of life with His own, God in Christ who made justification and reconciliation possible and actual (Rom. 3:23). Further, Paul speaks of the "will of God in Christ Jesus" (I Thess. 5:18). The promises of God are completely valid in Christ (II Cor. 1:18ff.). It was God in Christ, most crucially, who triumphed over the "principalities and powers" (Col. 2:15). The expression "God in Christ" points us to the effective action that took place at a moment *in history* on our behalf. In that light, nothing separates us from the love of God which is in Jesus Christ (Rom. 8:39). Moreover, the presence of God in Christ offers us a theological hint for the meaning of our presence in Christ.

We want to know how individuals of the twentieth century, individuals who have their being in a particular space and in a particular time can, together and individually, be in another individual, Jesus Christ, in whom God was present.

In Christ, Israel's covenant God came into history to climax His walk through time in partnership with man. In Christ, God opened the gateway to a new history by taking a hand—with absolute decisiveness—in history. In short, the incarnation, cross, and resurrection of Jesus, point us to God's way and God's being as the God of history and the God in history.

2. *Persons in Christ*

This is the category that concerns us most, though it does not stand alone. Perhaps the two most famous passages in which it can be found are these: "If anyone be in Christ, he is a new creature" (II Cor. 5:17). "There is therefore now no condemnation to those who are in Christ Jesus" (Rom. 8:1). Paul says elsewhere that it is his own deep desire to be "found in Christ" (Phil. 3:9). And again, Paul reads the relationship between Adam and the rest of us men in the light of the fact that we shall be alive in Christ: "As in Adam all died, so in Christ shall all be made alive" (I Cor. 15:22). In a way that antedates our actual existence in Christ, we were "chosen in him from before the foundation of the world" (Eph. 1:4). And while we were once babes in Christ (I Cor. 3:1), we are urged to "grow up in every way into him" (Eph. 4:15). Finally, just as men live in Christ, they die "in Him" (I Thess. 4:16).

3. The Church in Christ

Sometimes Paul speaks of the whole Church as being in Christ. Some of the salutations that he uses place the congregation in Christ (I Thess. 1:1, Phil. 1:1). And he talks to members as the "faithful in Christ Jesus" (Eph. 1:1; Col. 1:2). He speaks of the churches in Judea as "the churches of God in Christ Jesus" (I Thess. 2:14). When he speaks of the "freedom which we have in Christ Jesus," he apparently has the Church in mind (Gal. 2:4). He refers to the church as one body in Christ (Rom. 12:5). Being in Christ, the Church knows that sociological distinctions are irrelevant to its existence (Gal. 3:28).

4. The New Life in Christ

There are places where salvation in Christ is stressed as a corollary of our being in Christ. We are sanctified in Christ (I Cor. 1:2). We seek to be justified in Christ (Gal. 2:17). We are the Lord's freemen in Christ (I Cor. 7:22). We become "the righteousness of God" in Christ (II Cor. 5:21). The peace of God sustains us since we are in Christ (Phil. 4:7). In Christ, we live "to the praise of His glory" (Eph. 1:12). We are blessed in Christ, even as we are chosen in Him (Eph. 1:3). We are sons of God in Jesus Christ (Gal. 3:26). And it is in Christ that the blessing of Abraham falls on Gentiles (Gal. 3:8).

5. Life's Actions in Christ

Paul obviously thinks of the whole range of Christian life and practice as embraced within the reality of Jesus Christ. For Paul, the believer's speech, his thought, his hopes, his relationships, his attitudes, and his entire style of life are all set within his existence in Christ. A man marries a woman in the Lord (I Cor. 7:39). A Christian embraces another Christian in the Lord (Gal. 5:10; Phil. 1:14). All our ways are in Christ (I Cor. 4:17). Our speech is clear and decisive in Christ (II Cor. 1:19). We are enriched in Christ (I Cor. 1:5). We are wise in Christ (I Cor. 4:10). We are safe in Christ (Rom. 16:10). Our whole pattern of life is changed in Christ. The style, the dynamic, and the perspective are all defined by our status or location in Christ.

6. *The Apostle in Christ*

Though he does not set himself apart as being in Christ differently than other people are, Paul does identify his own actions as an apostle as actions in Christ. He notes that he became the spiritual father of the Corinthian Christians in Christ Jesus through the Gospel (I Cor. 4:15). He calls Timothy his child in the Lord (I Cor. 4:17). He takes pride in the life of other Christians, as an apostle in the Lord (I Cor. 15:31). As an apostle, he speaks the truth in Christ (II Cor. 2:17; Rom. 9:1), just as Christ speaks in and through him (II Cor. 13:3). He exhorts in Christ (Phil. 2:1). He labors in Christ (I Cor. 15:58; Rom. 16:3, 9, 12). He rejoices in Christ (Phil. 3:1; 4:4, 10). He hopes in the Lord (Phil. 2:19). He is weak in Christ (II Cor. 13:4), but in his weakness has power in Christ (Phil. 4:13) and is led in triumph in Christ (II Cor. 2:14). His ways are in Christ (I Cor. 4:17), and he is a prisoner in Christ (Phil. 1:13). He is bold in Christ (Philemon 8) and is established in Christ (II Cor. 1:21).

I have not mentioned every instance of the phrase "in Christ," but I have mentioned enough to indicate at least the variety of situations in which it is used. Sometimes Paul says "in the Lord," sometimes "in Christ," and otherwise, "in Jesus Christ." While it may be possible to distinguish aspects of his meaning according to whether he says "Lord" or "Christ" or "Jesus Christ," that is not our interest here. What we do see is that for Paul the Christian life is not merely a memory of a God-man who lived once and is gone. It is not an imitation of a good life. It is not a momentary ecstatic experience. The whole of life, from its fundamental being to its discrete actions, is surrounded by the reality of Christ. The pilgrim journey is not a burdensome trudge up a lonely road; it is a way that cuts through and is always within the environment of Jesus Christ Himself. Life begins, proceeds, and ends in Christ. He is the route and the country through which the route crosses. The Christian is always "in Christ."

B. THREE THEOLOGICAL PERSPECTIVES

B. F. Westcott said that "If once we realize what these words 'we are in Christ' mean, we shall know that beneath the surface of life lie depths which we cannot fathom, full alike of mystery and hope."[2] Westcott had a way of sensing where the large issues of

---

[2]*St. Paul's Epistle to the Ephesians* (New York, 1906; reprinted Grand Rapids, 1952), p. 186.

the Christian religion are found, and his intuition was surely accurate in this case. Being in Christ is not only the fundamental fact of the individual Christian's existence, it is a new reality within life itself. It is not a phrase that captures an incidental, side issue of Christian life, alongside of which man's real life is lived. It exposes the very root of life, the new life as it is created by and experienced in Jesus Christ. Westcott is right; if we can get a clear view of what it means to be "in Christ," we will have gained at least a glimpse inside the core of life's mystery and meaning.

But how can we capture such an elusive prize? The phrase by itself almost begs us not to take it seriously. How can one person actually be *in* another person, a person from whom, moreover, he is separated by two millennia and the gulf between heaven and earth? If Paul had spelled out his intentions in so many words, we could at least debate about the meaning of his expression. But as it is, he lets the phrase drop as though it would be quite clear to anyone who read it. He seems to think that anyone who knows what Jesus Christ means *to* the world will know what it means to be *in* Him. This is why we are forced to look at the phrase from the perspective of Paul's entire gospel. Paul lets the phrase drop, here and there, as a focus of his whole message about Jesus Christ. It represents a kind of "instant" proclamation of reconciliation with God.

To be "in Christ" suggests a strange realm of existence that few of us really suppose we inhabit. The lifelong reader of St. Paul, I suspect, conditions himself not to take Paul literally. It is a phrase with such powerful overtones of Christ-oriented piety and fellowship that it leaves us satisfied if we let it go at that. But Paul does not mean it to be a radical slogan with vaguely pious associations and no definite counterpart in reality. He must have meant the word "in" most seriously. He invested too much of his whole perception of Christ and His significance in this phrase to let us suppose that it can be merely a pious cliché. It crystallizes the essence of what Christian existence means.

Insisting that we take Paul's words seriously does not, however, give us a hint as to *how* to take them. Shall we engage in a philological study? Must we compare his use here of the preposition "in" with his use of it throughout his work, and then his general use of it with the way the Greeks of his time used it? Should we engage in a comparative study of man's religions to discover how varieties of people have thought (if they have) of one man's being *in* another—perhaps in a god? Or should we let

Paul's gospel of Jesus Christ, his understanding of who and what Jesus is and what He did, speak to us about this strange phrase that seems to capture all of the Christian experience? We should, I think, take the latter route. But before we begin, we ought to take a brief excursion through the forest of "in Christ" theologies. These are either theologies which undertake to define the Pauline words or theologies built on them. Any survey of "in Christ" theologies is likely to be oversimplified, because the route is impossibly complicated, the theologies closely interwoven. The categories which I am going to suggest are only rough ones, and sometimes individual interpretations fit partly in one and partly in another.

1. Mystical Union

First, there is the mystical interpretation. For a long time it dominated the field in one form or another. Mysticism is, of course, a tenuous, elusive thing. We really get nowhere by defining it in advance; about the best we can do is to try to get hold of what people think when they use the word. For our purpose, we can distinguish between two kinds of mystical interpretations: (a) the moralistic mystical and (b) the ontological mystical. What they have in common is the conviction that Paul's doctrine of union with Christ as a "being in Christ" involves an actual sharing of His life in some form.

a. Moralistic Mysticism

It was in 1892 that Deissmann published his study of the expression "in Christ," and modern interpreters have had to start in some way where he left off.[3] First of all, he took the preposition "in" as indicating locality. When one is in Christ, he is in Him as a man is in a room or in a city. Being in Christ is not a psychic experience, like being in a blue mood or in a state of bliss. Christ is a kind of place. But of course He is a person. Paul, as Deissmann noted, was the first writer to speak of being in a person. And while it was passing strange for any Greek reader to think of being in a person, the only way in which a Greek could possibly have read Paul was in a local sense; for being in something (with the dative case of the thing occupied) *had* to signify a place.

Now, we could respond here that we are not much interested in

[3]*Op. cit.*

how a Greek reader would understand Paul. A Greek could mis-
understand him as easily as we can. What we are trying to discover
is what Paul *wanted* the Greek or anyone else to understand. But
right now all we want to do is understand Deissmann. To Deissmann the fact that Paul pioneers the use of the word "in" with a
person, uses it this way very often, and does not explain it to his
Hellenistically oriented readers, leaves us with the unavoidable
conclusion that he meant to say precisely this: the Christian is a
man whose life is lived within a certain locale, and that locale is
Jesus Christ.

How this can make any sense at all is explained by Deissmann's
Spirit Christology. Jesus Christ, at His ascension, was evaporated
into a universal Spirit, diffused throughout the universe, and
turned into an air-like substance in which men can live and move
and have their new being. He, as Spirit, becomes the atmosphere
which we take inside of us and which we, as bodies, occupy
spatially. We are in Christ in a way somewhat parallel to the way
in which we are in God. As everyone, whether he knows it or not,
has his being in the universal Spirit of God, the man who opens
himself to Christ has his moral being in the Spirit who is Christ.
As Spirit, Christ has room for us all.

This, according to Deissmann, is Paul's mysticism. We live in
Christ; Christ lives in us. His Spirit is one with our spirit. But
Deissmann saves Paul from being a pure mystic. Paul is obviously
not a man who quietly waits for a "happening" to transport him
into ecstasy. He is the most morally directed person in history.
When Paul is "in Christ," he reacts morally, dynamically, and with
his whole being. Christ-mysticism is very different from oriental
God-mysticism. In Christ we do not lose ourselves passively in
deity; we are not swept into a world of visions; and we are not absorbed as a drop of water in the ocean of divinity. We are moved
to *act* as Christ acted; we are pushed into moral effort. Deissmann
calls Paul's "mysticism" a "reacting mysticism." In union with
Jesus, becoming one with His Spirit, we respond with moral en-
thusiasm. And this makes Paul's mysticism unique. Christ as universal Spirit is shot through with the moral character of Jesus.
Being in Him, we respond with the same moral urgency that the
earthly life of Jesus revealed.

We called this a moralistic mystical interpretation. The name
fits because in this view the significance of Jesus for the rest of
humanity is the availability of His moral power. The existence of
Jesus as a moral personality and the diffusion of His moral being

throughout the universe, as Spirit, combine to make Jesus Christ
meaningful to the rest of us. Not what Jesus Christ *did in* history,
but what He *became beyond* history is the key to His significance.
The incarnation of God is not the *leitmotif*, nor is the cross of
Jesus; but the ascension-evaporation of Jesus is. In any case, the
saving effect of Jesus is found in what He is, not in what He did.
And men are saved as they are located, at their own initiative,
within the Spirit-Being who once was and no longer is Jesus.

b. Ontological Mysticism

There is another kind of mystical understanding of Paul's
language which, though very different in form, reveals an under-
lying similarity to that of Deissmann's. It is of the same genus,
though a distinct species. Ontological mysticism is found in some
Catholic scholarship, though it would be misleading to lump all
Catholic interpreters in this category. E. L. Mascall provides a
good example of the ontological mystical approach.

Mascall is fond of saying that being a Christian involves one in
a change of life so radical that we can call it an ontological
change. The Christian, he says, is given a new footing for his
existence; his soul is elevated to a new level. When Paul says that
we are "new creatures" in Christ, he means nothing less than that
we are lifted out of the status of mere creatures and given a share
in the life of God.[4] Being in Christ must be taken ontologically
and realistically. "The Christian is a man to whom something has
happened, something moreover which is irreversible and which
penetrates to the very roots of his being; he is a man who has
been recreated in and into, Christ."[5]

The ontological change in man means that he has been given a
share in the status enjoyed by the humanity of Jesus Christ. Jesus
enjoys it by nature, of course, and we by grace. But the status is
the same. We are sons of God *in* the Son of God. And this means
nothing less than that we are infused with the divinized human life
of Christ Himself. Mascall does not, any more than any other
Catholic, suppose that this could just as well have happened
through a cross-less incarnation. The atonement is part of the
picture. But the cross and resurrection are simply necessary *means*
for the incarnate life of God to come to us. A debt had to be paid,

[4]*Christ, the Christian, and the Church* (London, 1946), p. 109.
[5]*Ibid.*, p. 77.

since we men are sinners. The crucified Christ had to live again to make His life available to us. But at the heart of things, stands the incarnation.

Our life in Christ comes, as may be expected, through baptism into His body, the Church. The Church, Mascall holds, is the sacramental institution which conveys the divine-human life to us. For this reason, incorporation into Christ means, in practice, incorporation into the Church. The Church is the social organism which forms Christ's earthly body now, as really as the organism of His discrete and single body was the body in which He walked on earth. Being in the Church, incorporated into it by baptism, the Christian is in Christ Himself. The sacramentalist wants us to take him quite seriously. "The *totus Christus* includes the Messiah and the *ecclesia*, Jesus and His Church, being the one organism of redemption," says L. S. Thornton.[6] We are not being told that the Church is a very strong *metaphor* of Christ. We are being told that the Church and Christ are ontologically one, that they are one in being. Thus, to share in the life that the Church gives is to share in the life of Jesus Christ. And to share in the life of Christ is to share in the life of God.

The claim that to be in Christ is to be in the Church is not, of course, limited to sacramentalist thinking. Many contemporary interpreters of Paul not at all inclined to the sacramentalist view agree that the "in Christ" formula is an ecclesiastical one, that when Paul says we are "in Christ" he intends us to think about being in the Church.[7] What distinguishes the sacramentalist is his conviction that it is in the Church that the purpose of the incarnation is achieved. The Church is the "extension of the incarnation." It is through the Church that the divine-human life is channeled into the world.

---

[6]*Revelation in the Modern World* (London, 1949), p. 127.

[7]Schweitzer says that Paul's talk of being "in Christ" is merely "a brachylogy for being partakers in the mystical body of Christ" (*The Mysticism of Paul the Apostle* [New York, 1955], pp. 122f.). Bultmann, too, insists that it is an ecclesiastical formula, though not exclusively that (*Theology of the New Testament*, I [New York, 1955], p. 311). Ernst Käsemann says that, in the deutero-Pauline letters at least, "being in Christ" means "being in the church" (*Leib und Leib Christi* [Tübingen, 1933], p. 183). Ernst Percy, too, insists that "being in the church is the same as being in Christ" (*Der Leib Christi* [Leipzig, 1942], p. 44.) This, then, is not at all an uncommon opinion among Paul's interpreters. The crucial question is what the body of Christ, as Church, means. I refer the reader at this point to the final chapter of the book.

To be "in Christ" is, then, to be in a given place; it is to be in
the Church. This conclusion fits what we have already discussed
as the Sacramental Christology. It is the conviction of a broad
spectrum of Catholic Christians.[8] And we must add that the
conviction is born of a desire to take St. Paul seriously: are we *in*
Christ as Paul says we are, or are we only *behind* Him as followers?

The very stuff of Christ's divine life is channeled through the
Church. This means that in Christ—as the Church—creation has
the possibility of being restored *and* elevated to a new level of life
never achieved by mere creatures. The last plateau is reached; we
are together, as a social body, lifted into the supernatural life. As
the animal organism was once lifted into the realm of spirit to
form man, so humanity is now lifted into Christ to form a new
race—deified humanity. Being in Christ, then, is not a flight from
the earthly into God; sacramentalism does not offer an escapist
mysticism. Sacramentalism sees created life as being taken up *en*
toto to a higher level. Theologians like Mascall have profound
respect for the integrity with which grace treats creation. *Gratia*
non tollit naturam, sed perficit: this is their favorite motto. As a
lower organism loses whatever life it had before being taken into
a higher form of life and finds its *own* life only within that higher
level, so humanity finds its truly human life within a higher, divine,
level. Being "in Christ" is an ontological reality; a genuine share
in divine life is given and this results in a change in metaphysical
status; being "in Christ," we are now, at the depths of life, "supernaturalized."

2. *Where the Action Is*

We have talked about two mystical interpretations of Paul's "in
Christ." To a moralistic mystic, like Deissmann, Paul means being
"in the Spirit" with a moral change as the result. To an ontological
mystic, like Mascall, Paul means being "in the Church" with an
ontological change as the result. For Karl Barth, Paul means being
where the action of Christ is going on. The great theologian of the
"wholly other," even in subdued talk about "the humanity of

[8]To mention just a few: Y. M. Congar, *Chretiens Desunis,* Paris, 1937,
pp. 59, 69, 94, etc.; H. de Lubac, *Catholicisme,* Paris, 1938, pp. 41, 44, 92;
E. Mersch, *Le Corps Mystique du Christ,* II, pp. 376f. Of course, the
present question among Roman Catholics is whether one can be in Christ
without being in *the* Church.

God," is not likely to be found burning the mystic flame. But it should be said that Barth's Christology does not prevent him from putting as heavy an accent on the significance of our being in Christ as anyone could. Union with Christ is, in fact, the beginning, the middle, and the goal of Christian reality. To ask Barth what Christian reality is, is to be told that it is union with Jesus Christ.

True, we hear him regretting that Reformed theologians ever used the word "mystical" in this connection.[9] He has no taste for a theology that finds Christ diffused in the universe. Nor has he any taste for a theology that deifies man. But for all this, he insists that union with Christ is the sum and substance of the Christian existence.[10] And union with Christ is being "in Christ."

Such union is for Barth a union of action. The fact that he discusses it under the heading of vocation shows how dynamic a reality he considers union with Christ to be. And as such it is in keeping with his anthropology and his Christology. Man is man in terms of what he *does*. Jesus is Christ in terms of what He *does*. The union of Christ and other men is understood in terms of what they *do* together.

Jesus Christ is He who speaks and rules. He speaks to men of His reality and theirs. He rules in grace for man's good. And those who listen and obey are caught up in His speaking and acting. If we are in Christ "our thinking, speech and action has its ruling and determinative principle . . . in the speech, action, and rule of Christ."[11] What this means is that the Christian is a man who lives within the sphere of the lordship of Christ, lives actively as a participant in the prophetic, priestly, and kingly offices of the Savior. Christ, in His Spirit, whom Barth elsewhere calls the "power of Christ," is present, doing the effective speaking and acting and ruling. But the Christian is involved too, as a partner— not an equal partner to be sure, but by grace a partner nonetheless.

What being in Christ amounts to, for Barth, is the *act*. It is the total action of the whole man within Christ's total service to the whole world. He is very willing to let this be understood as a spatial matter; the Christian is *in* Christ and Christ in the Christian. The gulf between heaven and earth is overcome. Christ is spatially present where the Christian is, and the Christian is spatially present

---

[9]*Church Dogmatics,* IV/1 (New York, 1936-58), p. 540.
[10]*Ibid.,* p. 548.
[11]*Ibid.,* 3, p. 548.

where Christ is, "not merely alongside but in exactly the same spot."[12] But this is all in terms of service, action.

"Fellowship," he ventures, is really too weak a word for being in Christ. So is "association." It is not a matter of teamwork. Christ creates and controls the sphere of action in which the Christian really finds his own being. But—and this is not negotiable—there is no identification of the Christian with Christ. There is no blending of natures, no participation in divinity by men, no blurring of the difference. "Their fellowship of life thus finds realization as a differentiated fellowship of action in which Christ is always superior and the Christian subordinate. Hence the principle controlling Christian existence . . . will always necessarily result from the fact that the Christian, as he lives in Christ and Christ in him, exists in this fellowship of action and its order."[13] Jesus Christ has a program of action. When the Christian is said to be in Christ, therefore, he is said to be with his entire life in the sphere in which Christ is operative as Lord.

The sacramentalist stresses *being* in Christ; Barth stresses *action* in Christ. The sacramentalist insists that one is *deified* by participation in Christ; Barth insists that one is brought into *service* by participation in Christ. The sacramentalist says that one is brought into Christ by the sacramental act of *baptism*; Barth says that one is brought into Christ by the *call* of God (vocation). The sacramentalist tells us that the goal of the life in Christ is the *supernaturalization* and *deification* of all life; Barth tells us that the goal of the life in Christ is *unanimity of purpose and desire* between the creature and his Lord. The sacramentalist can easily discuss union with Christ under the heading of sacrament; Barth finds it natural to discuss it under the heading of vocation.

A footnote should be added to this distinct contrast between Barth's thought and that of the sacramentalist. There are, in spite of the contrast, fascinating points of contact. The sacramentalist cannot ignore the possibility that the whole of creation is to be lifted into unity with Christ. Neither can Barth. The sacramentalist insists that the integrity of man's being as creature is not sacrificed through unity with Christ. So does Barth. The sacramentalist wants Christian existence to be understood as existence within a total structure of life. So does Barth. There is in the sacramentalist position a strong hint that man needed something to fulfill his being

12*Ibid.*, p. 547.
13*Ibid.*, p. 597.

as a creature, a something provided by Christ. Barth too would insist that man comes to fulfillment only through Christ. To both, each in his way, Christ is necessary to creation from the outset.

But they do differ in their understanding of how and when man and creation are fulfilled. To the sacramentalist the "supernatural-izing" grace of Christ insinuates itself into created life, not violating it, but boosting it to a higher level. The work of this infused grace is already going on, gradually transforming creation as really as nature gradually took on its present shape and form from earlier and lower ones. To Barth, the fulfillment is still elusive. "Created being as such needs salvation, but does not have it: it can only look forward to it."[14] Moreover, the fulfillment of creation will be a *new* creation, not a transformation of the old. One is hard put to find in Barth the notion of a fulfillment that actually happens in and to creation. The fulfillment is somehow present, salvation is somehow here, but never, or at least hardly ever, inside, part of, and actually possessed by nature. "Salvation," he writes, "is ful-fillment, the supreme, sufficient, definitive, and indestructible fulfillment of being." But—and here is a sentence that sets Barth off from the sacramentalist rather decisively—"Salvation is the perfect being which is not proper *to created being as such but is still future*" (italics mine).[15] The sacramentalist would point to such sentiments as proof that the Protestant does not really mean it when he says that the Christian, with his whole being, is in Christ —as proof that the new being in Christ is for the Protestant not really the Christian's being, but a being "out there" in the eschatological future.

3. *Within the New Situation*

The interpretation of the expression "in Christ" that I wish to discuss now has a great deal in common with both the sacramen-talist and the activist approach. Like the sacramentalist approach, it holds that something radically, even ontologically, new has come into existence with Christ; but instead of seeing the new thing as a stream of divine life that boosts created existence to a new level, it sees the new thing as a new order in history, a new environment, a new situation. Like the activist approach, it holds that being "in Christ" involves a summons to action

14*Ibid.*, 1, p. 8.
15*Ibid.*

as partners of Christ in the world; but instead of seeing the new thing as something future, or in God's mind, or only in "hope," it sees it as actually taking place with life on earth among men.

To be "in Christ" is to be in the new reality of a new historical order already present, created by Jesus Christ and kept alive by His Spirit. The question of where is not as important as the question of how. The stress is on the victory that Christ won over the powers of frustration and defeat, the "principalities" that had kept human life in bondage. It is also on the present lordship of Christ that is exercised on earth through His Spirit. Being in Christ, then, is to be within the rule of Christ, free from bondage, and within the liberating domination of the Spirit.

This interpretation of "in Christ" is of a piece with what we called Situational Christology. There is a strong element of hope in it, for the full historical achievement of Christ's rule waits for the eschaton. But it is already present wherever the Spirit dominates life. There is a strong element of faith in it, for the new situation was established behind the scenes of ordinary life and, moreover, plain verification of it is impossible. But even though it is "hid with Christ," it is real, experienced, and lived in the here and now.

For the most part, situationists do not much care to use the word "mystical" for our life in Christ. They strongly prefer to talk about being involved in a new historical order, a new movement, a new epoch, or as we have called it, a new situation. This is not meant to suggest that the personal relationship between the man in Christ and the person of Christ is inconsequential. Nor does it suggest that a real experience of life in Christ is unimportant. Christ is always the active head of the new order. His Spirit is always Himself in action within the new order. We are bound to Christ by the memory of His victory and the anticipation of His coming. But we are also bound to Christ by the present reality of His lordship. We live and move and have our being in a situation where the Spirit is closer to us than we can possibly realize intellectually. But the upshot is not that we are infused with life, but that we are incorporated into the new situation under Christ.[16]

[16]This is a point made by Fritz Neugebauer in his study of the Pauline phrase (In Christus [1958]). Neugebauer, to my knowledge, never makes use of the word "mystical" in his thorough treatment; the whole reality of being "in Christ" is understood in terms of salvation history. It is extremely difficult to shed the word. Deissner, who found nothing in Paul similar to the oriental mysticism current in Paul's day, likes the phrase "faith-mysti-

In Chapter One (Section D) it was implied that Paul's view of
our existence "in Christ" can best be understood within the framework of his Situational Christology. We will now, therefore, go
directly on to a hard look at some of the crucial passages in which
the formula "in Christ" occurs, in an attempt to show that this is
the case—to show that, taken in their contexts, the "in Christ"
passages are illuminated most meaningfully by the new reality that
Paul contends was introduced into history by Christ's victorious
ascendence as Lord. It should be emphasized here, perhaps, that
Paul also teaches a Christology of personal atonement; it goes
without saying that Paul believes Christ to have died in order to
propitiate God and to render satisfaction to His demands for a
just retribution on human sin. One surely ought not to *oppose* the
situational to the personal transactive dimensions in Paul.

C. FOCUSING ON PAUL

1. Life Outside of Christ

One way to find out what a Frenchman is like is to watch how
a Frenchman looks at the rest of the world. One way to tell what
life in Christ is like is to see how a man in Christ looks at life
outside of Christ. St. Paul's observations of life outside of Christ
are kaleidoscopic; they are many shapes and colors, and they keep
moving. Sometimes he catches the personal, existential contradictions and frustrations of that life. Sometimes he is more impressed
with the superhuman powers that control and confine personal life.
His vocabulary is forged in the struggles he has within the religious
situation of his own time and is therefore often like a foreign
language to us. We cannot possibly enter into all the complexities
of interpretation that have kept scholars preoccupied in recent
years. But perhaps we can grasp enough of Paul's general outlook
to cast some light on the new life in Christ.

Paul's favorite words for capturing life outside of Christ are

---

cism," designating an experience of Christ through faith (*Paulus und die
Mystik seiner Zeit* [Leipzig, 1918], p. 107). H. E. Weber talked about the
"mysticism of expectation" (*Eschatologie und Mystik im Neuen Testament,*
II [Gütersloh, 1930], pp. 75f.). Albert Schweitzer's book was called *The
Mysticism of Paul the Apostle* even though Schweitzer's understanding of
mysticism is set within eschatology. All in all, we do not get a step further
in understanding Paul by raising the question whether he includes mysticism or not; too much hangs on what is meant by mysticism.

"flesh," "law," "sin," and "death." But these are intertwined and interdependent. "Flesh" by itself no more characterizes life outside of Christ than does "law." And "sin," in Paul's mind, can be understood only in terms of the meaning of both "law" and "flesh." Together, in the effects each has on the others, they are the verbal net in which Paul catches the futility and hopelessness of life without Christ.

a. Life in the Flesh

Anyone demanding a clear and simple definition of "flesh" as Paul uses the word is doomed to disappointment. Yet the word appears everywhere. The apostle never bothers with precise definitions of it, and for his Hebrew readers probably did not have to bother. But what a confusion of meanings have been read into it in the long history of Pauline scholarship! I am not interested in reproducing all the colors on his canvass. But it is not hard to make a rough, working distinction. Paul's evaluation of flesh has two dimensions: (1) Flesh is the basic fact of human existence, to be accepted in humility and lived in gratitude; in this sense, it is the substructure of the moral life and has no prejudicial moral overtones. (2) Flesh is a chief characteristic of the life opposed to Christ and to the Spirit of Christ; it is a life in which a man not only is capable of displeasing God, but one in which it is *impossible* to please God. Let us take a longer look at each.

(1) Man in Weakness. This is the man who can be vexed by a thorn and who, paradoxically, finds his strength in accepting it in grace (II Cor. 12:7-9). He is the man who gets sick and dies (Gal. 4:13; I Cor. 15:50). Abraham was a man of flesh (Rom. 4:1), and so was Jesus (Rom. 1:3; 9:5). The Christian lives his life of faith "in the flesh" (Gal. 2:20), and while it is not as appealing as being "with Christ" (Phil. 1:22, 23), it is his opportunity to demonstrate the life of Christ even in so earthen a vessel (II Cor. 4:11).

Of course, the flesh is inferior to the way of Christ. The circumcision of the flesh cannot match that of the heart; but the circumcision of the flesh in itself is not evil (Rom. 2:28). The weapons of the flesh are paper tigers compared with those of the Spirit—the weapons of the flesh being human intelligence and will—but are not evil per se (II Cor. 10:2-4). For the same reason, flesh and blood are not the formidable opponent to the

Christian that the lords and powers behind the fleshly scene are
(Eph. 6:12). So, while inferior, the flesh in this sense is not bad.

In all this, Paul talks the language of the Hebrew who knows
that men *are* flesh. This is why he often identifies the ego of man
with his flesh. The flesh has desires (Gal. 5:17) and intents
(Rom. 8:6f.). Flesh stands for man, for weak, dependent man. It
means man whose existence needs a continuous inbreathing of
God; the moment God takes His breath away, flesh collapses.
As flesh, man is always on the edge of nothingness; to know this,
and to know it well, is to know oneself and, almost, to know
God. But to say that God's creature of flesh always needs God
is not to say that being flesh is bad.

(2) Man in Sin. As we have seen, being "in the flesh" is not
necessarily opposed to being "in Christ." It is true that in his
weakness, man is *open* to evil. In the first place, by virtue of his
body, he has an Achilles heel which angels do not have. For when
flesh is equated with weakness, the physical side of flesh is part
of the picture too. This solid but very vulnerable stuff we are
made of makes us special prey to sin. But, of course, our minds
and wills too are of the flesh; we are weak, mortal, and corruptible
clean through. Still, being a security risk is not the same as being
an enemy agent.

But Paul *does* in fact also put being "in the flesh" in the same
category as being on the wrong side in the great struggle for
ultimate commitments in the world. The bad side of the flesh is
exposed as being allied with the anti-Christian forces. Being "in
the flesh" here is far more than regrettable; it is a fatal identification with evil. In the first place, "those who are in the flesh
cannot please God" (Rom. 8:8). No Hebrew of the old covenant
would have dreamed of saying this: to him man *was* flesh, and
the way to please God was to face up to it. So, being "*in* the flesh"
cannot mean here the same thing as *being* flesh. "In the flesh"
means here "outside of Christ." To Christians, perhaps appre-
hensive of his indictment of the flesh, Paul quickly says: "But
you are not in the flesh, you are in the Spirit" (Rom. 8:9).

When one is "in the flesh" he lives "according to the flesh"
(Rom. 8:5, 7) and sets "his mind" on the flesh (Rom. 8:5). And
when this happens, his life bears fruit that is not only different
from but incompatible with the fruits of the Spirit (Gal. 5:16ff.).
But why? Why does the flesh war against the Spirit; why are "the
desires of the flesh against the Spirit" (Gal. 5:17)? Why is the

man who "lives according to the flesh" fated to die (Rom. 8:13)? That Paul is not talking merely about being sensuous or committing sensual sins is clear from the kinds of sin that living in the flesh produces: many of them are clearly sins of the spirit and mind (Gal. 5:17ff.).

Obviously, a new dimension is introduced into the life of man as flesh. Whereas once the pious man was the man who admitted and was glad that he was flesh—for this meant that he threw himself into the hands of God—now the man of flesh is precisely the sinful, condemned, and doomed man because he is opposed to God. Being in the flesh now means that a man puts his total stock in the flesh; makes it his "ultimate concern," his chief interest. Being in the flesh betrays where a man's heart is, where his hope and trust are planted. Being in the flesh reveals where a man's deepest loyalties lie and where the basic orientation of his life is found. The word "flesh," therefore, has come to stand for the spiritual environment in which a man willingly locates himself and by which he identifies himself. But that environment is not merely one that lacks something. It is an environment dominated and characterized by the powers of evil. It epitomizes the character of life in the unredeemed world; it is an epigram for life outside of and hostile to Christ. In its innocent sense, "flesh" stands for human life in its weakness, dependence, mortality, and corruptibility. In its bad sense, it stands for the weak life captured by evil.

Flesh as weakness could be a plausible foundation for the sacramentalist slant on human need. Flesh is fragile and precarious; it needs something else, a super-fleshly addition. Here, the contrast would be between flesh and God, with flesh needing something of God for its endurance and survival with God. Well, flesh obviously does need God; it needs God in, under, over, and around it always. But it needs the Creator to sustain it in life so that it can, in turn, respond to God in obedience and joy. Whether it is meant to have divinity within itself is dubious. This becomes clear as we notice how closely the distress and despair of life in the flesh is related not to its insufficiency in itself, but to its bad choice—its decision to try to be independent and self-sustaining with the help of a thing called the law.

b. Life under the Law

The law appears on the scene as another competitor to Jesus Christ, and life under the law as incompatible with life in Christ

(Gal. 5:4). Paul's fundamental thesis about the law is that its time
had come to an end: For Christ is the end of the law, that everyone who has faith may be justified (Rom. 10:4). To be under
the law is to opt for the "old things" that passed away when
everything became new in Christ (II Cor. 5:17). And this state
has the same ultimate frustrations and fatality as life "in the flesh."
In fact, they are but different-colored facets of the same tragic
reality.

Paul's attitude toward the law, as his feeling about everything,
was deeply prejudiced by his life stance within the new Christian
reality. He was not much interested in anything in the abstract;
what he wanted to know, as the decisive factor, was the bearing
a thing had on life in Christ. This is why he was concerned not
only with the *what* of a thing, but with the *how* as well; in the
case of the law, what he bore down on was not its material content,
but the *function* it had within a religious community. It was the
function that people gave the law that was decisive, not what the
law was in itself. For its function settled the question of how it
bore on men's relationship to God. Now anything—even the holy
law of God—that got in the way of grace was judged in terms of
its threat to salvation in Christ. This, it seems, must be kept in
mind as we try to understand Paul's complex and often passionate
assessment of the law.

Obviously, Paul's basic attitude toward the law is positive. This
is not surprising; the God of Jesus Christ is the God of creation
and the covenant *and* the law. As far as its content is concerned,
the law is "holy and just and good" (Rom. 7:12). Who would
expect the apostle to believe anything else? Paul knows that the
intent of the law is the fulfillment of love; the author of the hymn
on love is not inclined to complain of the plain purpose of God's
moral law (Gal. 5:14; Rom. 13:10). Christ is not the end of the
law in this sense; He is the one person who meant to fulfill and
did fulfill the law. Christ, far from ending the law, put it on its
proper footing (Rom. 3:31). And the Spirit's function within us is
to enable us to fulfill the genuine demands of the law (Rom.
8:4). *What* the law is, *what* the law reveals, *what* the law demands
is not only unassailable from the vantage point of Jesus Christ;
man must bow before it in total commitment as the revelation of
God Himself.

The *content* of the law gets unconditional assent. But the
function of the law is another matter. Here things become more
complex. There is an important distinction within the function of

the law. We can talk about its legitimate and intended function on the one hand and its illegitimate and distorted function on the other. We can talk about the function that God meant it to have and the function that people, at one time or another, invested it with. It would be hard to show that this distinction is spelled out by Paul in every case. But perhaps we can indicate it in rough outlines.

Let us take, first, its intended function. Was the law ever meant to be a means to save oneself? Paul says that the law itself witnessed to the righteousness that came by the free gift of grace (Rom. 3:21). How did it function as a witness to grace? This is not easy to say. The beginnings of the decalogue, of course, proclaim the fact that Israel's identity as the people of God rested in the mighty act of redemption from Egypt: "I am Jehovah thy God, who brought thee out of the land of Egypt." But Paul means the law to be taken as something broader than the decalogue: the whole religious system in the old covenant was the law, circumcision being its focal point. As such the law was a shadow of the real thing to come. More, it was a promise; it functioned as a harbinger, a pointer to the reality of divine grace.[17] This is why David and the congregation could sing of their *love for the law*. Now when the law functioned as a promise or a witness of better things to come, it had to be accepted as a conditional good; but when the reality came, this function was no longer necessary. Anyone in the Christian community who wants to restore the law to

[17]This is not always clear. Paul seems, in one place, to put Moses on the side of those who seek righteousness by the law: "Moses writes that the man who practices the righteousness which is based on the law shall live by it" (Rom. 10:5). This righteousness, preached by Moses, is opposed to the righteousness which is by faith (10:6). This, in turn, seems to oppose Paul's statement in Romans 3:21 that the law itself witnessed to the righteousness which is by faith. Is Paul putting Moses on the side of the Judaizers? Or could he be making Moses say what he himself would say: *if* you choose to live by the law, if you do determine to be a legalist, you had better go all the way with it, because on that basis you are going to be judged. Andrew Bandstra believes that Paul is putting Christian words in Moses' mouth: Moses is, in Paul's anachronism, speaking of Christians (Bandstra, *The Law and Elements of the World* [Kampen, 1964], p. 104). In another place, Paul uses Abraham's other wife, Hagar, as an allegory of spiritual bondage. He makes Hagar stand for Mt. Sinai, "for she is in slavery with her children" (Gal. 4:25). This seems to put the law (Sinai) in the camp against the promise. But Paul just said that the law could not conflict with the promise. Apparently, he slips Sinai into the allegory according to the definition that the Judaizers gave of the law; he is, for the moment, speaking the language of the legalists.

this function denies the fulfillment of the promise; he goes back to time B.C. and denies that Christ has come.

When Christians in Galatia were wooed back to the ceremonial law, their implicit denial of Christ surely formed part of Paul's vigorous protest (Gal. 5:4). And it may well be, as many commentators contend, that this is what Paul means when he affirms that Christ is the "end of the law." Christ, that is, fulfilled the law's promise; He is that to which the law pointed. To go back to the shadow, back to the sign, is to confess that Christ has turned out to be a failure, and we must look for another. At any rate, Paul says that in its time and for its purpose the law is good. But to continue that function now, in the time of Christ, is unthinkable. The law had a glory, but its glory is now eclipsed (II Cor. 3:14ff.).

But there is a negative function of the law that must also be approved. It is the law's condemnation of sin. To enter this part of Paul's theology of the law is to enter a maze of problems. Our purpose must be kept in bounds; we are trying to lead up to the law as a characteristic of life outside of Christ. But Paul says some important things about the law as the finger of judgment against sin. The law exposes acts of sin for what they are—rebellion against a living God. The law pins the sinner down, nails him at every corner; its sweeps the whole of life into its net and brands every infraction a culpable act of rebellion (Rom. 7:7-9). As it prohibits immoral and hostile acts, it reveals their true context. And at the same time it shows that everyone living under the law is under a curse; he is condemned (Gal. 3:10). Of course, the law condemned the *sinner*; it revealed God's deep indictment against him. But it did not manage to overcome *sin*; only Christ and His cross were up to this (Rom. 8:3). Yet insofar as it did condemn the sinner, with his sin, it did no more than God did in Jesus Christ. And this is a good and necessary function.

Leaving this discussion of Paul's positive attitude toward the law utterly incomplete, we do an abrupt about face to hear Paul's indictment of the law. Looked at from within Christ, the law is a bad thing. It is a prison, the dank dungeon of spiritual bondage (Gal. 3:22, 23). It is the jailor as well, the man who keeps people in chains (Rom. 7:6). The law is a domineering, restrictive guardian or pedagogue who keeps a child too long from the freedom of the mature (Gal. 3:24). It makes sin the worse (Rom. 7:13) and can even be branded as the power behind sin (I Cor. 15:56). In fact, the law destroys the souls of men (II Cor. 3:6).

No wonder Paul says to people who want to find salvation in the law, "You are severed from Christ" (Gal. 5:4). The law is not only a good thing now outmoded; it is a monster.

Here Paul is talking about the law as a concentrated anti-Christian power. The law, vicious and destructive, is the epitome of life outside of Christ. In this sense, Christ is the end of the law as its destroyer. He "cancelled the bond which stood against us with its legal demands; this he set aside, nailing it to the cross" (Col. 2:14). His crucification of the law was of a piece with his defeat of the "principalities and powers" (Col. 2:15). Apparently, the law had become a tool of the enemy; one of God's great goods had been stolen by the enemy and used to destroy God's creatures. But how?

At this point, we meet the strange coalition between flesh and the law of God. The conspiracy is terribly complex; the relationship between man and the law is dynamic, ambivalent, and shifting. But a few things are clear.

The law became a destructive power because of its alliance with the flesh. The flesh in one sense, we may recall, is man in weakness; it is man as he survives and accomplishes anything at all only with the underpinning and creative breath of God. But the flesh had, by the time the law was made explicit, already deluded itself with pretensions of independence from God. And so it had already capitulated and become sin. When the law came, it saw in the law a possibility of gaining status with God on its own; it made the law an instrument of self-righteousness. The law became part of a religious system which fostered man's sense of self-sufficiency. It became party to man's monstrous delusion.[18]

The law of God, as such, cannot be blamed. It was weak in this alliance, but it was weak only because it was given a function that it was never meant to perform. It had no power to enable the flesh to make good on its pretensions (Rom. 8:3). So, man's moral weakness, when it turns to the law as a device for moral pretension, turns the law into a moral Frankenstein.

This was the Judaistic legalistic system in its moral center. It was the religious system that Paul recognized as the enemy of Christ. The law had been turned inside out: rather than a witness to man's need of redemption, it had become a technique to save oneself. As this had occurred in history, the inner meaning of the

---

[18]See Berkouwer, *De Zonde*, I (Kampen, 1958), pp. 167ff.; and Bultmann, *Theology of the New Testament,* I, p. 264.

law had been forgotten: the letter is easier to use than the spiritual content of love. The prophets faced the horrible results of this legalism within Israelite society: they saw the barren, compassionless, unjust, and cruel effects within the community of religious legalism. So their indictments of the law were as severe as Paul's were. And they saw that the function of the law had failed because the people had turned from walking humbly before God and man (Mic. 6:8), as man in weakness, to the cruel pride that religious pretensions always create. They saw that only a new situation, one in which the Spirit replaced the code and got at the heart of man, would bring about a genuine change (Jer. 31:31; Ezek. 11:19ff.). They too realized that the law was inadequate to the function that men of flesh gave it in their delusions of strength.

What we have, then, is a situation in which the alliance between flesh and law creates a power which would destroy the soul. Within this situation, the real righteousness of God can never be discovered; faith—man's openness in weakness to God—is replaced by works, man's pretensions of self-achievement. This is the character of life outside of Christ. Although Paul has the Judaistic distortions before him,[19] the situation is parallel to every religious system in which man in weakness pretends to be man in strength, in which man in need of grace pretends to be man without need of grace. Paul sees the world outside of Christ as controlled and dominated by this alliance: moral law (or religious law) and flesh. When Paul talked about "the elements of the world" (Gal. 4:3; Col. 2:8, 20), he had in mind this collusion between flesh and law; for this collusion had created a moral system that gave the world its basic religious character.[20] In this sense, Paul saw the

[19]It has been shown that Judaism is a much more complex system than we would have known from Paul's indictment of it. There was always present within Judaism some sense that forgiveness was necessary and that the written law was not sufficient. See W. D. Davies, who gives a rather sympathetic account of Judaism (*Paul and Rabbinic Judaism* [London, 1955], pp. 321ff.). The Qumran community and its use of the law present a picture less legalistic than the Judaism that Paul knew. But Paul was not making fine distinctions. From within Christ, he radically opposed any system that left men on their own with the law to salvation by faith alone.

[20]Andrew Bandstra, *op. cit.,* p. 177. The law, Prof. Bandstra says, is called an "element of the world" specifically "as it operates in the context of the flesh." Here, God's "valid instrument" becomes occasion for and a power of sin.

moral and religious life of all men as bound to and structured by this fatal alliance.

The law (whether the decalogue, the religious system, or natural law) had become what people in their delusions of moral strength had made of it. Its function had been distorted. It had become quite another thing than a revelation of the free and living God, pointing to God's grace and promising God's redemption even while it exposed man's sin. This is why Paul, epigrammatically, can talk about being "under the law" as in violent hostility to being "in Christ" or in faith. The word "law" is a shorthand description of the whole situation men have gotten into. Paul is not abstracting law from life and condemning it as a thing; he sees it as it *functions* in the dynamic framework of man's sinful self-delusion.

But the law and the flesh result in sin. And sin ends in death. This is the fatality of the alliance. Flesh plus law equals death because flesh plus law leaves men in sin. It is this inevitable sequence that Paul probably has in mind when he talks about "the law of sin and death" (Rom. 8:2).[21]

c. Life in Sin

No one saw better than Paul did that a man is personally responsible for his acts. No corporate involvement in a social or political situation absolves the individual from his own responsibility. And no theological appraisal of the unity of the human race and its collective involvement in Adam's disobedience relieves the burden of his personal guilt. Being "in" a situation of sin has to do with men's inability to extract himself, not with a shifting of the burden of responsibility. Sin, for Paul, is personal hostility toward and flight from a personal God (Col. 1:21). And it is judged and

---

[21]It has always been hard to believe that Paul meant the "holy law" when he said that the Spirit had released us from the "law of sin and death." Calvin says that he would not dare to take this to mean God's holy law; he thinks rather that Paul is referring to something within the sinner's psychic penchant for sin (*Commentary on Romans,* 8:3). Dodd, too, takes it to be the subjective experience of sin's tyranny (*The Epistle of Paul to the Romans* [London, 1947], 8:3). Now I think it certainly involves subjective experience. But the law is that something "out there" which binds and controls this experience. While Paul is not speaking of the law in the abstract, he *is* talking of the law in its distorted function within the religious system of the man of weakness who is trying to use the law to gain moral independence. See Ridderbos, *Paulus* (Kampen, 1966), pp. 106ff.; I. Hermann, *Kyrios and Pneuma* (München, 1961); and Neugebauer, *op. cit.,* p. 92.

forgiven on a decisively personal level. For men are personally and privately, as well as corporately, engaged in practices and possessed of minds that are reprehensible and intolerable. There is no escaping the fact that for Paul every man, privately and personally, is responsible for sin. To be "in sin" is to be a sinner.

There are many dimensions to sin, many grades in the seriousness of sin, many kinds of specific sins. But there is also a universal *state* of sinfulness. This does not mean only that all men commit sins of various sorts, though it certainly means this much (Rom. 3:23). But the sinfulness of the human situation betrays moreover the fact that all men are somehow *bound* to sin. In one sense, God has allowed men to bind themselves to sin: He gave them over to a "reprobate mind." This is repeated several times in Romans 1: it suggests that God did not merely create men with freedom to sin, but that He abandoned them in a situation which they freely chose to enter. God, says Paul, "consigned all things to sin" (Gal. 3:22). This could mean that God "declared" all things to be sinful and it could mean that God assigned men to the situation to which they willingly assigned themselves. In either sense, He considers men to be imbedded in a situation that is sinful. Therewith, sin dominates men. It is not merely an occasional decision; it is a power that creates the atmosphere in which men live. It dominates their mind (Rom. 1:21), their will (Rom. 7:15-20), and their body (Rom. 7:24). Individual men are inextricably involved and hopelessly controlled by something which Paul telescoped into the word "sin."

To be "in sin" is to have one's whole existence as man dominated by sin. And since the situation is the human situation, globally, every man is a sinner. It is easy for Paul to objectify sin and personalize it too. Sin is a despot with absolute control over man (Rom. 5:21). It "entered" the world, achieved mastery over men (Rom. 6:6, 11ff.). Death is sometimes a retribution for sin and sometimes a natural fruit of sin (Rom. 7:9, 11, 25), but sometimes sin itself pays with death (Rom. 6:23). The man in sin is the man "sold under sin" (Rom. 7:14). He is its slave, though its obedient and willing slave. Paul is not telling us that sin is actually a thing or a person. He is telling us, however, that the human situation is so dominated by this characteristic form that it can be thought of as a personal power at work in the world. Being "in sin" is living "under the power of sin." We hear Paul saying that we "walked in sin" when we were "following the course of this world, following the prince of the power of the air, the spirit that is now at work in the sons of disobedience" (Eph. 2:2).

Being "in sin" therefore is to be in the human situation that is outside of Christ's redemptive lordship. Being liberated from sin is to be liberated from the power that controls the human situation in this "evil age." Of course, it is also to be liberated from personal sinful behavior. But the redemptive power of Christ is basically the power which liberates the sinner from his captivity by the demonic forces behind all particular sins (see Rom. 8:38, I Cor. 15:24, II Cor. 4:4, Eph. 6:12, and Col. 2:14).

Sin was not introduced by the fateful alliance between the flesh and the law. "Sin indeed was in the world before the law was given" (Rom. 5:13). But the collusion of flesh with law intensified and deepened the hopelessness of the sinful situation. For sinful flesh, flesh in delusions of independence, tried to fight its way out of its tangle of deceit by making use of a law that had no capability for the fight. And thus the sinful web caught man the more completely.

The hopelessness of sin intensified by the alliance between flesh and law is the overwhelming fact of life outside of Christ. Such a life leads to death because it involves men in divine judgment. It leaves men in despair or in delusion until Christ liberates them. And to suffer from either is to suffer from the sickness unto death. It is to be "dead in trespasses and sin." The only way out is to be transferred from the world under the "principalities and powers" to the world under the lordship of Christ. All of Paul's various ways of summarizing man's predicament point to the same total situation. When he says "being in the flesh" is hostile to being "in the Spirit," or that being "under the law" is incompatible with being "under grace," or that being "in sin" is impossible while one is "in Christ," he is pointing to the same situation. The interaction of all these deadly characteristics creates man's situation as it is controlled, betrayed, and doomed by the "powers of darkness" behind the scenes. This is why, within everything that Paul writes about Christ's death and resurrection, the decisive aspect for the creation of a new world in Christ is victory over the forces of evil.

It could with some plausibility be argued that man is bound to his sinful situation because, being *only* flesh, he cannot lift himself above it. And it could then be argued that Jesus Christ provides the sacramental infusion of trans-fleshly divine life that enables man to transcend this sinful situation. We will face this question when we discuss Paul's notion of "Christ in us." But our brief excursion into the life of man "outside of Christ" certainly suggests

the need for a radically new situation rather than a supernaturalized, divinized old one.

2. *The New Creature in Christ*

"Therefore, if any one is in Christ, he is a new creation; the old
has passed away, behold, the new has come" (II Cor. 5:17). This
is by all odds the best known of the "in Christ" passages and
without doubt among the most central. But it is really no more
than a frame around the phrase "in Christ." We see that being "in
Christ" means that a man is a new creature. Being a new creature
means that he has left the old creature completely behind. But we
are left to ask Paul what he has in mind with each of these abso-
lutistic categories. The verse does not explain; it only proclaims the
great expectation for the disciple of Jesus.

If ever the old rule against quoting texts out of context holds
true, it does here. Without the context, this manifesto of the new
creation could be used to lead us in many directions. By itself,
Paul's statement could be given the most unrealistic of moral ap-
plications. It could also be construed in strong support of mysticism. But while Paul talks here about a man's being *in* Jesus
Christ and about a radical alteration in such a man, the context
makes it clear that his main theme is neither of these. His subject is the act of God in Jesus Christ at the cross of Calvary.

The classic passage on the new creature in Christ begins with
a "therefore," and this word refers back to the crucifixion. The
event that changed things for people is the death of Jesus. The
place where the "old things passed away" and the new came into
being is Calvary, back there in history now gone by; "He died for
all, that those who live (having once died) might live no longer
for themselves but for him who for their sake died and was raised"
(vs. 15). The crucial moment is a moment in past history. The
crucial category is an event.

Reconciliation is firmly planted in this historical event. God
reconciled us to Himself by means of a particular occurrence at
a particular place during three particular hours that could have
been measured on anyone's clock. Reconciliation brings together
people who had been estranged. In this case, it brings a world
of people back into partnership with the God from whom they
had been alienated. This is how it happens that men become new
creatures. And it comes about because "hostility was brought
to an end" at the cross.

We are not groping in a world of ideas about initiation into the divine-human life of a universal Spirit. We are in a very clear set of historical events. Jesus did something that changed things between God and us. It is true that some translations of verse 16 can mislead us: "Wherefore henceforth know we no man after the flesh: yea, though we have known Christ after the flesh, yet now henceforth know we *him* no more." Readers have been known to jump on the last part of this sentence as disclaiming an interest in the historical Jesus. But such a move is precipitate. The RSV provides this discerning translation: "though we once regarded Jesus from a human point of view, we regard him thus no longer." This tells us that while Paul is not dissociating his gospel from the earthly Jesus, he is dissociating himself from earthly judgments about Jesus.

The measure that Paul takes of Jesus is not by ordinary canons. This is why he says he does not regard Jesus any longer "after the flesh." Men whose wisdom was limited to the "flesh" or "the world" judged Jesus deserving of hammer and nails. And now it takes the "wisdom" taught by the Spirit (I Cor. 2:13) to gauge the real dimensions of that "judgment." In short, Paul is not saying that the Jesus of history fails to interest him now that he has had a mystical involvement in the Christ of the Spirit. He is saying that what he knows of the historical Jesus is gained from a transcendent vista.

What he knows is that when Jesus died, the world came alive to God. Paul's vision of reconciliation is not crippled by an atomistic individualism. Paul is not cabined by a narrow theology which counts as gospel only the possibility of individuals escaping hell. He does not shrink his soteriology to the rescue of isolated souls from a forsaken world, nor his expectations merely to a hope in the moral development of the inner life of the soul. The entire world that God made, the world that men led away from God's love, the world that God kept on loving, the world to which God gave His Son—this is the world reconciled through Christ. Nothing less than the panoramic vision of a world recreated will capture Paul's vision of reconciliation.

What, then, is the new creature?

Paul speaks in the indicative mood. He is not urging men to *become* new creatures. Nor is he, expressly at any rate, telling us what they *may become* in some distant and perhaps remote future. He does not urge us to put aside the old and work ourselves into the new life. He appears to be stating a bald fact about

the *present* state of the man in Christ.[22] And it must be noted that
he seems quite unconcerned about what could only have been perfectly obvious to him—the fact that even he had not shed his "old
nature" and become wholly new. He retained in himself more than
a few embers of sin. Yet he states with utter surety that the man in
Christ *is* a new creation.

Where is the new creation? May we look for it in the changed
moral life of individual Christians? There, too, of course, but not
primarily. The new exists wherever Christ is known, confessed,
and served as the Lord of life. The new exists wherever men are
in fact reconciled to God. May we insist, as Neugebauer and most
interpreters do, that the new creation is the Church?[23] I think we
may. If I understand this thesis, it suggests that anyone who is
genuinely part of the community where the reconciliation of Christ
is preached and lived is part of that new movement in history
called the new creation.

What is understood here is that the Church is in embryonic
form the model, the avant-garde, of the recreated world. It
means that the new creation takes the form now of a community
aware of the new reality. And this means that Paul is saying something like this: If anyone is reconciled to God within the community of Christ, he is by that token in Christ; and anyone in
Christ is part of that new community which knows that its leader
and ruler is Christ. What is helpful about this interpretation is the
reminder that the new creature is social, just as the old creature is.
The man in Christ is never there by himself; being in Christ is
always an existence in communion. The new order of Christ is
present in the tangible social organism of the Church.

What Paul is stressing is the existence of a new creation through
reconciliation. The old order is doomed and as good as dead.
"With the old order passed away, the new has taken its place. That
these two should co-exist in one sphere is impossible. When the

---

[22]Calvin seems to suppose that Paul is talking in the imperative mood;
one ought to be a new creature. Calvin supplies what he thinks is Paul's
point: "if anyone is desirous to hold some place in Christ, that is, in the
kingdom of Christ, or in the church, *let him be a new creature.* By this
expression he condemns every kind of excellence that is wont to be in much
esteem among men, if renovation of the heart is wanting." *Commentary on
Corinthians,* Vol. II, II Cor. 5:17. Calvin assumes that Paul is talking about
the inner moral condition of individuals. This is why he cannot assume that
Paul is simply stating a fact about affairs as they are in Christ.

[23]Neugebauer, *op. cit.,* p. 112.

new arrives, the old must be disrobed of power."[24] This, Paul is proclaiming as a cosmic *fait accompli*. As Geerhardus Vos said: "There has been created a totally new environment, or, more accurately stated, a totally new world. . . . The whole surrounding world has assumed a new aspect and a new complexion. . . ."[25] The creative center is the cross. The dominant person is Christ. The arena is history. The Christian is a man in the new world. He has "been transformed into a new world, a world which differs *toto genere* in all its character, its whole environment . . . from the present world."[26]

All this does not pinpoint with finality how we should interpret the "in Christ" part of the passage. But it does give a sign. It points us in the direction of the historical cross, an event, as the determining factor; it points us to history. Schweitzer was right: "like a lighthouse that throws its beam upon the ocean of the eternal, the Pauline mysticism stands firm, based upon the firm foundation of the historical manifestation of Jesus Christ."[27] The most famous of the "in Christ" passages is rooted in the non-mystical world of Pontius Pilate, Roman soldiers, public executions, and garden tombs.

Further, we see that the new creation is tied to reconciliation. What God did in Christ at the cross of Calvary was to break down the wall that divided men from Him and therefore from one another. The new world is the world of reconciled men. Anyone who is part of the reconciled world order, in which Christ is preeminent as the dominating personality, is "in Christ."

Since being "in Christ" is not an escape from history, but a participation in the new reality in history, the person in Christ is in agony. For while being "in Christ" involves the relocation of a person within a whole new order of existence in history, he can find little in actual history that indicates the radical righteousness and love characteristic of the new creation. The "old things" have not all passed away. The "new" has come only ambiguously at best. And the saints on earth cry even more agonizingly than their brothers under the altar: "How long, O Lord?" (Rev. 6:9f.)

If being "in Christ" were a mystical or idealistic experience of the soul or mind within the life of divinity beyond history, we

[24]Seesemann, in Kittel, *Theologisches Wörterbuch zum Neuen Testament,* V (Stuttgart, 1933), p. 716.
[25]*Pauline Eschatology* (Grand Rapids, 1961), p. 47.
[26]*Ibid.,* p. 150.
[27]*Op. cit.,* p. 379.

could escape the agony. Were it the truncated apocalyptic of extreme fundamentalism, the failures of historical promises would only generate in us a deep skepticism. Were it an existentialist category of personal decision, undetermined as to form and norm, we would not be bothered by the apparent contradiction between the "new thing" in Christ and the actual existence around us of the "old things." None of these perspectives actually looks for, believes in, or assumes the reality of the new creation as an authentic reality within the history of our present world. But if we assume, as we must, that the Christian has here and now been liberated from the kingdom of darkness and given asylum in the land of light, that the "powers" have fallen, that the "god of this age" has been defeated, that "old things have passed away and the new has come," we are in agony. But it is the agony of one who knows that things have really changed and are going to change; only the man who knows in faith that something has happened and is going to happen is likely to cry, "How long?"

3. Freedom in Christ

Scholars have sometimes seen in Paul two minds struggling for possession of his theology, the prophetic mind and the mystical. The prophetic mind was the Hebrew in Paul. The mystical mind was the Greek. According to the prophetic mind, God was the holy and just Judge who pardoned us. According to the mystical, God was the One who shared His life in Christ with us. The prophetic mind proclaimed justification by faith. The mystical mind offered union with Christ through the Spirit. The prophetic mind preached forgiveness through the juridical atonement made at the cross. The mystical mind offered new experience through the Christ who had become Spirit. The prophetic mind said that Christ was "for us." The mystical mind said that we are "in Christ." And for many scholars it has been a fascinating game to prove that one mind or the other was at work in a given instance, or that both were reconciled into a synthesis.[28]

No single sentence shows that Christ "for us" is not in tension with our being "in Christ" more clearly than does the famous opening verse of Romans 8. There is therefore no condemnation

[28]Neugebauer presents a lucid summary of several attempts to work with Paul in this manner, *op. cit.*, pp. 9ff. Davies dispels quite effectively the notion of a Hebrew-Greek dichotomy in Paul, *op. cit.*, p. 320.

for those who are in Christ Jesus. Here we have the language of
the courtroom ("no condemnation") combined with the language
of mysticism ("in Christ"). Freedom from condemnation is for
those who are in Christ. But what is the relationship between
these two factors? Taken by itself, Romans 8:1 does not give us
any light on the meaning of "in Christ." Nor does it tell us how
being in Christ releases anyone from condemnation. Almost any
theological outlook can bring this sentence into its service as long
as it isolates the verse from others. But, of course, it does not
stand alone, and it cannot be taken by itself.

The seventh chapter is primarily a picture of human history
under the lordship of the "powers of darkness." Man here is under
the control of a situation beyond his changing or undoing. He is a
man "sold under sin" (7:14). There is a "law of sin" (7:23) to
which a man "in the flesh" is captive. This "law"—or prevailing
power—dominates, frustrates, and dooms human life. Not even
the good law of God can help in this situation; indeed it only
makes matters worse. Even when a man, in his deepest humanity,
approves the law of God and hates sin, he is powerless to commit
himself to that law because he is ruled and weakened by the other
law. Man is shackled to the situation. This is why Paul ends his
description of the futility and bondage of life with a desperate
"Who will deliver me?"[29]

The anguish is answered by God in action. Paul's song is
"Thanks be to God through Jesus Christ our Lord" (7:25). More
specifically, the situation has changed and man is released from
the "law of sin." "For God has done what the law, weakened by
the flesh, could not do: sending his own Son in the likeness of
sinful flesh, and for sin, he condemned sin in the flesh" (8:3).
This is the action that changed the old situation into the new one.
When Paul says that Christ "condemned sin," he is not talking
about so weak a thing as moral disapproval. The old law did that,

[29]It seems inescapable to me that Romans 7 is *not* a picture of the
twisting and turning of the man in Christ as he wrestles against his "old
nature." Of course, Paul is looking at the "old situation" in Romans 7 from
the perspective of the new situation "in Christ." He is not necessarily
describing his personal experience, but the experience common to the native of the old order. Nor does this mean that every verse in Romans 7
applies, the most obvious exception being verse 25. If the reader is interested in exegetical roll calls, I may say that I am here following Bultmann,
Theology of the New Testament, I, pp. 244ff., 266, *et al.*, and Ridderbos,
Romeinen (Kampen, 1959), pp. 142ff. For a creative presentation of a
via media, see Bandstra, *op. cit.*, pp. 138ff.

and won man's agreement; everyone agrees that it is better to be good than to be bad. Everyone in his deepest conscience approves the good, even "delights in the law of God" (7:22). When Paul says that Christ "condemned sin," he means that Jesus doomed sin as a power, that Jesus disarmed and dethroned it as the prevailing force in the new age and sentenced it effectively to exile.

But the effect of the cross is far more than negative; it introduced the new age of the Spirit. In Romans 8 Paul goes on to depict life in the new situation in terms of the Spirit; he mentions the Spirit some twenty times. Here we must recall everything that has been said about Christ and the Spirit. We must recall that in the new covenant of freedom the "Lord is the Spirit." Christ is Lord, and His lordship is effective because the Spirit functions as Christ the Lord on earth.

Thus, when Paul describes the new situation as governed by the "law of the Spirit," he is also saying that the new situation is the historical scene of the lordship of Jesus Christ. The "law of the Spirit" dominates the new situation as the "law of sin" dominated the old. The "law of the Spirit of life in Christ Jesus" has set us free. Now the Spirit dominates even as He liberates; He leads even as He sets us free; and He enables us to "fulfill the just requirements of the law" even as He liberates us from the "condemnation" of the law and sin.

Clearly, freedom in Christ does not retire us from service to the moral law; Christ does not make the law an obsolete vestige of a more primitive religious age. What He does do is change our way of looking at the law. And so the law itself looks differently to us and functions differently for us. Once, in our stupidity, we expected the law to function as our ally. And we thought that with the help of the law we could conquer the moral life. But we were weak and the law was unable to protect our flanks. In fact, the law helped to trap us, and we were defeated, unconditionally. But Christ created a new alliance: now we are under Him as Lord, and we are in the new situation where the Spirit exercises His lordship. The Spirit enables us by His own powerful influence to "fulfill the just requirement of the law."

Now the whole face of the law is changed. Now the law looks like the living Christ, who Himself fulfilled the demands of the law. The content of the law is the same: the life of total love. But the function is quite different. Now the law means the service of Christ who set us free. And obedience is a matter of being "led by the Spirit." The law is now the way of life within the lordship of

Christ. That man is free, indeed, whose life is "in the Spirit" and not "in the flesh." He is free from something so that he can be free for something; he is liberated from condemnation so that he can freely serve in the Spirit.[30]

Let us celebrate this freedom! Let us not be intimidated by its abuse. License must not tempt us to go back under the law. The way to answer license is not to proclaim a new legalism. This was not Paul's way when he faced the false demand for freedom in Corinth; it should not be the Christian's way when he faces the phony demands for freedom rampant in our age. We should not encourage people to distort the function of the law again. We should point them to the Christ, whose victorious death condemned sin and whose lordship opens the way to true morality under God. Our way must still be Paul's way, even though the situation outside of Christ takes on a new form today.

So we have in Romans 7 and Romans 8 two basic divisions in human history, implacably opposed and mutually exclusive. The first is tragically guilt-ridden; the second is joyfully guilt-free. The first is an alliance between man in his weakness and the law in its impotence to overcome man's weakness; the second is an alliance between man in his weakness and the Spirit in His power to overcome man's weakness. The first is bondage to sin; the second is freedom in service. The first stands condemned; the second stands liberated from condemnation. The first ends in death; the second ends in life. Between the two situations stands the cross of Jesus Christ, where our liberation and the liberation of history were achieved.

Who is the person "in Christ"? He is the person for whom sin has been condemned by the cross and who has been brought into the new life situation of the Spirit. He is the man who has been liberated from the "law of sin and death" and given permanent asylum in the situation where the "law of the Spirit of life" is in force. He is a man in the new situation within human history, in which Christ is Lord and the Lord is Spirit. Therefore he is liberated from the doom that fell on sin at Calvary because he does not come under its jurisdiction. It must be clear that being "in Christ" means being within the dominion of Christ, under His lordship as it is made good on earth by the Spirit.

Surely the theology of Christ "for us" cannot be in tension with

---

[30]I recommend as a delightfully incisive discussion of Christian freedom Henry Stob's *The Christian Concept of Freedom* (Grand Rapids, 1957).

the theology of existence "in Christ." Paul is not of two minds. Only if we let ourselves think of Christ "for us" in a purely personal and juridical way and then let ourselves think of being *in Christ* in a purely personal and mystical way, only if we *let* them be at odds will they be at odds at all. But if we think of Christ "for us" as having accomplished something against the power of defeat and doom and as having established the new order of His Spirit, we will see that reality "in Christ" follows as an inevitable effect.

To be "in Christ" is to be part of the new community where the Spirit of holiness and life is the dominant power and guiding norm. His creative, life-giving and life-styling action is the way Jesus Christ exercises His lordship. It is the way of love and peace and assurance. And from this new situation, nothing can separate us, nothing at all; for it is the situation in which we are kept by "the love of God in Christ Jesus our Lord" (8:39). And to be there, where He is, is to be "in Christ."

4. In Christ and in Adam

Christ and Adam represent the beginnings of two conflicting histories of man. Each in his way is so crucial to human destiny that Paul finds it meaningful to say that men are "in Adam" just as he says they are "in Christ": "For as in Adam all die, so also in Christ shall all be made alive" (I Cor. 15:22). Here, we die in Adam and are alive in Christ. In Romans 5, Paul draws the parallel in the contrasting colors of sin and grace, guilt and forgiveness. But the two passages merge; for death is the corollary of sin and life is the corollary of pardon. As members of the old, sinful humanity, we are in Adam. As members of the new, forgiven humanity, we are in Christ.

Our concern with the existence of man "in Adam" is to see how this reality helps us understand how we are "in Christ." Paul does not give us a simple doctrine of our being "in Adam," at least not a doctrine that is clear to a modern Western reader. His interest, of course, is theological; he is not talking cultural anthropology or racial biology. So we would be foolish to construct a theory of the unity of the human race and apply that theory to the doctrine of unity with Christ.

We must also recall that St. Paul looks at everything from his vantage point in Christ; this was true of the law and it is true of Adam. When he says that we are "in Christ" as we are "in Adam," he brings in the parallel because he first sees man as in Christ. "Paul," says Berkouwer, "does not analyze the world of death and guilt and then turn to seek a remedy for it; but he holds up the reality of grace against the background of a world of death. Adam stands in the light of Christ. Christ is the center and theme of the whole argument. Adam only stands for the darkness into which *this* light has dawned."[31] Barth says the same: "Paul does not go to Adam to see how he is connected with Christ; he goes to Christ to see how he is connected with Adam."[32]

This is clearly the case. Paul's premise and his argument is that Jesus Christ did awaken from His own death and that His resurrection means that we too will rise again. But he does make the analogy between our inclusion in Christ as a consequence of His resurrection and our inclusion in Adam. And he must have assumed that the analogy would make sense to his readers; thus he must also have assumed that being "in Adam" would not be a totally strange notion to them.

So, while Barth is right in warning us against coming to the "in Christ" doctrine with our own theory of the unity of the human race in Adam, as though we could explain being "in Christ" by means of our theory about Adam, this should not keep us from asking what *Paul* had in mind with his "in Adam" analogy. Nor should it prevent us from asking what light the analogy plays on the reality of our new existence "in Christ." Further, the "background of the world of death" is clearly meant to help us understand the universality of the creative effect that Christ's resurrection had on human history.

The comparison is this: one man brought death to all and another man brought life to all. The first Adam brought death. The last Adam—the final or eschatonic Adam—brought life. How did the final Adam bring life? Paul gives a double answer. The final Adam brings life by the *event* of His own resurrection. And He brings it by the fact that He became *the life-giving Spirit*. By His resurrection He overcame the power of death. In becoming the life-giving Spirit, He became the creator of new life. Each of these is indispensable. If Christ were not risen, the message of hope would be false (I Cor. 15:14). If Christ were not the life-giving Spirit, there would be no possibility of our overcoming mortality. Is there in the first Adam a parallel to each of these factors?

[31]*De Zonde*, II, pp. 290ff.
[32]*Christ and Adam* (London, 1956), p. 17.

There is to the first, but not to the second. Adam too was decisive in his effect on man's history by virtue of an *event*. This we learn from Romans 5. He brought death into history by his *act* of disobedience. By "one man's disobedience many were made sinners" (Rom. 5:19). And sin results in death.

The fact that sin results in death explains why in I Corinthians 15, Paul says that if Christ is not risen, we are yet in our *sins*. Being in sin is contrasted to being made alive because being in sin is equivalent to being doomed to death. I Corinthians 15 must be read as a companion to Romans 5. They do not say different things; they complement each other. When in Romans 5:19 Paul says that many are made righteous by the obedience of Christ even as they were made sinners by the disobedience of Adam, he is only bringing out another facet of the same reality he emphasizes in I Corinthians 15 where he says that we are dead in Adam and made alive in Christ. The two facets are joined in Romans 5:21: "As sin hath reigned unto death, so might grace reign through righteousness *unto* eternal life by Jesus Christ our Lord."

The parallel between Adam and Christ, then, is focused on the decisive *events* in which each was the central figure. Adam is not the first man simply because he was first on the scene. He is not the originator of the old simply because he was the first psychic or biological man. Paul's interest here is not cultural or biological; his interest is theological. Adam is first in the significance of what he *did in response to God's demands*. And Christ is final in the same sense.

So in one respect Adam and Christ are parallel, though opposite in their significance. In the second respect, they are not parallel: "The first man Adam became a living being while the last Adam became *a life-giving Spirit*" (I Cor. 15:45). We have already discussed the importance of this verse for the work of Christ in the present time. Here we need only note that Paul makes this contrast to show that the present physical constitution of man is no criterion for assessing the possibility of a resurrection body. All Paul tells us here is that we cannot judge the possibilities of the future by the creation of Adam; for now, in the new situation, we have an association with another kind of power. Jesus Christ, the new and decisive head of the new race, is the life-giving Spirit. The only criterion for measuring the possibilities of having resurrection bodies is the power of Christ as Spirit. Adam is here disqualified from relevance to the question.

The parallel between our being "in Adam" and our being "in

Christ" must be understood, then, in terms of the historical consequences of the decisive actions of each. Adam by his act brought
history under a new control, with a new destiny. Christ by His act
also brought history under a new control, with a new destiny. To
be in the situation which each key man created is to be "in" that
man. The situations are absolutely different. They are different in
their outcomes. But they are also different in their manner. In the
new situation in Christ, the Final Man *remains* personally active.
Within the history begun by Him, He remains at work as the Spirit
who actually makes men alive to the new reality and shapes them
to the standards of the new situation.

But we must ask one more question. If we say that Paul's
doctrines of existence "in Adam" and "in Christ" refer to our
existence in the historical community and situation begun by each
and dominated by the effects of each, we are saying that the two
men *represent* the race of men within each situation. There must
then be a fundamental unity of mankind to make it possible for the
actions of Adam and Christ to determine the destiny and character
of men in history. And Paul must have assumed that his readers
shared his deep intuition of this. What does tie us so profoundly
to Adam?

Perhaps we should not try to answer this question; perhaps we
should simply accept the deep sense within us and the obvious
biblical assumption that we are all bound together in common
humanity as limbs are vitally connected in one body. Anders
Nygren says that our share in Adam "rests on the fact that our race
stands in *organic* unity with Adam."[33] C. H. Dodd thinks Paul
looks on us all as existing in "a sort of mystical unity" with Adam
and one another.[34] Davies says that Paul assumed a traditional
rabbinic doctrine that the physical body of Adam—its constitution
and the way it was made—"was symbolic of the real oneness of
mankind."[35] Ridderbos is content to talk about a "divinely ordained
structure in creation and redemption" that makes possible a repre-
sentation of the whole by a single member.[36] Do these observations
really tell us anything? That Paul—that the entire Bible—looks on

---

[33]*Commentary on Romans* (Philadelphia, 1949), p. 237.
[34]*The Epistle of Paul to the Romans*, p. 79.
[35]*Op. cit.*, p. 57.
[36]*Romeinen*, p. 114. Bultmann, as would be expected, thinks that Paul,
in talking about the unity of the race in Adam, is "unquestionably under
the influence of the Gnostic myth" (*Theology of the New Testament*, I,
p. 251). He agrees, however, that "the universal fallenness of Adamitic
mankind to sin and death is beyond all question in Paul" (*ibid.*, p. 253).

man not as a conglomeration of atomistic souls, but as a corporate oneness is clear. And that Paul can let one individual represent the whole is based on this assumption. We can be "in Adam" in the sense that we belong to the human situation whose character and destiny is shaped and formed by his decisive actions.

Perhaps the popular phrase "corporate personality" is as helpful as any to indicate the relationship of one man to the rest of men. Among the Hebrews, the solidarity of the clan or community meant that one individual and his acts could represent the whole. Adam, then, stands for the situation or community of men as it exists under conditions set by his crucial act of disobedience. "As Adam stands at the head of αἰὼν οὗτος [this age] as the first man, so the risen Christ stands at the head of the αἰὼν μέλλων [coming age] as the Initiator of the perfect redeemed creation of God."[37] Behind this fact there is the assumption that the community is bound together with the one individual in so basic a way as to make it possible for the individual to change the character and standing of the whole community. The individual is a specific personality, but he stands for the corporation. In a sense, he *is* the corporation.[38]

Being "in Adam" is then a matter of being in the community he represents. As we have seen, he represents the community of mankind in terms of his significantly disastrous action. He created a situation in which all men subsequently find themselves. To be in that situation, to be conditioned, controlled, and confined by it in a theological sense, is what is meant by being "in Adam." This is formally parallel to what is meant by being "in Christ." As Oepke says: "Believers are removed from the sphere of the first Adam, which is that of sin and death, into the sphere of the second Adam, which is that of righteousness and life."[39]

We have said enough, I think, to show that the parallel between

[37]Jeremias, in Kittel, *Theological Dictionary of the New Testament*, I, p. 143.

[38]"The group could be thought of as functioning through an individual member who for the time being so completely represents it that he became identical with it" (H. H. Rowley, *Re-discovery of the Old Testament* [Philadelphia, 1946], p. 216). Of course, the notion of "corporate personality" could be abused so as to cancel out individual responsibility. Berkouwer reminds us that the faddish use of "corporate personality" could suggest that men are only pawns in a cosmic struggle. He does not deny communal involvement; but he wants to stress the other side, that "communal guilt is *manifest* in the way of *our own* guiltiness" (*De Zonde*, II, p. 303).

[39]Kittel, *Theological Dictionary of the New Testament*, II, p. 542.

Adam and Christ—and our existence in each—is a matter of the historical consequences of their actions for the rest of the human race. We are not dealing with a mystical identity with them personally. Nor is it a case of being germinally present in Adam's sperm or physically present in the human nature of Jesus. Rather, we are dealing with the fact that what Adam *did* and Christ *did* had a chain of consequences that radically affect the situation in and under which other men live. If any theory about the mystical unity or the biological unity of the human race helps to underscore this reality, it may be useful; but it is not the exclusive key to an appreciation of the fact. To be in Adam is to be a member of the human race whose life and history are basically affected by what Adam did. We see this because we know that to be in Christ is to be a member of the new race of men whose life and history are basically determined by His redemptive acts of death and resurrection.[40]

5. Elect in Christ

> Blessed be the God and Father of our Lord Jesus Christ, who has blessed us in Christ with every spiritual blessing in the heavenly places, even as he chose us in him before the foundation of the world, that we should be holy and blameless before him. (Ephesians 1:3, 4)

No other sentence that Paul wrote carries more mystery into our union with Christ than this doxology. And the doxology can easily be spoiled by trading the mystery for a crisp formula. The Christian faith is better off when it bows before the mystery of eternally antecedent love than when it carries off the prize of a logical formula and kills the doxology. Still, the words are in front of us. And words are meant to help our understanding as well as to kindle our devotion.

---

[40]Paul does not mention faith in this context, just as he omits it in the chapter on "dying with Christ" (Rom. 6). This is hard to take at first glance. James Denney refuses to take it at all: "St. Paul does indeed represent Christ as the head of a new humanity . . . but the mere existence of Christ does not constitute the new humanity. It is only constituted as men in faith freely identify themselves with Him" (*The Christian Doctrine of Reconciliation* [New York, 1917], p. 305). But his alternatives are wrongly put. There is no such thing for Paul as "the mere existence of Christ." Christ is what He is *in* His significance as the head of a new humanity. Only as He is the head of a new humanity is He the Christ, the Eschaton Adam, at all. Granted this, we can then say that we are in that humanity only *in faith*.

We approach Paul's words with this question: what does the doctrine of election tell us about our life in Christ? This is the reverse of the question that one ordinarily asks of this text: what does the fact that we are chosen in Christ tell us about the doctrine of election? But the two questions are interwoven. And, in a sense, we are forced to ask them both at the same time. For each question, if asked separately, implies that we already have the answer to the other. So, we had better ask again about "*election* in Christ" and also ask if it illumines the reality of our *being* in Christ.[41]

First we must observe that Paul sings his song to electing love from within the reality of life in Christ. He begins from where we are—in Christ. We are, he says, blessed in Christ and are present with Christ "in heavenly places" (1:3). This is what he mentions here. But, of course, his thought reaches out to all that life in Christ means for faith and hope. He speaks from the perspective of hope as well as of faith. He is now "in the heavenly places": this is the language of faith. "Heavenly places" points to the new creation that is really, but not comprehensively present. So it is the language of hope: the "heavenly places" are where we are *hid* with God in Christ. It points ahead to a future reality that Paul mentions a few sentences later—the reality of "all things" united in Christ, things on earth as well as in heaven. The surprising reality is that we, sinners, are already included in the new reality.

Only a sense of wonder and the experience of surprise inspire songs. A man is not moved to sing by commonplaces. The inevitability of the syllogism does not inspire a doxology. A man sings when he wonders; his songs are born of mystery. And the wonder here is that men *like us* are "in the heavenly places with

[41]That the nature of our union with Christ was explained by Paul's doctrine of election was firmly believed by Albert Schweitzer. "Once it is perceived," he writes, "that we have to start from the conception of the predestined solidarity of the Elect with one another and with the Messiah, the mystical body of Christ is at once explained" (*op. cit.*, p. 117). This is too large a claim, it seems to me. But it does have point. Taken in its whole breadth, to include the goal of election as well as the fact of it, to include God's purpose to unite all things in Christ by means of His resurrection, it does tell us something truly significant about union with Christ. But Schweitzer's entire book was weakened, in my judgment, by finding in the "pre-ordained solidarity" of the Messiah and His people the key to understanding Paul's "mysticism." There is too much of real history, including our experience and discovery of God in history, to make *pre*-ordination the key to Paul.

Christ." Knowing himself and the ordinary reality of common sense, Paul is overwhelmed by the extra-ordinary reality about himself and his world in Christ. How does one account for this reality, this "being in Christ"? There is no accounting for it. There is no *reason* in heaven or earth why we should be so blessed.

It is a gift. Paul ran from Christ; Christ pursued and overtook him. Paul resisted Christ; Christ disarmed him. Paul persecuted Christ; Christ converted him. Paul was an alien; Christ made him a member of the family. Paul was an enemy; Christ made him a friend. Paul was "in the flesh"; Christ set him "in the Spirit." Paul was under the law; Christ set him in grace. Paul was dead; Christ made him alive to God. How does one give reasons for this? He does not give reasons; he sings: "Blessed be God who blessed us . . . even as he chose us in him."

The reason for saying this is to remind us that Paul is not philosophizing about the eternal plan of an absolute deity. He is on his knees—stricken by grace, overwhelmed by love, and made new by Christ. And he sings because he knows now that all of this is only of God's free desire. What he says of election in Christ is said as a song, a confession, a hymn of wonder. What can one say in the face of such a gift but that God is in Himself eternally merciful. Love is not a *reason*; it is always a mystery.

The next thing we should say is that the phrase "before the foundations of the world" should not bother us at all. A lot of needless sophistry is spent on this phrase. We are, for instance, often reminded that there is no "before" or "after" in God. But are we so sure of this? We know God only as He comes to us. And He comes to us where we are, in history, with all of *our* "befores" and "afters." We find Him responding to the present moment with new action. We find Him remembering the past in anger and sorrow, but also in affection and commitment. We find Him promising to do surprising things in the future. Why should we not assume that time is very real with God; He deals with it, uses it, and comes into it. There is a genuine "before" in God. But, of course, Paul is not interested here in calendars or timetables. He is not dating election. But what better way could be found to say that God's election is not provoked by historical accident or human merit than to say that it was made "before" the world was made?[42]

---

[42] "'Before' indicates that the divine act of salvation, preached to us by the gospel, is free from what we know to be arbitrary and capricious" (Berkouwer, *Divine Election* [Grand Rapids, 1960], p. 150).

We must now turn to the fact that our election was *in Christ*
from before the worlds were made. God wanted us to be His human
partners. He decided *freely* to act on our behalf, and chose to enter
our lives with His healing presence *in Christ*. The most obvious
remark to be made at this point is that Christ *too* was elect. And
to say this is only to repeat what the New Testament says again
and again. The first known public witness said that Jesus' death
was predestined (Acts 2:23; 4:28). "This is my Son, my chosen,"
Luke reports the Father as saying (Luke 9:35). God loved Him
too before the world was founded (John 17:24). He is the Lamb
of God, elect to be slain for man's atonement (I Pet. 1:20). And
like Melchizedek He was a priest with no earthly antecedents to
account for him (Heb. 7:16). Moreover, he was *appointed* "the
heir of all things, through whom he [God] also created the world"
(Heb. 1:2).

He was elect as the *concrete* individual doing the specific task
that He was chosen to do. But we must also note that His election
was not only as the *concrete* individual Jesus Christ; He was also
elect as the *comprehensive* Christ. We would not fully grasp
Christ's election were we simply to say that the person and work
of the man Jesus were ordained by God's free decision. The Jesus
of concrete history occurs in a comprehensive context. Paul is
always concerned with Jesus in His total significance, in His grand
context. That context is, first of all, the election of Israel. Israel is
God's chosen; out of all the nations of the earth, she was God's
unique concern. "You only have I chosen out of all the families of
the earth," says Jehovah (Amos 3:2). Israel may have distorted
and twisted the meaning of its own election, but it could not undo
the fact of it.

Israel is living witness to who God is. Her whole history witnesses to God as the *electing* God, the God who freely decides to
enter into union with man. The core of Israel's election, centered
amid the twisting convolutions of its changing historical fortunes,
was this: it was to be God's people and Jehovah was to be its God.
A common Chaldean, distinguished by no religious or moral superiority, heard it and witnessed to it at the beginning: "And I
will establish my covenant between men and you and your
descendants after you throughout their generations for an everlast-
ing covenant, to be God to you and to your descendants after
you. . ." (Gen. 17:7). Generations later, with enough time between to allow for the rise and fall of several civilizations, it was
asked: Who is this God? And the answer was: "I am the God of

Abraham" (Exod. 3:6). Again, Israel is witness to who God is. He is the God who freely comes to partnership with a man, commits Himself to covenant union with a people. God is the electing God.

The essential meaning of Israel's election is emphasized again and again in the Scriptures: God and His people in vital community. We could speak of community as the purpose or end of election. But it crystallizes the meaning as well as the goal. When Jeremiah in Israel's greatest gloom speaks a word of witness to Jehovah's faithfulness, this is his theme. When all is made new again, he says, and the law has become a Spirit instead of a letter, it will indeed be as Jehovah promised to Abraham: "I will be their God, and they shall be my people" (Jer. 31:33). Jeremiah's conviction is echoed by prophet after prophet. And it is echoed in new forms in the New Testament until, in the vision of the Apocalypse, John hears the great voice from the throne crying, "Behold, the dwelling of God is with men. He will dwell with them, and they shall be his people, and God himself will be with them" (Rev. 21:3).

The electing God is He who freely decides to give Himself as man's partner. And to all men who enter His community, the message comes as it came to the original elect company:

> For you are a people holy to the Lord your God; the Lord your God has chosen you to be a people for his own possession, out of all the peoples that are on the face of the earth. It was not because you were more in number than any other people that the Lord set his love upon you and chose you, for you were the fewest of all peoples; but it is because the Lord loves you, and is keeping the oath which he swore to your fathers (Deut. 7:6-9).

These words have the peculiar flavor of a specific historical setting. But clearly they apply to all men called into the companionship of God.

Israel's besetting failure was its eagerness to presume on the specificity of God's election—its significance to Israel—and to ignore its comprehensive context. From the beginning, however, Israel's election was set within a universal intent. To that same Chaldean to whom God came with a specific promise, the universal intent was also made known, briefly and fleetingly, almost in passing, but still very clearly: "and by you all the families of the earth shall bless themselves" (Gen. 12:3). The election of

Israel was never, from its inception, revealed as a narrow, restricted privilege for a single, isolated people. Israel's temptation to forget the challenge for the sake of the promise only made it lose its claim on the promise: "You only have I chosen from all the nations of the earth," said Jehovah; "therefore will I punish you" (Amos 3:2). The surest way to distort God's election is to turn it inward on one's self as a reason for relaxed self-indulgence. When this happens, we are no longer dealing with Israel's election.[43] Israel was elect so that the election of the world could be achieved. God chose Abraham so that through him the nations of the earth would be blessed. And where Israel turned from God's fundamental thesis, it failed to achieve the large purpose of its own election.[44]

Israel is part of the larger context of Jesus Christ. We cannot speak of Christ without speaking of Israel, and we cannot speak of His election without speaking of Israel's election. For who is Jesus, but the "seed" that was promised to Abraham? And did not Paul call that promise the "preaching of the Gospel" to Abraham (Gal. 3:8, 16)? Israel was elect as Jehovah's servant for the blessing of the nations; Jesus is the culmination of Israel's election, for He is the "suffering servant of Jehovah" for the salvation of

[43]See H. H. Rowley, *op. cit.,* pp. 83ff. Like Paul and the Christian community, Israel knew of its election only in the historical experience of God as He came into history as Israel's covenant partner. Election was known as God's free decision of love only as Israel experienced and appropriated that decision in action. Had Israel, if we may conjecture, refused to follow Moses out of Egypt, it would have known nothing of election. Moreover, and conversely, its own history had meaning only as it discovered and appropriated God's election. Partnership with God was the meaning of Israel's history; and that partnership was experienced only as God freely initiated it. When Israel lost the knowledge of God's election— its freeness (that is, its complete independence of Israel's merit) and its purpose—Israel lost the meaning of itself and its history. So the Christian knows election only in the light of the *historical* cross and the *here and now* reality of the new creation. But, conversely, he knows the meaning of Christian history only as he bows before God's free *electing* grace.

[44]Of course, Israel's election was a privilege as well as a summons to service. Israel's was the law, the oracles, and the covenant, "and of their race, according to the flesh is the Christ" (Rom. 9:5). And who is to say that it will not have a time and place in the election of God again? "As regards the gospel they are the enemies of God, for your sake; but as regards election they are beloved for the sake of their forefathers. For the gifts and the call of God are irrevocable" (Rom. 11:28, 29). Who can tell what that "irrevocable" call may yet mean in history? After all, they became enemies of God for *our sake.*

the world. What He performs by His cross and resurrection, what He achieves in history, is what Israel's election was all about. He established a covenant "in His blood" that cannot fail. And the core of His covenant is the same as the core of Israel's covenant—God and man in reconciled partnership (Isa. 42:1). He is the Chosen One who brings light to the blind and freedom to the captives (Isa. 42:7). He is the Light to the Gentiles (Isa. 42:6). He is the harbinger of peace.

This thought must be brought back to our election in Christ. God's election is His "plan for the fulness of time, *to unite all things in him*" (Eph. 1:10). Christ, in whom the world was created, was elect as the Christ "to reconcile to Himself all things whether on earth or in heaven, making peace by the blood of the cross" (Col. 1:20). He is elect as the one in whom a new creation is brought into being through the reconciliation of men with God at the cross. He is elect as Head of His body, the Church, which is the present-day harbinger of the coming new creation. This is the comprehensive sense in which we must think of the election of Jesus Christ. Christ the concrete individual, the Man for others, is elect. But *His election, like Israel's, and with Israel's, is the decision of God to create a new world of men in partnership with Him. When we think of Christ's election, we must think of God's comprehensive decision to have a "new creation."*

Thus, when we think of ourselves as elect in Christ, we must think of ourselves as elect in the *comprehensive* Christ. This means that we must understand that when Paul says "Christ" he includes the specific, concrete person and His specific cross, but also His universal goal and its universal achievement. We are in Christ in God's decision, but that very decision is to unite "all things" in Christ. God's free commitment to man, which is His election, is the gift of Himself in Christ for the universal restoration of men and things in Him. The Christ of the cross is God's elect Christ. So is the Christ in whom all things are recreated. And we are elect within that concrete and comprehensive Christ.

If we reflect on our "election in Christ" in this way, we will be spared from the frightening abstractions that have so often plagued the doctrine of election.[45] We will never think of election as a

---

[45]See Berkouwer, *Divine Election*, pp. 153f. where he says that Ephesians 1:4 is the text which, more than any other, keeps us from "abstractions and determinism in which the traits of the living God, the Father of Jesus Christ, are obscured by the hiddenness and the menace of inscrutable fate."

grace-less, love-less decree to select some individuals for heaven
and to reject other individuals for hell. The election in Christ
is not a matter of numbers. Whether every member of the human
race were included or only a minuscule number, the same truth
would be captured in the phrase "chosen in him before the
foundations of the world." Paul is talking, as we said, as a man
dumbfounded that *he* and *we* were included in God's election. He
is singing of the mercy of God that included us; he is not speculating on why certain others are not included.

If we think of our election in this way, we can also avoid the
sharp edges of the problem of whether Christ is the *executor* of our
election or the *foundation* of it. This question has been discussed at
great length since Karl Barth restored to respectability the notion
that Christ is the foundation of our election.[46] We could put this
vexing question in this way: Is Christ's election prior to ours, or is
our election prior to His? Were we to say that our election is prior
to Christ's election, we would be forced to say two regrettable
things. (a) We would say that election is not really gracious. The
only grace of God we know is His grace in Christ, and if we are
elect prior to Christ, we would be elect without grace. (b) We
would be saying that Christ is only the executor, the one chosen
to properly and justly bring God's elect to salvation; hence, we
would deny what St. Paul says in Ephesians 1:4. On the other
hand, if we say that Christ's election occurred before the election
of His people, we would imply two equally regrettable things. (a)
We would imply that the Savior was elect of God without a decision to elect *people*; and a Savior without people is a contradiction in terms. (b) We would imply that the election of people is
not really a free decision, but rather was cajoled or persuaded. To
think of God being persuaded to elect or, worse, cajoled to elect,

---

[46]*Church Dogmatics,* II/2, pp. 94ff. In order to rescue election from the
notion of an arbitrary decree, Barth insists that Christ is the electing God
as well as the elected Savior. This could be taken in a reasonable sense.
But by Christ as the electing one, Barth means the historical Jesus. As far
as I can see, there is no biblical warrant for this notion. But apart from
this, it must be credited to Barth as well as to Berkouwer that Calvinists
have been forced to take great care lest their doctrine of election be that
of a frightful decree made by God apart from Christ and therefore apart
from grace. Barth insists that "before [Christ] and without Him and beside
Him God does not elect or will anything." Calvin himself makes this
clear; it is, he says, "impossible" that God should elect us except in Christ
(*Institutes* iii.24.5). Berkouwer demonstrates that Calvin gives no evidence
of believing in an election apart from grace (*Divine Election,* pp. 141ff.).

is to qualify the freedom of God's decision and so to render it less than gracious.

And so we must say that Jesus Christ is not an afterthought of election, the means of getting us *properly* to God. Nor is He the One who persuaded God to elect us or who made us look good enough for God to want us.

We are elect *in* Christ. How hard it is to *say* what this means! Christ and His Christians, the Lord and His subjects, the King and His kingdom, the Reconciler and the reconciled, the Leader and His followers, the Head and His body are elect together. Bavinck says: "The community and Christ are together in the one decision; they are, as one community, the elect."[47] Perhaps this is what we should be content to say. Bavinck is also willing to say that Christ is the cause or the foundation of our election; but he means by this that Christ is the person by whose willing death the elect people are wooed and won, brought over into the new creation from the old, liberated from the powers that bound and doomed them. But as to God's free decision, we may be content to say that God wanted a new creation with people in it who were His people, and *this* was His decision. He elected a kingdom *with* a King, a body *with* a Head, a people *with* a Leader, a universe *with* a Lord, and sinners *with* a Savior. He elected us in the comprehensive Christ, the Christ who was—in faith—first defined as "Lord of All."

Being chosen in Christ means that we can no more be the object of God's agapic desire apart from Christ than a fraction can exist without an integer, a part without a whole. He is the circle in which we are included. He unites the whole of which we are individually parts. He is the elect Head of whom we are the body. To confess that we are chosen is, then, to confess that our new being is in Christ fundamentally and eternally; and that is to say that we are included in the new creation in Christ only through God's agapic, free decision of love. To make the discovery that one is in Christ is, at the same time and with the same wonder, to confess that one is in Christ because God in love freely desired a new creation in Christ, with him as a member of it.

What, then, does election by God's free agapic decision tell us of union with Christ? It tells us that the new order begun at the cross and resurrection, which sweeps into the here and now under His lordship and in the power of His Spirit, and which will culminate

[47]H. Bavinck, *Gereformeerde Dogmatiek*, II (Kampen, 1911), p. 421.

in a new earth where all things are reconciled, is rooted, not in time present, not in our prestigious achievements or grand designs, but in God's own eternal desire in love to give Himself in partnership with men and to restore a situation where we will be "his people" and He will be "our God" and Christ shall be all and in all.

D. SUMMARY

We have walked a long and arduous mile in search of what Paul means by the expression "in Christ." Yet our study is anything but exhaustive. We have seen enough, however, to provide a strong hint of the category in which Paul thought when he used the expression in all its contexts. For lack of a better word, we can call the category "history." A new historical situation was created for men by Christ; to be in that situation, which began at Calvary and climaxes in the "new earth" to come, is to be "in Christ." We have seen that being "in Christ" is not, at least primarily, a deeply subjective moral experience, nor a mystical experience of elevation into deity, but existence within a radically new situation in the continuing turmoil of human history.

The reality of being "in Christ" must be fixed in what Jesus Christ *did, is doing,* and *will do.* He overcame the powers that dominated human history and led it through frustration toward what promised to be a fatal end. He was established as Lord of a whole new order in history and He exercises His lordship here and now as Spirit. Being "in Christ" is the same reality as being "in the Spirit," because the Spirit functions within history for Christ the Lord. The phrase "in Christ" is an epigram for the total reality of the new community under Christ's lordship, a community called by His voice, ruled by His Spirit, and forming the embryo of a total new race and a whole new creation united and renewed by Him.

We can summarize some of the main thoughts of this chapter this way:

(1) Central to an understanding of reality "in Christ" are the cross and resurrection. It was in His death and resurrection that Christ acted decisively on behalf of the world: He undid the power of sin and cancelled its claim on us, He defeated the "powers" behind our situation outside of Christ, and He began a new history with a new destiny for all who are incorporated in His new order.

(2) The new situation gets its character and style from the

controlling and liberating action of the Spirit, who is Christ in action as Lord on earth. This is why being "in the Spirit" is the same as being "in Christ."

(3) The new situation is so radical and so complete, so inclusive of life in all its dimensions, that it can be called a "new creation." While it will not be complete until the fullness of time, it is in a sense already present because the Spirit of the Lord is here and at work. This is why Paul can speak of *all* his actions as being "in Christ."

(4) Within the new creation, man is liberated from the judgment that falls on the situation outside of Christ. But even as he is liberated *from* the condemnation which comes of his fatal allegiance to the "powers" of the old world, he is also liberated *for* service by the action of the Spirit within the new world.

(5) The unity of men "in Christ" is analogous to their unity "in Adam" because both Christ and Adam began an order of life by their decisions and actions. The old humanity is dominated by the destructive effects of Adam's actions. The new humanity is dominated by the creative effects of Christ's actions.

(6) Paul's characterization of life "outside of Christ" as life "in the flesh," "under the law," and "in sin" illuminates what he means by life "in Christ." These words—"flesh," "law," "sin"—crystallize the whole of history under the moral and spiritual influence of evil. As *they* represent the whole dynamic of the historical order outside of Christ, so the name "Christ" represents the whole new reality governed by Christ as Lord.

(7) Divine election is God's decision to re-create the world in Christ. We are elect within God's loving desire and sovereign decision to establish, dominate, and realize a new creation, a creation which has Christ as the center, the Lord, the imminent power. Our position in the new creation is rooted in the loving freedom of God's decision.

In all this, I have been trying to suggest that being "in Christ" means being part of a program as broad as the universe and as deep as life. The new creation is not merely the renewal of individuals, though this must be given its due. The familiar text about being "new creatures in Christ" should not be waved too easily as a slogan for what happens "in me" when I am converted. The design of Christ's new creation is far too grand, too inclusive to be restricted to what happens inside my soul. No nook or cranny of history is too small for its purpose, no cultural potential too large for its embrace. Being in Christ, we are part of a new movement

by His grace, a movement rolling on toward the new heaven and
new earth where all things are made right and where He is all in
all. We are, of course, still vitally a part of history, the world, and
its community. But it is just *this* world which is hastening toward
and "groaning for," not its final annihilation but its final redemption. All that characterizes the old, the passé, the defeated,
will be swept out; but what belongs to God will be renewed and
reunited in Christ.

Chapter Four

With Christ

Jesus Christ calls men into partnership with Him in the ongoing program of reconciliation; He calls them to be *with* Him, with Him as His followers and His colleagues. But in a fascinating shift, Christians are asked by Paul to think of themselves as actually having been Christ's partners in the crucial events of *past* redemptive history, in His death and resurrection. Paul invites us to understand that we not only are on His side in the world's competition for commitment, but were fellows in His decisive venture for the world's redemption. He tells us that we were not only died *for*, but actually died ourselves, and that we are not only beneficiaries of His resurrection, but were raised along with Him. To be *in* Christ is to have been *with* Him when He died and arose.

A. BEGINNING WHERE WE ARE

Some ways of being with Christ are not difficult to understand. In a moment of bravado, Thomas the disciple urged his friends to join him and go with Christ to die with Him (John 11:16); he meant this literally—though not, of course, seriously. And while it has mysteries of its own, Paul's hope of being with Jesus in heaven is at least understandable. "My desire," Paul wrote, is to be "with Christ, for that is far better" (Phil. 1:23). Being with Christ is a comforting prospect and one full of exciting possibilities. For every Christian, being with Christ *is*, in fact, the future. "Then," says Paul, "we who are alive shall be caught up together with . . . [those who have already died] to meet the Lord in the air; and so we shall always be *with* the Lord" (I Thess. 4:17). The future holds some sort of personal proximity to Jesus Christ that is lacking now. But it would be misreading Paul's mind to think that the present is for him devoid of real association *with* Christ. As

James Stewart notes, "It is not because he has had so little of Christ that he yearns for more. It is precisely because he has had so much of Christ that he is sure God intends him for the perfected experience."[1]

Moreover, a vision of companionship with Jesus is a truncated version of Paul's outlook on the Christian future. Paul's yearning to be with Christ was a yearning for the fulfillment of life itself, for the total release of all his creative energies, and for the climax of the whole new creation. What he wanted, one may assume, was the completion of the "growing up into Christ" that began when he became a Christian. But he did know that life in the new creation established by Christ was unthinkable without a personal communion with Him. In this sense, then, being *with* Christ meant being in His presence, "seeing" Him, and finding first hand that "in everything He is indeed pre-eminent." What Paul wants, in short, is not merely a sight of Jesus "in person," but a life in the company of Him "in whom all the fulness of God was pleased to dwell" and in whom "all things, whether on earth or in heaven," were finally united.

But our principal interest is in another kind of being with Christ. Our concern here is the participation we had in the redemptive events of the past. A few instances of Paul's remarkable vocabulary serve to introduce his thesis:

> We were buried with him by baptism into death. . . . We know that our old self was crucified with him. . . . So you also must consider yourselves dead to sin. (Rom. 6:4, 6, 11)

> I have been crucified with Christ. (Gal. 2:20)

> If with Christ you died to the elemental spirits of the universe. (Col. 2:20)

> For you have died, and your life is hid with Christ in God. (Col. 3:3)

> But God . . . made us alive together with Christ . . . and raised us up with Him. (Eph. 2:4-6)

> And you were buried with him in baptism, in which you were also raised with him through faith in the working of God. (Col. 2:12)

> If then you have been raised with Christ. . . . (Col. 3:1)

[1]*A Man in Christ* (London, 1935), pp. 201f.

We must realize how important these words are. Only the man who has in fact died and risen along with Christ is the new man. Only such a man has a share in the reconciled new humanity. All of Paul's exhortations to practice the new life presuppose the reality of our participation in Christ's death and resurrection. And since the new creature is nothing less than the real manhood of man, a share in Christ's death and resurrection is the New Testament condition for being human. The way to genuine humanity is the way of death and resurrection along with the one new man, Jesus Christ.

There are two biases that we ought to try to avoid before we become involved in Paul's thought. One is the notion that Paul is plucking us out of our time and place and setting us back around A.D. 30 with Christ. At least we need not *assume* that Paul sees Christians as somehow being with Christ at the literal moment of His death and resurrection, dying with Him on some invisible cross and rising with Him from some invisible tomb. One should perhaps be realistic at least until he is certain there is something in our being with Christ that does overcome our limitation to the here and now. The realistic view might be this: I am living in the twentieth century, and every moment sends me a bit farther in time from the cross and resurrection. Jesus was there, alone, in the time and place God chose. He was there, at that time, and I am here, at this time. My own past is still part of the mysterious reservoir of my memory; but the past in which Jesus lived and died is beyond my reach. Perhaps, counting on my election in Christ, I can believe that God "saw" (i.e. imagined) me dying and rising with Christ. And I may put myself back in some distant era by flight of imagination. But in my flesh and blood reality, I am limited to my own allotted time. I have to live in the present.[2] I may be a member of a race *represented* by another, like Adam or Jesus Christ, but as an individual member I have to play my part here and now.

One feels an instant sympathy with Bonhoeffer's bold remark: "Jesus is not *a* man. He is *man*. Whatever happens to Him happens to man. It happens to all men, and therefore it happens also to us. The name Jesus contains within itself the whole of

---

[2]One thinks here of Lessing's famous "ugly broad ditch" of time that cuts us off from the past. I do not think we need call it ugly, but it is broad and it is real.

humanity and the whole God."[3] But, one may still ask, is the
destiny of mankind sealed by the fact that Jesus is *the* real man
and therefore the whole of mankind? And is my own death and
resurrection *with* Christ summed up in the very objective fact of
His universal manhood? What, we may ask, does it mean to say
that He *contained* the whole of humanity? And is it true that He
was not *a* man?

The other bias we should avoid is the notion that Paul means
simply that we die and arise in our own moral life, that our individual decision—either in conversion or in rededication—to stop
living a selfish and sinful life and to start living here and now a
God-oriented life is our dying and rising with Christ. On this view
what the Reformers called mortification of the flesh and vivification of the spirit constitutes the reality of dying and rising with
Christ. Our decision to live an authentically spiritual life would be
an analogy of Jesus' real death and resurrection.

But Paul calls us to a decision for life here and now on the basis
of having in fact died and risen with Christ *in the past*. That is,
he tells us that we should turn our backs on sin because we have
already died to it. And he tells us that we should seek the life of
the risen Christ because in fact we have already risen with Him.
He sets the imperative squarely on the foundation of the indicative.
To turn the Christian's past into his present spiritual vocation is to
misconstrue Paul's thought badly. It is an evasion of Paul's realism
to assume that when he says I died with Christ, he only means
that I *ought* to die morally in a way roughly analogous to Christ's
literal death. Our death and resurrection is not a little reproduc-
tion of His death and resurrection; it is an event that somehow
actually happened to us as it happened to Him. At least we ought
to begin with this literal reading of Paul.

We shall not suppose, therefore, that we are limited to thinking
that the event of dying and rising with Christ is either (a) an event
that happened to us contemporaneously with the death and resurrection of Jesus in the first century, or (b) an event that happens

[3]*Ethics* (London, 1955), pp. 10f. T. W. Hahn's approach is somewhat
like this. Jesus died in a specific time and place, and it is there at that
time and place that we died with Him. Hahn evidently tries to put
Kierkegaard's problem of our contemporaneity with Christ into Paul's mind.
As difficult as Paul's doctrine is, Hahn seems to make it infinitely harder
(*Das Mitsterben und Mitauferstehen met Christus bei Paulus. Ein Beitrag
zum Problem der Gleichzeitigkeit des Christen mit Christus* [Gütersloh,
1937]).

to us simply within our own moral experience, as a conversion
from one manner of life to another. Each of these cancels the
other out and they seem to offer the only alternatives. So if we
refuse to begin with either of these assumptions, we are faced
with the job of looking very hard at Paul to see if there is another
way. The place for us to begin is Romans 6. For here Paul sets
out our actual death and resurrection with Christ in its most
striking, as well as its fullest form.

The chapter appears in a context that stresses Christ's death *on
our behalf*, apart from us and *for* us. Christ did what we could *not*
do, with Him or without Him: "While we were yet helpless, at
the right time Christ died for the ungodly" (Rom. 5:6). And by
what He did, all of us are set within the reality of God's free favor
and acceptance. *One* man's act brought "acquital and life" (5:18).
This act, for us and apart from us, an act in which we could not
share and to which we could contribute nothing at all, this act set
straight the moral imbalance between God's demands and man's
failure, and opened the door into the household of God for us.
Unconditional and unequivocal, the status we have with God is
the gift of grace because Jesus has "trodden the wine press *alone*"
(Isa. 63:3).[5]

Now, should anyone suppose that what he does personally is
not particularly important since Christ did so much, Paul has this
to say: How can we choose to live in sin when, in fact, we died
to sin? Suddenly the focus has shifted. It has shifted from the
status we have with God in grace as a result of *Christ's* death to
the moral obligation we have before God as a result of *our* death.
"How can *we who died* to sin still live in it" (6:2)? Paul knows

[5]Paul uses three crucial terms which stress the "out there" character of
Christ's action on our behalf. (a) "Justification." This is taken from the
juridical world. The key word is *dikaiosune*, or righteousness. (b) "Expiation." This word is taken from the cultic world of the Old Testament. The
key word is *hilasterion*, or propitiation. There is an ambivalence in this
concept. Propitiation suggests an effect on God—literally a pacification, or
appeasement, or perhaps a cooling off. Expiation suggests an effect on
man—literally a covering over of sin and, hence, an annulment. (c) "Redemption." This is taken from the pagan slave market. The key word is
apolytrosis, or ransom. We need not think merely of a *payment* made to
ransom or emancipate the slave. It can mean an *act* of intervention for
someone's liberation. The Israelites, for example, were ransomed from
Egypt (Deut. 7:8) and from Babylon (Isa. 51:11) by an act (see C. H.
Dodd, *The Epistle of Paul to the Romans* [London, 1947], pp. 49ff.). It is
this last dimension of Christ's work that the letter to the Romans stresses
as the key to Paul's doctrine of the union between Christ and the Christian.

that sin is indeed more than possible for a Christian. But he wants
to tell us that it is impossible for a Christian to live as though the
sinful life were a legitimate option for the Christian man. It is impossible in view of the Christian's death to sin. The fact of our
union with Christ in His death makes a decision to live in sin a
grotesque absurdity.

Union with Christ closes the door on one world, just as it opens
the door on another. We cannot have both worlds. When Paul
faces up to the notion that God's grace would ring out the more
clearly against the sounding board of human sin, he rejects it not
simply because it is improper, but because it is utterly absurd. And
this is what leads him to spell out our actual death and resurrection with Christ. We are to consider ourselves dead to sin and
alive to God (6:11), because in fact we are.

B. WITH CHRIST IN DEATH

A good place to begin our reading of Romans 6 is at verse 10,
which says something about Christ's death to sin: "The death he
died he died to sin, once for all, but the life he lives he lives to
God." Jesus died to sin; He who "knew no sin" but who was
"made sin for us" died to sin. And since He died to sin, Paul says,
"sin will have no dominion" over us (6:14). In what sense did
Jesus die *to*, with respect to, sin? It is true that He died because
sinful men could not tolerate sinlessness in their presence; but this
is not Paul's theme here. It is true also that Jesus died on behalf of
sinners, so that they might be forgiven; but neither is this Paul's
point here. *Sin* was the object of Christ's death; Christ did something to sin, so that it could not hurt or destroy Him thereafter.
Sin is in the dead past as far as Jesus is concerned. He had condemned it (Rom. 8:3) and executed its death sentence. It could
not touch Him anymore.

This is admittedly a strange way to talk about sin. We are
hard put to think of sin as other than subjective motives and
actions; unlike Paul, we are so dominated by psychological interest
that we tend to concentrate only on our acts of sin. But for Paul
sin is a force or power outside of us, a power that can make a
prisoner of man. In fact, Paul talks about Jesus dying to sin in
the same way he speaks of Christ dying to death, to the world,
and to the law. He died and therefore, for instance, "death no
longer hath dominion over him" (6:9). He died and thereby
abolished "the law of commandments and ordinances" (Eph.

2:15). He nailed the bond with its legal demands to the cross (Col. 2:14). When that one man out there, separated from us in time and space, died for all, He died to sin, to the flesh, to the world, and to the law—meaning that He put the principalities and powers of the old world order to flight and sent them underground, where they still subvert the new authority, but do so without any power over Christ or any power to enslave any citizen of the new regime. Jesus died to sin, just as He died to the other objective elements of the hostile world powers.

Now just as Christians died with Him to sin, they also died with Him to these other facets of the old world. And just as sin in this context stands for the corrupting power of the old regime, so do the others. We died with Him so that "we might no longer be enslaved to sin" (6:6) or under the dominion of sin (6:14). We died with Him, and the result is that we are dead to the law (Rom. 7:4; Gal. 2:19), dead to the world (Gal. 6:14) and its beggarly elements (Gal. 3:9), dead to the flesh (Col. 2:11), and dead to sin (Rom. 6:2). We have noted several times that for Paul these are all forces of the evil age which came to an end with the death of Jesus. They are the forces which control, confine, and frustrate human life. Just as we refer to organized crime by several names— the "underworld," the "syndicate," or sometimes the "Mafia"— Paul assumes that he is talking sense when he refers to the power of the cosmic enemy with such words as "sin," "death," and "flesh." So when Paul says in Romans 6 that Jesus Christ died to sin, he is pointing to one facet of His victory over the old world power. And when he says that as a result of His death we are dead to sin, he means that we are liberated from the control of the powers of the old age.

In Romans 6, then, sin is objectified as the *rule* of evil over life. It is like a secret police force haunting us, tracking us, preparing to knock on our door in the middle of the night to claim us. It is Big Brother of 1984. It is like a man pressing a law suit against us. It is like a straitjacket that binds us. Being dead to sin is to have all these things made impotent, without power to control or threaten us. Being dead to sin, we are given asylum and citizenship in a totally new country, with new laws and new rulers; the old world has no claim on us and no power to extradite us for judgment. For not only are we given citizenship in a new order, but the old order itself has been overthrown.

Dying with Christ, then, is not a daily process of self-denial and cross bearing. It is an absolute, final, and unconditional event. We perhaps do not live as men who died to sin; but this only demonstrates that we betray our origins. A political exile from Red China may speak with a Chinese accent, enjoy Chinese food, and have nightmares of the secret police; similarly, we may still sound like sinners, enjoy acts of sin, and dream of judgment. But in fact the Chinese person is dead to Chinese law and Chinese police. For the exile to live under Chinese law while he enjoys American citizenship would be an absurdity. For the man who died with Christ to live under the domination of sin is an even greater absurdity.

With this, we are getting close to Paul's understanding of union with Christ in His death. It is not a mystical lifting of our temporal limits, giving us a contemporaneity with Christ at Calvary. Nor is it a matter of our self-denial in discipleship. It hinges on the objective, situational change in the cosmic balance of power that Christ accomplished at Calvary. He crushed the old powers for us. And in His death He changed the power structure: "For to this end Christ died and lived again, that he might be *Lord* both of the dead and of the living" (Rom. 14:9). The old powers cannot touch Him anymore, and they cannot touch us either—and for the same reason: they are undone. This means that, for our status and our identification, we are considered as having died with Christ.

C. WITH CHRIST IN LIFE

The cross and resurrection are the negative and positive sides of the one redemptive event. Christ was crucified in weakness but lives in the power of God (II Cor. 13:4). In His weakness, He defeated the "power" and introduced a new order of life existing in His power. And as we are identified with Him in His death, so we are also risen with Him that we too may live to God (Gal. 2:19) or, what is the same thing, may live to Christ (II Cor. 5:15) and hence know the "power of His resurrection" (Phil. 3:10). The factuality of our resurrection with Him is as firm as our participation in His death.

Does this fact of being risen with Him refer to the future or to the present? The answer is that it refers to both. In one place Paul says that God "made us alive together with Christ . . . and raised us up with him, and made us to sit with him in the heavenly places in Christ Jesus" (Eph. 2:5, 6). This clearly says that our partnership with Christ in the resurrection has already taken place and is a fact of the present. This meaning is confirmed by the fact that Paul urges his readers to live the risen life: "If [or, since] you have been raised with Christ, seek the things that are above" (Col. 3:1). In Romans 6, however, the apostle points more specifically to the future and bases his urgings on it. We were buried with Christ "so that as Christ was raised from the dead . . . we too might walk in newness of life. For if we have been united with him in a death like his, we shall certainly be united with him in a resurrection like his" (Rom. 6:4, 5). We cannot, however, pit Romans against the other letters; Ephesians 2:7 and Colossians 3:4 refer to the future, and Romans 6:11 speaks of the present risen life of the Christian. So there are both present and future dimensions in the fact of our participation in Christ's resurrection.[6]

In some sense, then, we are people whose history includes a resurrection along with Jesus Christ. What can this mean? The resurrection of Jesus involves far more than the resuscitation of a corpse. Jesus Christ came alive to a new situation, for Him and for us. He now lives and functions as Lord with the power of God. Thus, sharing in His resurrection implies far more for us than a guarantee that our corpses will one day be resuscitated. Coming alive to God (Rom. 6:10) means that we gain a new point of orientation, a new goal and thus a new direction. More, it means that we live by a new power (Phil. 3:10) within a new life order. Raised with Christ means that we are "in Christ" with all that this implies. We are dead to the destructive powers and threats of the old order and are free to live in a new setting, under new conditions and with a new style of action. Coming alive with Christ, we share the quality and style of His life. And this is far more than the neutral fact of immortality. It means that we come to live in freedom (Rom. 8:2), in righteousness (II Cor. 5:21; Gal. 2:17), in power (II Cor. 4:7-15; Phil. 3:10), in hope (Rom. 8:11; II Cor. 4:14), and in confidence (Rom. 8:39)—to mention just a few of the qualitative dimensions of the new life.

What Paul wants us to understand is that when Christ arose, a new situation was created with a totally new character and a totally

---

[6]It is not quite true to say that Paul describes our being with Christ in death as an accomplished fact, whereas he describes our participation in His resurrection as "the gradual proximation to a final goal" (Roy A. Harrisville, *The Concept of Newness in the New Testament* [Minneapolis, 1960], p. 65). The responsibility to grow in the risen life is also based on accomplished fact. We can reckon ourselves alive to God only because we have already in some real sense become alive to God.

new future. He wants us to understand that we do not create the
new situation by our decision, that its future does not rest with our
diligence, that its character is not determined by our consistency.
To speak of coming alive with Christ is to say that we are assigned
to the new reality introduced by Christ's resurrection. Now we
have to keep on choosing to be what we have already become. And
what we have become, in the first instance, is a member of the
new situation in which Christ rules as Lord.

This insight is crucial. When Paul proclaimed the resurrection
of Christ, he did it as a man who knew himself to have been risen
with Christ. Had he thought that the significance of Christ's act
for him depended on his decision or his consistency, he would
not have broadcast it as good news decisive for all time. In fact,
Christ's resurrection was the event that released him from the
anxieties of his former "do it yourself" morality, that released him
from the powers that frustrated his efforts and at the same time
bound him to his own egotistic moralism. He could look forward
to sharing in "the power of the resurrection" (Phil. 3:10) because
he was part of the resurrection reality. Markus Barth is quite right:
"The co-resurrection of sinners is either included in Christ's
resurrection, or else there is no witness, no faith, no reality to His
resurrection."[7] That is, without our inclusion in it, Christ's resurrection would be only an incidental miracle having no more
power in it for us than the resurrection of Lazarus has.

When we speak of Christ's resurrection, we are speaking of the
beginning of a new life situation. And we can speak of it in the
Christian sense only if we are part of that new situation. There is
no resurrection of Christ *for me* unless I am included with the
living Lord in His new order of life. How this can mean that I
"was risen *with* Him" can best be discussed by going on to consider the function of baptism.

D. BAPTISM AS BURIAL AND RESURRECTION

We cannot, finally, pretend to have heard Paul's message
about dying and rising with Christ unless we face the problem of
baptism and its bearing on our situation. Union with Christ in His
redemptive action occurs for us at the moment of our baptism. It
is this association between our union with Christ and our experience of the sacrament that plants our feet firmly in the present

---

[7]*Acquittal by Resurrection* (New York, 1964), p. 56.

time and practically rules out the trans-historical notion of contemporaneity with Christ in the past. We did not die with Him
about A.D. 30 at Calvary outside Jerusalem, but rather in our
own time at the baptismal font in our local church. There is no
getting around Paul's plain language and, evangelical shyness
about sacramental efficacy notwithstanding, there is no avoiding
the fact that it is in baptism that we are both buried and raised
with Christ. The problem is *how* it happens.

Our task is not to develop a doctrine of baptism at this point,
but rather to try to understand how baptism is related to union
with Christ. One of the notions that has beclouded the discussion
of baptism through the years is that baptism has to do primarily
or even exclusively with what happens *in me*, with occurrences
inside my soul, with a change in my character. This is the stubborn
fiction that has caused doctrines of baptism to polarize around two
extreme positions. One of these is the Catholic doctrine of baptismal regeneration and the other is the doctrine that baptism is a
dramatic testimony to a regeneration that has already happened
in me. By way of contrast, let us put a typical sacramentalist and
a typical Baptist statement side by side.

The person baptized, says a popular Catholic handbook, is
given an "indelible mark."

> Plunged in the living stream, cleansed by that running water . . .
> he is absolved from original sin, as well as his own sins. . . . Sanc-
> tifying grace is infused into him, and henceforth he participates
> in the life of grace of the incarnate Son of God. . . .[8]

Baptism is the miraculous event in which the deified life of the
Incarnate is infused into our souls, wiping the spiritual slate clean;
it takes away the old life, obliterates it, and starts us on a new
road in a new condition. Dying and rising with Christ is a thing
that happens inside our souls, first of all, as an ontological event.

> The point is that with the incarnation something new has begun
> to be, namely human nature hypostatically united to the Person
> of the Word of God; . . . and the organic communication of this
> recreated human nature to men and women as their personal

---

[8]N. G. M. van Doornink, *A Handbook of the Catholic Faith* (New
York, 1956), pp. 260f. The phrase "indelible mark" is from Thomas'
Summa Theologica, Q. 22, Art. 9 (*character indelibilis*) and presents the
problem of what happens to a baptized person who becomes apostate.

possession is (at any rate normally) brought about by baptism. . . .[9]

What baptism does, it does to the ontological depths of the person,
and what it does to him there is to give him a real share in the
divine life of the incarnate Lord. This is Sacramental Christology
carried through to baptism.

Protestants have often reacted against the sacramentalist view
while accepting one of its premises about baptism. That is, some
have assumed that baptism is related primarily to what happens
in us and to us. But while Catholics say that baptism is a
causal instrument, these Protestants say that baptism is only a
dramatic testimony. They say "faith and not baptism" just as
Catholics say "baptism and not faith." A fine example of this sort
of Protestant reaction to the Catholic idea is that of James Denney.
Denney wonders how "this striking and original idea of a union
with Christ in His death and resurrection" could have occurred to
Paul in connection with our baptism. Baptism, he writes "is for
. . . [Paul] a *picture* of what faith really is." Essentially "there is
nothing in Paul's gospel but Christ and faith, and faith, it cannot
be said too often, is the unreserved abandonment of the sinful
soul to Christ . . . it is the soul's self-identification with Christ
in His death and resurrection, the two great events in which
His saving faith is summed up."[10] Denney insists that the
baptism Paul talks about in Romans 6 is "that of believers solemn-
ly and publicly declaring their faith in Christ." It follows, of
course, that our "death and resurrection with Christ are not in the
rite of baptism, apart from faith . . . they are in the gospel . . .
and in the rite only through the faith which accepts the gospel."[11]
Denney's description of faith is admirable. But, he is doing just
what the sacramentalist does: locating the significance of baptism
in the interior life of the Christian man. And, for the same basic
reason that the Catholic says baptism is the instrument of our
mystical union with Christ, Denney says that it is only the symbol
of our faith in Christ.

Both the sacramentalist and the Baptist position contain an ele-

[9]E. Mascall, *Christ, the Christian, and the Church* (London, 1946), p.
96. Mascall, an Anglo-Catholic, is a more thoroughgoing sacramentalist
than are some Roman Catholics, who deal more seriously with Pauline
eschatology.
[10]*The Christian Doctrine of Reconciliation* (New York, 1918), pp. 315ff.
[11]*Ibid.*, p. 316.

ment of truth about baptism. The Catholic is true to Paul when he insists that baptism initiates one into the body of Christ. The Baptist is right when he insists that baptism has meaning for a person only in the context of faith. But both positions assume that baptism is related primarily to what happens to a person subjectively. The Catholic says that baptism creates within a person a clean heart by *infusing* into that heart the life of Christ. The Baptist says that baptism only testifies to the faith that has already brought about a clean heart. But, in fact, if we are to see baptism entirely as Paul presents it, we must see that it points beyond what happens within a person.

One more thing we ought to note is that baptism does not, for Paul, provide us with the same experience Christ had in dying and rising, or an experience closely similar to it. A notion popular among radical critics for a time was that the baptism Paul talked about was a pale imitation of the Hellenistic mystery rites of initiation.[12] In these Hellenistic rituals, the initiate symbolically reenacted the death and resurrection of the god of the cult. When he underwent the ritual, he was given an experience parallel to that of the god. However, the experience was only a temporary rapture, sometimes lasting only for the time it took to perform the initiation. For that ecstatic moment, and perhaps a little longer, he was given a share in the immortality of the gods.

But the notion that Paul's doctrine of baptism was borrowed from the pagan cults is simply an assumption. And this assumption rests on the flimsy supposition that a formal similarity in the cult must have meant a material identity, which is like saying that since both Jews and Buddhists worship in temples, their gods are the same. Moreover, as Albert Schweitzer pointed out, the mystery cult was based on what everyone knew was a myth about the rising of the god, while Paul's doctrine is based on the historical actuality of the cross.[13] Finally the theory has even the slightest credibility only so long as we can believe that the function of baptism is primarily that of dramatic imitation. But Paul does not say that baptism is a symbolic imitation of Christ's burial and resurrection. Baptism is also related to "putting on" Christ (Gal. 3:27), and

---

[12]Cf. R. Reitzenstein, *Die Hellenistischen Mysterienreligionen* (Leipzig, 3rd ed., 1927). See also K. Deissner, *Paulus und die Mystik seiner Zeit* (Leipzig, 1918), pp. 1-20.
[13]*The Mysticism of Paul the Apostle* (New York, 1955), p. 23.

here the symbolism of going down and coming up is quite absent.[14] Baptism is initiation into Christ, but not an imitation of Him.

Paul does locate our dying and rising with Christ in our baptism. There is no denying this. But there is also no denying the real time lapse between our appearance at the baptismal font and Christ's death on Calvary. As Anders Nygren says, "Paul has not ceased to take time into account. He knows very well that Christ died at a precise point in human history, and that a certain period of time had elapsed between that event and the date Paul writes this epistle to the Romans."[15] There is no way of getting Paul's intentions straight unless we firmly recognize the lapse of time between the cross and our baptism. Baptism is not a magic leap into the past; it is a sign that points us to the past and identifies us with its effects in the present.

We must remember that when Paul is writing to people who he assumes are believers, he simply asserts that they were buried and raised with Christ when they were baptized. Schweitzer must have jolted some of his readers when he said that baptism introduces a person into the events of redemption "without any cooperation or exercise of will or thought on his part."[16] This is, as we shall see, an overstatement. Baptism occurs within a context of personal faith, including that of the person baptized. But Schweitzer is right in calling attention to the fact that Paul never mentions faith or commitment in Romans 6. And while we cannot keep personal faith out of the picture for very long, Paul does give us the lead in isolating baptism from faith for a while, only to get its special significance in focus. Letting baptism speak for itself, we are really letting the total effectiveness of Christ's accomplishments speak for themselves. This is what Schweitzer does, in effect, when he says: "Baptism is for . . . [Paul] a being buried and risen again, because it takes place in the time of Jesus Christ, who was buried and rose again. It effects what the mysticism of being-in-Christ accepts as the effect of redemption."[17] That is, it is not

---

[14]See H. Ridderbos, *Romeinen* (Kampen, 1959), pp. 132ff.

[15]*Commentary on Romans* (London, 1952), p. 238.

[16]*Paul and His Interpreters* (London, 1912), p. 225.

[17]*The Mysticism of Paul the Apostle,* p. 19. As to baptism being a symbol of a fellowship with Christ previously begun by faith, Schweitzer says: "Of such fine distinction Paul knows nothing. He simply asserts that it is with Baptism that . . . the dying and rising again have their beginning." Schweitzer is right about Romans 6. But unfortunately he isolates Romans 6 from the rest of Paul's teaching about our entrance into Christ's redemption.

baptism that transcends time. It is the cross and resurrection that created a new situation in time. Baptism introduces individuals to that new situation.

But *how* does baptism initiate us into the effects of Christ's death and resurrection? How are we baptized *into Christ, into His death,* so that we can be said to have died with Him? We get a hint from another initiation by baptism. Paul says that the Israelites were baptized *into Moses:* "I want you to know, brethren, that our fathers were all under the cloud, and all passed through the sea, and all were baptized into Moses in the cloud and in the sea" (I Cor. 10:1, 2). This awkward reference to baptism provides a significant clue as to how Paul thought about Christian baptism within the large arena of the new creation in Christ.

Paul is thinking about the Exodus as the redemptive event by which God liberated His people from the old order of Egypt and created them as a new community within history. The God of the Exodus is the God of the new community. The crossing of the Red Sea was an act of baptism. The people were baptized "in the cloud and in the sea," which were visible signs of God's presence. The passing of the people through the sea stands for God's sacramental identification of the people as His community and for the people's acceptance of that status within God's redemptive program. Now in the whole event of the Exodus, Moses was the dominant and characteristic person; he was what theologians call these days the "representative personality" of the redeemed and redemptive community. So we have three elements: redemption by God in the Exodus, commitment to the redemptive act by the people as they crossed the Red Sea, and Moses as mediator, as the representative of God to the people and of the people to God.

Being baptized into Moses, then, meant an initiation into the redemptive program of which Moses was the dominant personal figure. In taking that decisive step into the sea, the Israelites accepted their liberation from bondage under one power and their entrance into a national destiny and divine calling of their own. They died to Egypt with its power to prevent them from fulfilling their covenant destiny. They came alive to God as His covenant partner, His people, called to be a blessing to all peoples. They died and rose again with Moses. And so they became the community of God under Moses, a new body with a redemptive purpose for the whole world. Their baptism sealed and signified them as that new community.

But all future generations of Israel were participants in that same redemptive action. Removed from Moses by the gulf of time, the generations to come would nonetheless be "with Moses" in death and resurrection. This would be possible because they too were members of the community created by the Exodus and sealed by the crossing over under the cloud. In that community, the redemptive effects and purpose were realized, and so its members would be baptized into Moses even though they did not literally come out of Egypt with him.

The Passover was the liturgical means by which the national experience of liberation (that is, of death and resurrection) could be appropriated by each individual within the community. An individual Israelite could be a true member of the community only as he was pointed to the event of redemption. That is, since the community had meaning only as the redeemed community, the individual's participation in the community had meaning only as he participated in the redemptive meaning of the community. But on the other hand, he participated in the redemptive meaning only as he participated in the actual existence of the community.

The Passover liturgy contains some illuminating dialogue on this point. It shows how the Jewish individual was to think of himself in terms of the community and to think of himself and his community in terms of its origins in an act of God that took place long before. The youngest person at the Passover celebration asks, "Why is this night different from all other nights?" And the response is this:

> We were slaves to the Pharaoh in Egypt and the Lord our God brought us forth from thence with a strong hand and outstretched arm. If the most holy, blessed be He, had not brought our fathers from Egypt, then we, our children and our children's children, would have been slaved to the Pharaohs in Egypt. . . .[18]

The explanation goes on:

> In every generation each one of us should regard himself as though he himself had gone forth from Egypt, as it is said (Exod. 13:8): "And thou shalt shew thy son in the day, saying, This is done because of that which the Lord did unto me when I came forth out of Egypt."[19]

---

[18]From the *Mishna Pesahim* cult of the Passover. Cited by W. D. Davies, *Paul and Rabbinic Judaism* (London, 2nd ed., 1955), pp. 104ff.

[19]From the *Revised Haggada* (London, 2nd ed., 1955), 21ff. Cited by Davies, *op. cit.*, p. 104.

The calendar-bound modern man has a problem with this beautiful indifference to time. The Israelite who lived a thousand years after the Exodus could say, "*We* were slaves to the Pharaoh in Egypt and the Lord our God brought *us* forth." For him, being a living member of the community created by the Exodus made him a participant in the Exodus. Being part of the redemptive program made him a participant in the original redemptive action. The Israelite was not a mystic. Nor was he a romantic without a sense of time. What he understood was this: every new generation was a continuation of God's community by participation in what God *did* through Moses. To share in the effects of the redemptive action was possible only by being a member of the community that the action created. But to share in the effects was, so to speak, to be a participant in the action itself. Every Israelite had to think of himself as though he himself had gone forth from Egypt.

To be baptized into the death of Christ, and so to die and be raised with Him, is to share the life of the community that was created by the redemptive acts of the cross and the resurrection. The parallel is natural, since the Exodus was a very real anticipation of redemption through Christ. At the Exodus, God destroyed the power of Egypt to keep Israel in bondage and to destroy it as the covenant community. At the crossing of the Sea, God introduced the people into the new situation, free from Egypt and alive to a new history and a new calling. All this was oriented around Moses, the servant of Jehovah. At the cross, God defeated the spiritual powers who otherwise kept God's people in bondage and destroyed their ability to function as God's covenant partner. At baptism, God initiates individuals into the new community, free from the destructive powers and made alive to a new history and a new calling. All this is oriented around Christ, the Servant of Jehovah. The difference is that baptism is repeated in the case of each individual, while the Passover was the means by which the individual Israelite was given a share in the collective baptism of Israel.

In short, to talk of being "baptized into Moses" was for Paul a way of saying that one was initiated into the community created through Moses, the new community of redemption. And this was what is meant by being "with Moses" at the Exodus. Being baptized into Christ has the same pattern of meaning.

This thought is strongly suggested by the fact that Paul says at one time that we are baptized "into Christ" (Gal. 3:27; Rom. 6:3) and at another that we are baptized "into the body" (I Cor.

12:13). What better way could be found to show that a person
baptized into the community is given a share in the significance of
Christ's death and resurrection than to say that baptism makes
him a member of Christ's body? For the "body of Christ" is the
new community where Christ's redemptive action is believed,
celebrated, and experienced; it is the community which carries on
the reconciling action of Christ through its ministries. To be
baptized "into the body" is the same as to be initiated into the new
age or new creation; it means to be placed "in Christ," with all
that we have already seen this to mean. Being baptized "into the
Body" and "into Christ" and dying and being raised "with Christ"
in baptism all come down to the same reality.[20]

What Paul says in I Corinthians 12:13 is of a piece with what
he says in Romans 6 and Galatians 3:27. To be baptized "into
Christ" is to be baptized "into the body." This is not a mystical
notion, at least not in the ordinary sense. Nor is it a matter of
sacramental infusion. The baptism into Moses is the clue.
Baptism means the introduction of a person into the community
that began by and lives out of and serves the purposes of the resurrection of Christ; it means being made part of the new historical
movement that received its impulse from Calvary. The baptized
person comes alive within the community to the lordship of Christ.

He thus becomes a member of a community with a calling as
well as a promise. As part of a community with roots in the
saving acts of Christ, he has a new calling and a new obligation as
well as a new privilege. He faces, of course, real dangers. For he

[20]See Ernst Percy, *Der Leib Christi* (Leipzig, 1942), p. 28: "Dying with
Christ in baptism . . . [means] that the believer is brought into what Christ
accomplished at the cross—which can only mean that he is incorporated
into Christ Himself. . . ." Stig Hanson does not dispute anything I am
saying, but he does bring in a dimension that I do not. He writes: "It is
against the background of Christ as the Second Adam that we wish to
understand the Body of Christ and the importance of baptism. . . . As Adam
is not conceived as an individual, but represents all humanity, with which
he forms a unity, one body, similarly Christ does not stand alone, but
represents a New Humanity, with which He forms one Body, a unity.
Individual man is baptized into this body . . . and as a member of His
Body, he belongs to an entirely new sphere of life, a New Aeon. On
account of this, he may benefit from what Christ as a representative has
accomplished. . . . Thus baptism imparts communion primarily with Christ,
but as Christ is . . . the representative of a collectivity, baptism implies
communion also with other persons joined to Christ." *The Unity of the
Church in the New Testament* (Uppsala, 1946; reprinted in Lexington,
1963), pp. 77f.

is tempted to renounce his calling and his responsibility. He is tempted to dissociate himself from the implications of the cross. He may reject his status within the community that lives by divine grace; he may wish to go back under the law of his own self-attained morality and thus alienate Himself from Christ (Gal. 5:4). But the temptation and the danger are real only because the participation he has within the community that lives by Christ's death and resurrection is real.

I am buried with Christ and raised with Him, then, when I become a participant in the effects of His death and resurrection. The effects of His saving acts are known and experienced and realized in the new community called His body. Within that community, I become involved in the actual events which created it. That is, these events are no longer wholly external events of the past for me. I am part of the history begun by them. My whole existence is determined by them, and my existence as a new creature is thinkable only within the community which is the "one new man" created by our Lord's resurrection (Eph. 2:15).[21]

The distinction between "internal" and "external" history may be useful here. There is a sense in which most past events are external to me; they do not make me what I am and are not part of my life. For instance, I am able to think about the fall of Egypt's 18th dynasty without thinking myself personally involved. But as an American I can hardly think of Valley Forge and the Battle of Gettysburg without identifying myself with them. For I am a member of a community which owes its existence and continuity to the Revolutionary and Civil wars. I have a share in all that makes the American political community; though my parents

[21]In a book on Christian worship, J. J. von Allmen shows a rare grasp of the relationship between the Christian cult and the saving acts of God in history. He says this, for instance: "The history of salvation thus continues, efficaciously operative, in the form of an *anamnesis* of its central event. What then took place in a substitutionary way on behalf of the whole world is shed abroad by the power and work of the Holy Spirit, to become the ontological reality of those who rejoice in it and live by it." Baptism, in particular, Allmen writes, "consists, on the one hand, in efficaciously applying what God has done *illic et tunc* in Jesus Christ to the *hic et nunc* of such and such a man or community—the Holy Spirit thus mediates Christ to us—and, on the other hand, in efficaciously referring the *hic et nunc* of such and such a man or community (or event) to the *illic et tunc* of what God has done in Jesus Christ at Golgotha and in the garden of Joseph of Arimathea—the Holy Spirit brings us into communion with Christ" (*Worship: Its Theology and Practice* [New York, 1965], pp. 41, 40).

were immigrants, I was given my political existence by Washington's army at Valley Forge. Insofar as they created a new nation, they created me. And in that sense, I was involved at Valley Forge. As Richard Niebuhr puts it: "The ultimate nature of an event is not what it is in its isolation, but what it is in its connection with all other events. . . ."[22] This is true of the event of the cross and resurrection of Jesus Christ.

The apostle proclaims the death and resurrection of Christ not as isolated events, but as events creative of a new world order. Otherwise he would not have bothered to proclaim them. Only as a member of that new order, as a man alive to his own new existence in it, does Paul preach the saving acts of God in Christ. And he wanted the members of the Church to understand Christ's death from the same position—as members of a new community within a new world order established at the cross and resurrection. When he said that baptism initiated us into the community, he wanted that event to be seen in the light of the community's real meaning as the new creation of God. This helps us understand why it was natural, and not at all far-fetched, for him to say also that in our baptism we are buried and risen with Christ. For he means to say that our existence within the community is planted in the historical actions by which the community was created, on which it rests, and in the light of which it goes forward into the future. The time between the discrete event of the crucifixion is not annulled; but I in my time am located and identified as one whose life is defined by that past event and the new situation which it brought into being. This is what Paul is saying in II Corinthians 5:14: "Because we are convinced that one died *for all*; therefore *all have* died."

To die with Christ in baptism is possible because Jesus Christ is the *fulness of time*. He and His saving acts are contemporaneous with us only because what He did changes the *meaning* of time. He does not eradicate time, nor does He release us from the limits of time. But He does radically change the meaning of our existence in time. Jesus died in the distant past. Our baptism occurs in a fleeting moment in the present. But the cross and resurrection of time past do bring Jesus Christ into the ever recurring present. They do this not merely because Jesus lives in the present—though

[22]*The Meaning of Revelation* (New York, 1960), p. 83. It is Niebuhr who suggested the distinction between external and internal history. See the chapter on "History as Lived and Seen," *ibid.*, pp. 59ff.

without this fact nothing would be real about either our baptism or our faith—but because Jesus is the crucified Lord of the present time in that His saving acts in a moment forever past brought about a new meaning for the present. This present time is the time of freedom, of victory, of hope, and of the possibilities of love. It is the time of the new creation in Christ. When we are baptized in His death and resurrection, we are ushered into the effects and power of His death and resurrection. The new era, the new order, began back there. Brought into the new reality by baptism, we are stamped as people who are then and there dead to the things Jesus died to—sin, death, the law.[23]

E. CHRISTIAN SELF-IDENTITY

We must now ask about the relationship of baptism to faith. Personal faith and the sacrament of baptism are correlatives; they exist in creative tension with each other. This relationship must be kept in mind when either is talked about. Of course, the reality of faith goes considerably beyond this context, but never is the subject of faith closer to the existential character of personal decision for Jesus Christ than it is here. Here, faith is the Christian's identification of himself as being in Christ, as being in the new creation. And since baptism is God's method of initiating a person into the new creation, baptism is centrally involved with the decision of faith. After saying that the members of the congregation were buried and raised with Christ in their baptism, Paul concludes with a call to faith, a faith that is really an identification of themselves: "So you also must *consider yourselves* dead to sin and alive to God in Christ Jesus" (Rom. 6:11).

When a person has been baptized into Christ's body, he has been identified by God and by the community as a member of the new creation in Christ. He has been taken into the believing, praying, worshipping, witnessing, serving, and expecting community.

[23]What I have said is quite in line with Oscar Cullmann's view. For instance, he writes: "The event of Golgotha stands from the point of view of time and salvation in the same relation to Baptism as to the event of the Eucharist. This means on the one side that Baptism is no kind of repetition of that historical once-for-all event, but an ever new event, which whenever a member is 'added,' reminds us that salvation history continues in the present time. On the other hand, it means, of course, that this present event is entirely determined by the once-for-all event at Golgotha. . ." *Baptism in the New Testament* (London, 1950), p. 35.

He has been brought into the communion where Christ's death and resurrection are proclaimed. He is now where the Spirit is at work through the ministries of the community. He is where the bread is being broken and the risen life of Christ shared anew. He is part of the new order of things. He is a member of Christ's body and has Christ as his head.

Now he is told that he may, that indeed he must, identify himself in the light of this new order. He must identify himself as a person who died and arose with Christ. We have here the question of who and what and where a man understands himself to be. The baptized person is told to understand himself as *having died to sin.* He is not told simply that he *ought* to die to sin; he is told that he ought to die because he has already died to sin. The imperative rests on the indicative. The first imperative for the baptized person is to affirm the indicative.

The baptized person is told to consider himself as having a past that is utterly gone, never to rise up within him again. The former self, the old man, is not merely paralyzed, crippled, emaciated, or dormant. The sinner is not merely pacified, narcoticized, or suppressed. He is not, like the wayfarer, left half-dead. He is killed. He falls victim to the radical and final judgment of God. He is dead to sin, to the flesh, and to the law, and will one day be dead to death. And he is alive to God—and therefore must consider himself, identify himself, as such.

I can make this absolute judgment about myself only by faith and in hope. Outside of faith and hope the radical new identity that I assume would be utterly ridiculous. I *believe* that Jesus Christ destroyed the power of sin and established a new creation; and in faith I identify myself with the new order that He created. I *hope* for the realization of that new creation within the historical order; and in hope I identify myself with that coming realization. The realities of my present empirical self are too obvious for me to pretend that I am now, morally and psychically, separated from sin and alive only to the Christ-life. Nietzsche's "ugliest man" still clamors for recognition within my personal existence; I know he is there. But when he demands that I recognize him as my true self, my present identity before God and my future identity before man, I am summoned and allowed to deny his claim. But I deny that he is my true self only as an act of faith and hope.

This is not moral escapism. I am more or less sensitive to the demon that Dostoevsky says is alive inside every one of us. I look that sin-permeated empirical self full in the face. But I refuse

to say, before God, that it represents my genuine self. My real
self is that one who is "hid with God in Christ" (Col. 3:3). My
sinful self, still hanging like a parasite on my back, is part of the
old things that have passed away (II Cor. 5:17). When I identify
myself as a Christian man, I must stake claim only to the new
creature in Christ that I am in faith and in hope. My true self—
the self in Christ and the self of the future—is defined by the
reality of Christ's victory over the powers that would, were they
able, establish my sinful self as my true self.

Each day, I am summoned anew to see myself in the light of
Christ, to see myself a new being. The dead self has a way of
kicking its way into my mind. In moments of faithlessness, I am
tempted to think that it is my real self, and that I therefore am
still part of the old world and still under judgment. The old self
is still asserting its will to dominate my life and my appraisal of
my life; but if I then wonder "who shall deliver me" I am called
back to faith in Christ.

It should be clear that this radical new understanding of the self
is not gained by observation of some moral improvements one
makes within himself. For every sign that he is a new man, there
are several more signs that he is not a new man. The Christian
gains self-knowledge by identifying himself with the new reality
established by Christ. More, he gains it only by identifying himself
with Christ. That is, he believes in what his baptism stands for:
his initiation, with his whole being, into the new creation in Christ.
He accepts as the final word about himself the word which God
spoke over him in the baptismal sign: you are a member of the
body of Christ.

Baptism occurs in a context of faith, communal and personal.
The body of Christ believes for, prays for, and loves the baptized
person as a member of Christ. That is, baptism occurs in a community where the Lord is at work in His Spirit. The faith of other
people, the faith of the community, the faith of his family is the
context in which, first of all, a person is baptized. But his baptism needs for its final validity his own affirmation. He must see
himself as a man whose destiny is sealed by Jesus Christ. He must
consider himself to be a person who is in fact within the new life
order whose Lord is Jesus Christ. He must, that is, *accept* the
meaning of his own baptism. He must accept the sign of identification that God and the Church placed on his forehead. This is why
Karl Barth's sarcasm about the thousands of baptized Europeans
who became Christian in their sleep is quite understandable. Where

baptism does not take place within the community of active believers, and where the baptized person does not faithfully accept
himself as a person in Christ, there is no real baptism. A man
breaking bread and sipping wine at a French cafe is not thereby
celebrating the death of Christ. A child with water poured on his
forehead at play is not by that token baptized into Christ's death.
The context of faith, before and after, is the *sine qua non* of a real
and effective baptism because it is the context in which the new
creation is recognized and accepted.

This is why a person is never called to believe in his *baptism*.
He is called to faith in Christ. But he is called to the Christ with
whom baptism united him in the community of faith. He is called
to faith *by* his baptism. If baptism is only a dramatized testimonial
of my prior faith, it falls when my faith fails: it is no stronger than
my faith. But baptism says to me that God initiated me into the
new order of things. And when I personally doubt the reality of
my Christian self, when the past, dead self seems too real to me, I
can recall my baptism and be assured that God once identified me
as a member of His new creation. My baptism says to me: Jesus
Christ did in fact die and create a new life for you.

I understand myself as having in baptism died to sin and risen
as a new creature in the same act that I believe that Jesus truly
became Lord of life. Bultmann is right in seeing baptism as a
summons to self-understanding. When he says of baptism that "it
makes the salvation occurrence present for him just as the Word
does, only this time with special reference to him, the one being
baptized, as valid for him," he makes good exegetical sense.[24]
Baptism certifies to me that the death of Christ was the death of
myself to sin and to death. When I acknowledge the intent of my
baptism I am really affirming something profound about myself: I
am understanding myself in terms of Christ's death and resurrection. I identify myself as a naturalized citizen and active member
of the new regime in Christ. I have, in Paul's words, understood
myself as "crucified with Christ."

But Bultmann has made a crucial decision about the meaning of
Christ and His cross. In his decision to accept the scientific world
view as a norm for interpreting the reality of Christ, he rules out
the actual reality of the new order of human history begun by the
death and resurrection of Christ. There is, for him, no actual Lord
Jesus today. There is no actual new creation outside an individual

[24]*Theology of the New Testament* (New York, 1951), p. 312.

existence. So there is no real self-understanding *in Christ.* There is only a self-understanding in hope, a hope based on the possibility that I may on my own, partially and in spurts, actually be the authentic spiritual being that I must understand myself to be. Bultmann is so profound in his insight into the necessity of faith as a new understanding of the self that his refusal to believe there is genuine objective *ground* for the new understanding is one of the truly sad facts of modern theology.[25]

Christian self-understanding has a reference outside of the Christian person. First the Christian person identifies himself with Jesus Christ in His death and resurrection. Then he identifies himself with the new reality established by Christ; that is, he says and understands that what is true of life in the new creation is true of him. Then he identifies himself with the new community, the body of Christ. His self-understanding is an appraisal of himself in the light of his new environment, his spiritual and cosmic situation.[26]

This keeps him, or ought to keep him, from delusion about his

[25]I am not suggesting that Bultmann has *no* interest in the Jesus Christ "out there" in past history. But it is clear that for him the Jesus "out there" cannot be the source or power of my faith here and now. Bultmann's saving event is the "now and then" event of my faith; it is my decision to reassess myself that is the saving event. The only newness that appears in history is the newness of my self-understanding. (See, among many possible references, the *Theology of the New Testament,* pp. 302ff.) In shying away from the significance to baptism that is *prior* to faith, evangelical Baptists can unwittingly place themselves in Bultmann's camp. While they confess the historical reality of Christ, they tend to make personal decision the center and basis of our participation in the Christian life.

[26]A reading of John Calvin provides an interesting commentary on the relation of baptism and Christian self-identity. In one place he says: "It ought to be held as a fixed principle among us, that all that is out of Christ is hurtful and destructive. Whoever is a man in Christ is, in every respect, a perfect man" (*Commentary on Ephesians,* 4:13). But this perfection is claimed only as an act of faith and hope. "It is worthy of our observation that our life is said to be hid, that we may not murmur if our earthly life. . .differs in nothing from death, but that we may patiently wait for the day of revelation. And in order that our waiting may not be painful, let us note those expressions, *in God* and *with Christ,* which tell us that our life is out of danger, although it is not visible" (*Commentary on Colossians,* 3:3). Our baptism calls us, Calvin says, to identify ourselves with the "perfect man" who is as yet "not visible." Paraphrasing Paul's word to the baptized person, he writes: "Take this view of your case—that as Christ once died for the purpose of destroying sin, so you have once died, that in the future you may cease from sin" (*Commentary on Romans,* 6:1-11).

empirical self. He would make an utter fool of himself before God
and his fellow men were he to pretend that his life here and now
witnessed clearly to his new being in Christ. He does not identify
his redeemed person with the person people meet, associate with,
do business with, or even worship with. In fact, this is something
he mostly keeps to himself. He speaks of it when he prays. On
his knees he calls on God graciously to remember that his sinful
self is really the self that died, and to remember his real identity
in Christ. But when he is on his feet, talking to men, he points
them only to the cross of Christ.

Summary:

Being with Christ in His death and resurrection comes down to
this: by baptism one is made a member of the new order of life
that was begun when Christ died and rose again. The new order is
visibly present and its work is done within Christ's community, His
body. Baptism into the body of Christ is therefore the initiation of
a person into the historical effects and the ongoing work of Christ.
The present reality of His community is tied so uncompromisingly
to the event that created the community that to be part of the history of the community is to share in that event. This is the
peculiarly biblical—call it Hebrew, if you wish—way of thinking
about one's role and place in history. The time lapse remains, but
it is just not very relevant. What is relevant is the connection
between past event and present reality, the meaning, urgency, and
responsibility that the past gives to the present. We die with Christ
in baptism because God identifies us with the creative event of
Christ's death and therefore with the creative effects of His death.
    Baptism does not make faith irrelevant. It makes faith neces-
sary. But baptism has its significance prior to faith and therefore
is a visible sign which, along with the gospel, summons us to
affirm what God has already affirmed: participation in the new
reality for us.
    In short, when I affirm that my baptism has indeed initiated me
into the new community of Christ, I am affirming that I am "in
Christ." The reality of "being with Christ" in His death and resurrection is only another facet of the reality of "being in Christ." The
former identifies me especially with the events that created the new
reality. The latter identifies me especially as a member of the
new reality itself.

Chapter Five

Christ in Us

Being in Christ points to our inclusion within a new order of life established at the cross and resurrection and continued under the lordship of Jesus. Dying and rising with Christ points to our identification with the redemptive events of the past. We must now consider the subjective and personal reality of Christ dwelling within our lives. The phrase "Christ in us" opens up the other side of our union with Christ, the inward transformation of our lives to conform to the life of Christ. L. S. Thornton sees this two-sided character of union with Christ well. "By union with Christ," he writes, "we first die to the old life of sin through our transference from the old order to the new, and then there begins a process of assimilation to the new life which issues in resurrection."[1]

Brought into His new *order,* we are also transformed to His *character.* "God does not mock us," writes Thornton. "If he has brought us into the position of sons in his family, he has also taken corresponding steps to transform us spiritually, so that the inward reality of our life may correspond to the objective fact accomplished."[2] The step He has taken is the new step downward for Jesus Christ. Once incarnate in human flesh, He now becomes the Christ who takes up residence within the body called the Church and within every individual who is a member of it. Now, we must let St. Paul lead us into an understanding of how we are made new in subjective fact by the risen Christ as He lives within.

[1] L. S. Thornton, *The Common Life in the Body of Christ* (Westminster, 1946), p. 122.
[2] *Ibid.,* p. 124.

A. WHAT PAUL SAYS

Talking about Christ within us does not come as easily to Paul as does talking about our being in Christ. The phrase "Christ in us" or its equivalent occurs less often in Paul than the phrase "in Christ." But while it does not come as often, the concept of the indwelling Christ is nonetheless powerfully present in Paul's thought. For instance, we have the classic verse in which Paul identifies himself, individually, as one in whom Christ lives: "I have been crucified with Christ; it is no longer I who live, but Christ who lives in me; and the life I now live in the flesh I live by faith in the Son of God" (Gal. 2:20). The fact that Paul says this in the middle of a discussion about his release from the destructive situation under the law should not prejudice us against accepting the full force of its experiential and subjective thrust.

In other places, Paul drives home the fact that the indwelling of Christ is not a special apostolic privilege, nor the claim of an elite within the church, but is the assumed premise about every Christian. "Do you not realize that Jesus Christ is in you?—unless indeed you fail to meet the test" (II Cor. 13:5)! "Any man who does not have the Spirit of Christ is none of his" (Rom. 8:9). Paul's prayer that Christ may dwell within the hearts of people in the Church (Eph. 3:17) is meant to be inclusive.

Christ dwells within the Gentile Christians as a body; to all saints "God chose to make known how great among the Gentiles are the riches of the glory of this mystery, which is Christ in you, the hope of glory" (Col. 1:27).

Associated with the "Christ in us" passages are remarks Paul makes about having the "mind of Christ." He urges the Philippians to have in them the same mind that was in the self-emptying Christ (Phil. 2:5). He insists that he himself speaks from the mind of Christ (I Cor. 2:16). The power of Christ, too, is part of the picture. Paul speaks of himself as "striving with all the energy which . . . [Christ] mightily inspires within me" (Col. 1:29). He also talks about the congregation at Corinth being assembled "with the power of our Lord Jesus" to perform an excommunication (I Cor. 5:4). These passages are not as difficult to interpret as those about our having Christ within us, but they are part of the believer's experience of Christ Himself.

The notion that *God* dwells within us does not come naturally to Paul at all. Only in two instances does he say that God is in us. Both of these are quotations of sorts from the Old Testament. In

one instance he is talking about the incongruity of marriage between Christians and non-Christians. Marriage with unbelievers is
as incongruous as the presence of idols in God's temple. The
analogy is a good one, he says, "For we are the temple of the living
God" (II Cor. 6:16). From there he translates the covenant
promise in Leviticus 26:12 to read that the Lord promises to
"live in" and be among His people. In the other instance he is
concerned with worship and the need for communication in the
liturgy. When everyone shares in the "prophesy" and anyone
can understand, an outsider will recognize that "God is really
among you." But if some are babbling to themselves, the stranger
will only suppose that the Church is a congregation of idiots.
Here Paul is culling from Isaiah 45:15.

Speaking of our presence in God is as uncommon to Paul
as speaking of God's presence in men. Once, in Acts 17:28, he
quotes a Stoic passage saying that we "live and move and have our
being" in God, but he drops the phrase and never brings it up
again. Paul is christocentric in his whole theology of our relationship with God. He does not have a doctrine of union with God.
God was in Christ, but it is Christ who is in us.

The notion that the Spirit dwells in us is, however, as common
in Paul's letters as the notion that God dwells in us is uncommon.
We cannot possibly mention all the times Paul says that the Spirit
is either within us or at work on us, but a sampling will at least
indicate his propensity for this thought.

"But you are not in the flesh, you are in the Spirit, if the Spirit
of God really dwells in you," Paul says in Romans 8:9. The Spirit's
indwelling is the assurance of ultimate resurrection; for the Spirit
is the Spirit of God who raised Jesus (8:11). We spent a great
deal of time in the second chapter on the relationship in Paul's
thought between the Spirit and Christ, and what was said there
should be recalled here. For the indwelling of the Spirit and the
indwelling of Christ are one and the same thing in Romans 8. It
should be noticed too that the expressions "Spirit of God" and
"Spirit of Christ" are also interchangeable in this passage.

As Paul once said that we are the temple of God, he also says
that we, as the temple of God, have the Spirit of God within us (I
Cor. 3:16). A little later, he calls our bodies the temples of the
Spirit (I Cor. 6:19).

The presence of the Spirit provides the Christian with confidence and accounts for his virtue. The Spirit within us brings
love into our lives (Rom. 5:5). The Spirit within establishes our

status in Christ (II Cor. 1:22). His presence guarantees our immortality (II Cor. 5:5). The Spirit within enlightens the mind to the things of God (I Cor. 2:12). The Spirit assures our spirits that we are the sons of God (Rom. 8:16). The Spirit, says Paul, enabled him to make sound judgments (I Cor. 7:40). To be sure, the indwelling of the Spirit is not stated explicitly in these instances, but in each the implication is strong.

Several things become clear as we scan Paul's vocabulary: (1) There is no clear distinction between Christ dwelling in Christians and the Spirit dwelling in them. (2) There is no hint that Paul is using metaphor, as though he really means only that an impersonal power is at work on us to make us somewhat Christ-like or Spirit-like. (3) It is clear that the Christ who is in us is the person named Jesus, the concrete individual who died and rose again. The name Christ is not a pious reference to the moral and religious life of the believer in Christ. Unless we take this fact seriously, we will rob the Christian life of its heart and its mystery. Nor is there anything in Paul's vocabulary to suggest that he thinks of Jesus Christ, the Person, as having dissolved into Spirit. We are given a basis for interpreting the Spirit in terms of Christ; we are not given material for supposing that Christ has Himself evaporated.[3] (4) The presence of Christ and the Spirit within Christians is not limited either to a few Christians or to odd moments. The presence of Christ within is normal for all Christians. The Spirit does provide the body of Christ with specific ministries which all do not share. But the same Spirit is present in all. And He is present in all as the normal reality of Christian existence.

B. WHAT PAUL MEANS: THREE POINTS OF VIEW

When St. Paul says that Jesus Christ lives within men, he is obviously talking about a fundamental dimension of Christian life. But the language is either extraordinarily unclear or extraordinarily difficult. What sort of reality is affirmed by Paul's strange language? Is Paul affirming a reality concerning Jesus Christ or only a reality about ourselves and our faith in Christ? Is he saying something

[3]Here Wikenhauser's language is not wholly clear: "Paul could use the expression which he does, because he regarded Christ triumphant as a spiritual Being free from the limitations of time and place which bound Christ during his life on earth" (*Pauline Mysticism* [New York, 1960], p. 89). This is true only if the phrase "spiritual Being" does not suggest that Christ is any the less concrete and individual for being "unbound."

about the specific individual named Jesus and His invasion of our lives? Or is he witnessing to the vivid and lively experience of our faith?

Of course, the two thoughts do not compete with each other; if Paul has in mind a genuine invasion by Jesus Christ into my life, he can point to a deep experience that I have as a result. But on the other hand, he may be talking only about my faith or my piety and not about an actual invasion from the outside. That faith is for Paul a correlative of "Christ within" needs no saying. He prays for the Ephesians that Christ may dwell in their hearts "through faith" (Eph. 3:17). But the question is whether faith is a reception of something or someone from outside of the person who does the believing.

If that "something or someone" is the risen Jesus Christ, if faith is a form of personal consent to an actual invasion of one's very being by Jesus Christ, we are faced with the very sensitive task of understanding what Paul means. We can, of course, side-step this effort if we assume that Paul could not really have had the concrete individual Jesus in mind when he said that Christ "lives in me." Schleiermacher, for example, had no serious problem with it; for him, Paul's language was the pious affirmation of his own deep dependence on the universal immanent spirit which Paul poetically gave the name of the one man who most clearly and consistently lived in dependence on it. To Tillich, it would appear, Paul's language belongs to a galaxy of symbols that are more or less adequate for one's discovery of unity with the ground of all being. To Bultmann, "Christ in me" is mythological talk to convey one's awareness of need for help from the outside in the challenge of living an authentic, personal life. In such instances, a decision has been made, prior to a consideration of this specific matter, that there is no Jesus Christ "out there," that there cannot be—for reasons basically extraneous to Paul's theology—and that therefore there is no need for a modern person to bother himself with the problem of how Paul means us to understand him.

Those who assume that human faith witnesses to an objective reality find various ways to explain the meaning of the indwelling Christ. In this context, the objective reality affirmed by faith is the reality of Jesus Christ as a historical figure of past time and as the actually existing Lord of the present time; but more, it is the reality of Christ who somehow takes up a post within human life. The word "objective" admittedly is inadequate. We are dealing with an "objective reality" that has to do with our inward lives, our depths. But the word is used here to indicate that what happens inside of us happens by way of someone from the outside entering our lives. It is a way of saying that the Christian experience of the indwelling Christ is not merely an experience of ourselves, even though it is surely that too.

What follows is a brief look at three ways of understanding the reality of Christ within. What each has in common with the others is a conviction that we are dealing with Jesus Christ, a concrete Being. Further, each believes that the person Jesus Christ actually does impinge on our persons in such a way that Paul's language about His being within us is very fitting language to describe what happens to or in us as a result of Christ's direct involvement with us. But, given this common conviction, there is a significant difference between them.

1. The Divine Life Infused

In the first chapter, I characterized one kind of Christology as sacramentalist. I meant to indicate a way of thinking about Christ that sees His significance in terms of the incarnation, humanity taken up into a new level of existence by union with God. Consistent with his Christology, the sacramentalist tends to think of "Christ in us" in terms of an infusion of the divine-human life created by means of the incarnation. He does not suppose that Jesus Christ is vaporized as Spirit. Nor does he think that Jesus Christ is related to us merely as other human beings are related to us. Somehow, the incarnate life of the Son of God is transferred to and absorbed by our souls.

The sacramentalist does not mean that the Christ-life is a sort of stuff added to human life like air blown into a balloon, or insulin injected into the blood. The Christ-life is not a new substance added to the soul. It is more like a power that pushes the soul upward on the ladder of being. The result of having Christ within, then, is not the addition of a spiritual superstructure on the human personality.[4] Nor does the Christ-life dissolve and destroy the hu-

---

[4]True, Catholics have often presented nature and grace in a dualistic way, causing Protestants to criticize them for a two-story view of man (see Brunner's simplistic criticism in *Man in Revolt* [London, 1939], p. 94). But Karl Rahner criticizes Catholics for the same view: "In short, the relationship between nature and grace is thought of as two layers laid very carefully one on top of the other so that they interpenetrate as little as possible." In this way, sinful man who has lost grace differs from pure nature

manity of man, replacing it with the life of the God-man. It goes somewhat differently. But how?

One Catholic theologian who worked out a very grand theology on the premise of Christ within us is Matthias Scheeben. He starts with the assumption that men and God have a kind of innate kinship; their two natures are not separated by "an infinite qualitative difference" but are naturally drawn together by native affinity. No man can rise to union with God on his own. But, as a woman needs to be fulfilled by man, the human soul is naturally receptive to the life of God. And it is never fully content until it is filled.

Scheeben's thought does sometimes suggest the "superstructure" view. Man's natural life is the substructure; the divine life is added to it. There is, says Scheeben, a "new creation erected on the substructure of the first creation; a new establishment and foundation of a new, immensely higher life, for which no germ or seed was found in nature."[5] This, however, is simply Scheeben's way of saying that the new life of Christ within is really new, not just a refurbishing of the old. The change is not one of redirection, but of elevation; it is not the reorientation of life around a new object, but the rebuilding of life on a new level. That new level is the divine life.

The new life was begun at the incarnation. The humanity of Jesus was privileged as no other can be; it had been assumed into the very being of God and had become deified as a result. But the life that resulted can be shared. The incarnation created a center of supernatural life from which shares can be miraculously distributed to others. To be given a share in the life of Christ is to take part in the sharing of the Father's life with the Son in the eternal birth of trinitarian existence. In the communication of Christ's life, we are infused with the divine life itself. And so, we become divinized.[6]

"as the man who has lost his clothes differs from the man who has never had any" (*Nature and Grace* [London, 1963], p. 7).

[5]*Nature and Grace* (St. Louis, 1954), p. 102. Scheeben (1835-1888) published this book in 1861. It is one of his earliest works. His greatest book is *Mysterien des Christentums,* 1865. The republication of his works testifies to his renewed influence in Catholic scholarship.

[6]"Because this principle is so excellent an image of the Godhead and, in its capacity of vital faculty, imparts divine life to us, it raises us to an inconceivable nearness and relationship to God. The higher we mount above our own nature, the closer we come to . . . the divine nature. We draw so close to it and become so like it that we may be said to be divinized and actually are" (*ibid.,* p. 113).

The key word in all this is "life." Life is experienced on many levels. Each living thing shares it on its own level. Human life, being rational and communal, is at the highest level in the natural order. But human life reaches upward to a still higher level. It has a capacity for participation in a higher life. Yet it cannot rise to this level any more than a bird can fly without wings. This life must be given by grace. It is the prerogative of God and is located, in a manner suitable for us, in the life of Jesus Christ. It is given to us by a miracle of the Spirit.

What is given is the divine life. Of course, it is not forced on us. Nor is it given in such undiluted form as to efface our humanity and make us gods in the strict sense. What we receive is the divine-human life of Christ; it is the humanity of Jesus as it has been infused with divinity through the incarnation. "Since the Christ is both God and man," says Mascall, "the Christian, by incorporation into Christ, has received a share in the life of God Himself. He has been made a partaker of the divine nature, the nature of God who is trinity."[7] Mascall, we should quickly say, is actually about as far from pantheism as anyone can get. He insists that the infusion of the divine life within us happens without erasing the "radical and indestructible difference of kind" between God and man.[8]

Man remains a creature, just as Jesus in His humanity remained a creature. But, in a way that fits his inalienable creatureliness, he shares with Jesus a genuine infusion of the life of God. Something happens to him at the depths of his being to make him as new a creature as an animal body is made when it is taken up into human life as the body of man. The analogy between the organic elevation of animal life into human life and lifting of human life into the divine life is not haphazardly chosen. Most modern sacramentalists see the whole organic structure of life in these terms. The Christian reality of participation in God's life is the final stage of organic development; only it occurs not by the upward push of nature, but by God Himself lifting humanity to its new and climactic stage.

The sacramentalist wants to say that Christian existence is a new ontological reality. Emile Mersch says this:

> To be a child of God . . . is an ontological reality, so great as to be of a different order from every created magnitude, to over-

[7]Mascall, *Christ, the Christian, and the Church* (London, 1946), p. 109.
[8]*Via Media* (London, 1956), p. 121.

flow our intellectual categories, to be truly mysterious, to be capable of definition as regards what it is in itself only in terms of that which defines God as He is in Himself.[9]

What he means is that the reality of Christ within is a reality that can be explained only as the reality of God's own life siphoned through the humanity of Christ.

When we try to pinpoint what it is that comes within us, we are hard put. Life, of course, is a thing that is hard to define even in the most primitive biological terms. Biologists speculate among themselves about what life is; the best they can do with precision is to describe how specific living things *act* and *react*. So we should not be surprised if the sacramentalist is unable to be precise about the true nature of the life into which we are elevated to share with God. It has analogies on the organic level, but the analogies relate to the how rather than to the what. So we do not get a distinct picture of what it is that is within us.

We can see, however, that we are not dealing with the *person* of Christ. As long as we think of the person, we are forced to think of someone outside, who relates to us pretty much as other people relate to us; He would confront us, but not indwell us. In fact Wikenhauser points to this as a mark that distinguishes the genuinely Catholic viewpoint from the Protestant.[10] The Catholic sacramentalist suspects that as long as we think of the Jesus Christ within as a person, we are forced to think in terms of a relationship between two distinct beings, and thus a relationship which is basically one of separation.

On the other hand, the sacramentalist does not mean to tell us that the divine life is a sort of invisible stuff in an invisible package nestled alongside of our souls. Grace is always a power that affects the substance of our souls; it is not a substance itself. The divine life as it affects us is not a thing added to our souls. When we are given a share in the divine life, something *happens* to our souls, and by its net effect, to our entire life. It begins at the center of our being and works outward. We are not merely made God's partners; we are deified. There occurs a "real com-

---

[9]"Filii in Filio," *Nouvelle Revue Theologique* (July, 1938), 825.

[10]"They [Protestants] consider that Paul's fellowship with Christ is merely a relationship between two persons, no different from the relation which exists between any human being and someone whom he respects highly, except that it is a religious bond" (*op. cit.*, p. 103).

munication of the life of God to the human soul" and with it a
"real supernaturalization of our human nature in its essence."[11]

At this point, what we have is not merely a view of Christ and
His indwelling, but a view of man. No responsible sacramentalist
would suggest that man deified is thereby a proper object of worship. Nor does he assume that his thoughts automatically become
God's thoughts and his ways God's ways. What he does hold is
that man functions supernaturally. He is able to love, to obey, to
realize inward holiness and social justice, and above all to "see"
God. He is a son of God and a member of Christ's body. These, of
course, are effects of the primary event of deification. But if one
believed that man's inability to act as a Christian were due not to
a tragic incompletion of nature, but to a violent decision of the will,
he would not need to believe that man's nature would have to be
supernaturalized; he would need to believe that man's will needed
to be revitalized and redirected. In short, the doctrine of deification is a necessary corollary of the sacramentalist view of man.

If you begin your effort to understand Christian reality with a
prejudice against natural man's ability to live the life God destined
for him, you are likely to say that the gift of grace is the gift of a
new ingredient in the natural life, an ingredient which in effect lifts
the natural to a notch above nature. But what does this really come
to for the sacramentalist? It does not essentially eradicate man's
humanity. It does not unequivocally deify him. Nor does it *add* a
substance to his reality. What does it come to, then, but a divine
power which radically, that is, at the roots of life, enables him to
live a Christianly virtuous life?[12] Sacramentalists say that the gift
of grace *substantially affects* the human soul. One cannot help

[11]Mascall, *Christ, the Christian, and the Church,* p. 81.

[12]By way of ruling out the notion that super-nature is a loose addition to
nature, like an extension added to a house, Scheeben writes: "In this way
supernature is the vital power and inclination toward a definite end that
are imparted by a higher being. They surpass the vital power and aspiration of nature; but because they confer no new essence and no substance,
they must be attached to the natural vital power and aspiration and have
them as substructure. And because the new vital power is not added in
such a way that it exists alongside the natural one but is adapted to and
received by the latter, which it merely raises to a higher sphere of activity,
another objection vanishes; namely, that the essence is substantially
changed by accession of the new power" (*op. cit.,* pp. 34f.). Scheeben
admits—as all Christians admit—that the Christian virtues are the effect
of divine power; he, however, finds it necessary to *define* that power in
terms of the *deification* of man.

wondering, then, how much essential difference the sacramentalist creates between himself and other Christians with his talk of deification through an infusion of divine life. We shall have to talk about the "other Christians" in order to find out. But this is a nettlesome anthropological problem. We would not care to find fault with the notion that man is *substantially* changed by union without discussing what kind of being man is and what a *substantial* change would involve for him. At root, our difficulty with the sacramentalist is anthropological. But what we wish to say here is that he qualifies his "deification" doctrine strongly enough as a rule to suggest that the *function* of the word "deification" is to stress very clearly that union with Christ really, basically, and at the point where it matters most, *changes* a man.[13]

2. Christ in Us Means Christ "for Us"

The sacramentalist takes the preposition "in" very literally; but the Christ who is actually in us turns out for the sacramentalist to be an *effect* on us called participation in divine life. The viewpoint I wish to consider now wants to honor the full *person* of Jesus Christ in this inner relationship. Though it would be unfair to say that Barth and Brunner approach the subject of Christ-in-us out of *reaction* to mysticism, it is clear that both are convinced that any notion of the Christ-in-us that draws our attention away from the Jesus Christ of complete personal individuality and of decisive action in the past is likely to lure us away from the gospel.

The Word of God, Brunner emphasizes, points us to Calvary. And Calvary proclaims that we are justified by Christ. The cross says in effect: "You are judged, forgiven, and adopted as children." We respond as we identify the event of the cross as God's judgment on and affirmation of ourselves: "Yes, this is what I am, judged, forgiven, and adopted." Our affirmation of faith is our identification with Christ. Brunner says: "One might actually say, faith and Christ are synonymous, at any rate in the sense that 'to have Christ' and 'to believe' are one and the same thing."[14] This, according to Brunner, is what Paul means by Christ living in us. The Christian *believes* that God accepts him as he accepts Christ. "For faith consists precisely in thinking not one's self, but God's self-communication in Jesus Christ alone important."[15]

[13]See Additional Note 5, pp. 262-263.
[14]*The Christian Doctrine of the Church, Faith, and the Consummation* (London, 1962), p. 174.
[15]*Ibid.*

Faith is present when a man gives up his own pretentious claims to morality, admits he needed to be died for, and accepts God's judgment on him. That act, daily renewed and acted upon, is what Paul meant by Christ "in us."[16] Christ is *for* us—out there at Calvary. We affirm this. Brunner consistently rejects the idea of an ontological change within man on which he can rely, the idea of an indelible mark on the soul. He firmly rejects the idea of an infusion of divine life within us. Christ "in us" has everything to do with what happened outside of us.

> 'Christ in me.' How very easy it would be to confuse this with mysticism. And yet, how can we make this mistake? Are we not here concerned with Christ crucified, the sacrifice which has been offered once and for all, apart from anything I have done? With something which is really, actually, and outwardly a brute fact, with no 'inwardness' about it, a death? That with which I am united is the absolute opposite of mysticism.[17]

Christ speaks to us from the cross and we answer in faith. The intimacy of this personal response—the essence of revelation—is the be all and end all of Christ "in me."

To the sacramentalist, Brunner is the kind of Protestant who talks about union with Christ but does not really believe it. But Brunner does believe in a union with Christ, one that respects the integrity of the two parties in the union. Christ is in His place. We are in ours. He speaks and we answer. Our answer is a decision of faith to let ourselves be identified with the Christ "out there." He did something for us. And with that, God is for us here and now. But the Christ with whom we are identified remains the Christ of Calvary—the only Christ there is. We believe with a faith that brings our whole personality into acting obedience and Paul dignifies our faith with the phrase "Christ in us."

Karl Barth's understanding of Christ's presence in us is more complex than Brunner's, but is essentially the same. Barth tries harder to take the word "in" seriously. The word, says Barth, shows that "Christ is spatially present where Christians are, and that Christians are spatially present where Christ is, and not merely alongside, but in exactly the same spot."[18] But the question of space is not crucial; the Spirit of Christ makes space irrele-

---

[16]*Ibid.*, p. 205.
[17]*The Mediator* (London, 1934), p. 527.
[18]*Church Dogmatics*, IV/3 (New York), p. 547.

vant. Barth, we may recall, holds that the Spirit is Christ Himself, attesting to Himself here and now, summoning people to new obedience to the Christ "out there."[19] In short, the crucial question is not where Christ is (He is *here* in Word and Spirit), but what He is doing. This is why, in talking about the "Christ in us" passages, Barth writes:

> It has always involved an unwise and . . . an attenuating exposition of these verses to speak of an extension of the incarnation. . . . We are concerned rather with the extended action in His prophetic work of the one Son of God who became flesh once and for all and does not therefore need any further incarnation.[20]

The key words are "action," "prophetic work," "once and for all." There is one Jesus Christ "out there," who became incarnate. But His action goes on. And His action is a work of witness.

The reality of Christ in us, then, points to the *work* of Christ going on in history. It means that Christ is calling us to be united with Him. Union with Him is our vocation, our human destiny, our calling to be men; for to be a genuine man is to be God's partner in action. Christ is in us! This means that Christ is summoning us, not from a distance, but close at hand, through the Spirit that is Himself. And when we respond, in the obedience of faith, we have Christ in us.

Addressing himself directly to Paul's statement in Galatians 2:20, Barth writes:

> Christ lives in the apostle in such a way that he has to say of himself that he no longer lives, that is, in himself and apart from the fact that Christ lives in him, but that he now lives in faith in Him who gave Himself for him, this being his own most proper life to which, as one who still lives in the flesh, he can do justice only as he believes in Him.[21]

This is not the most lucid of theological statements. But the gist is clear. Apart from his identity with Jesus and His cross, Paul does not really live as a genuine human being. And he can do justice to Christ's being the center of his life, the point of orientation, only by *believing* in the Christ who died for him.

Christ does not enter us in some moment of silent, unconscious,

[19]*Ibid.*, 1, pp. 522, 648.
[20]*Ibid.*, 3, p. 543.
[21]*Ibid.*, p. 543.

passive receptivity; we cannot be united with Christ in our sleep. We are *called* to live the life of Christ within us. We are called every day anew. And we are called not to contemplate our sanctified souls, but to listen to and obey Jesus Christ. We are called not to an elevation of our being, but to a life of partnership in the prophetic work of Christ.[22] We are dynamically ordered to live out Galatians 2:20. Union with Christ is not the *assumption,* it is the *goal* of Christian living.

Christ always retains His own identity and His own position. He is "absolutely isolated from all others." But the wonder of His grace is that He chooses not to be considered simply in His own self. He chooses to identify Himself with us in all the frustrations of our fleshly lives, but particularly in the service we are called to perform with Him. He is in this the One who commands, who gives, who goes before: He is always free. But He comes to be our partner in His freedom. When He comes, there is "an encounter in time between two personal partners who do not lose but keep their identity and particularity." He keeps His identity as Lord. We keep our identity as disciples. He "speaks, acts, and rules."[23] And we listen, obey, and then speak.

Barth is consistent. In his Christology, he defines Jesus Christ in terms of action. In his doctrine of union with Christ, he defines our life in terms of action, co-action with Christ. Here, the identity of Jesus Christ—personal, lordly, free—is maintained. The centrality of the Christian's vocation as partner with Christ is kept. The concept of faith is one of active obedience. The Christ *in us* is the Christ *for us,* not only on Calvary, but in the daily renewal of His willingness to be on our side and at our side. Christ in us? When we think of this, we should think of Christ as Lord, the one around whom we center our lives; think of His summons to us, of His direct lordship over us, and of His willingness to make us partners—obedient partners to be sure, but partners in His action.

All this is, of course, substantially different from the sacramentalist point of view. And yet there are some formal similarities. Like the sacramentalist, Barth insists that man's destiny as a human being is to live the life of Christ within; he agrees that

[22]"The purpose for which Christians are already called here and now . . . is that in the self-giving of Jesus Christ to them, and theirs to Him, they should enter into their union with Him, their *unio cum Christo* (*ibid.,* 3, p. 540).

[23]*Ibid.,* p. 547.

only in union with Christ is man genuinely human. But Barth does not give an inch on the fact that it is *Christ* who is in us. What is in us is not a distilled version of the divine life; it is the concrete individual, Jesus Christ. Nor does he let himself come within a thousand miles of talk about the substance of man's soul being permanently altered; man is summoned daily, in the dynamics of the Word and Spirit, to follow and obey, to become a partner in action. The sacramentalist will not compromise on the word "in." Barth will not compromise on the word "Christ." And this is the impasse between them.[24]

Luther stands on Barth's side of the impasse. While in his comment on Galatians 2:20 he surely sounds as mystical as anyone could be, his thought in the main puts the comment in a different light. In his commentary on Galatians, Luther does talk about Christ and Paul as becoming wholly one, so that Christ takes over Paul's life in the most personal sense.[25] But Luther's major premise remained consistent: "One thing and one alone is necessary for life, justification and Christian liberty."[26] This is the single and marvelous doing of Christ. It was accomplished at the cross and, after the cross, is accomplished by the Word; the Word is always the Word of the cross. The Word acts. It does now what Jesus did while He was on earth. It heals. It heals by proclaiming forgiveness and peace and liberty. So the Word coming to us is Christ coming to us in the power that sets men free. Proclamation, action, healing—these are the dynamics of the situation in which men are united with Christ.

---

[24]James Denney, who was surely no Barthian, said something about Paul's "I live, yet not I" that comes close to Barth's meaning. These words, he writes, "do not mean that Christ . . . has become the constituting reality of Paul himself, so that Paul virtually ceased to be, his old personality vanishing, and that of Christ appearing in its place. . . . Whatever union with Christ does, it enables a man to become himself, the true self with the individuality for which God created him. When Paul says, 'I no longer live, but Christ liveth in me' he is not declaring his pure passivity or abnegation of striving henceforth, but the completeness with which Christ is taking his personality into His service" (*The Christian Doctrine of Reconciliation* [London, 1917], p. 307).

[25]"Christ therefore . . . thus joined and united into me and abiding in me, liveth this life in me which now I live; yea Christ himself *is* this life which now I live. Therefore Christ and I in this behalf are both one" (*Galatians* [London, 1953], p. 168). Luther's commentary on Galatians was delivered as a series of lectures at Wittenberg in 1531.

[26]*On Christian Liberty,* from *Luther's Primary Works,* ed. Wace and Bucheim (London, 1896), p. 257.

When our response to the Word is the response of our whole self, of our wills, we are true believers. Our faith becomes one with the Word. And since faith is the deep movement of the soul, our soul becomes one with the Word. As "iron exposed to fire glows like fire," the soul glows with the truth of the Word. Faith affirms what the Word affirms; the Word affirms that we are free men through the cross of Christ, and in faith we become what the Word declares us to be. This is what it means to have the Word dwelling in us richly. And since the Word acts now as Christ acted once in the past, it also means to have Christ dwelling in us.[27]

Luther is not shy of a real sharing in Christ; we become "little Christs" as a result of His dwelling in us. But what this means is that we act toward our neighbor as Christ acted toward us.[28] We become "little Christs" by sharing with others the love He showed to us, by giving ourselves to others as He gave Himself for us. Even Paul's goading us to "put on Christ" is read this way by Luther. Christ "put us on" when He died for our forgiveness; we ought to "put our neighbor on" in the same sense—we ought to give ourselves in service for him.[29] The whole "mystical" indwelling is seen in this light. In faith, we affirm Christ *for* us; we identify ourselves with Him and His cross. And doing this, we cannot but live the agapic life of sacrifice for others. Our labor for others is indirectly Christ's labor for them; Christ, then, is living in us. But the "in" always means the lively identity we make with His atonement on the cross.

We can summarize the difference between the two views which

[27]*Ibid.,* p. 262. Luther says that Christ in us makes us one with Christ as a man becomes one with a woman. A man has all things in common with his wife. So it is with Christ and the Christian. "Christ is full of grace, life, and salvation; the soul is full of sin, death, and condemnation. Let faith step in, and then sin, death, and hell will belong to Christ, and grace, life, and salvation to the soul. For if He is a husband He must needs take to Himself that which is His wife's, and, at the same time impart to His wife that which is His" (*ibid.,* p. 264).

[28]"As our heavenly Father has freely helped us in Christ so ought we freely to help our neighbor by our body and our works, and each should become to the other a sort of Christ, so that we may be mutually Christs, and that the same Christ may be in all of us; that is, that we may be truly Christians" (*ibid.,* p. 283).

[29]"He put us on, and acted for us as if He Himself were what we are. From us . . . [the good things from God] flow to those who have need as a covering and intercession for the sin of my neighbor, which I am to take on myself, and so labor and endure servitude in them as if they were my own; for thus has Christ done for us" (*ibid.,* p. 286).

we have discussed in terms of the following questions. (For lack of a better word, let us call the second view the "actionist view.") (a) What is it that is *in* us? The sacramentalist says that it is divine life. The actionist says that it is the concrete, acting person called Jesus Christ. (b) In what sense is the word "in" to be understood? The sacramentalist says that it is to be understood literally, in that we actually live the divine life in our created existence. The actionist says that it is to be understood metaphorically, in that it connotes the close association between Christ and us in the service of God and man. (c) What happens to us as a result? The sacramentalist says we are lifted to a new, supernatural level of life. The actionist says we are brought into the family of adopted children and called into a life of service. (d) In short, what does a man have in union with Christ that he did not have outside of union with Christ? The sacramentalist says *deification*. The actionist says *partnership with Christ*.

3. Christ Rules Within

If John Calvin can be called the theologian of the Spirit, he can also be called the theologian of the indwelling Christ. Union with Christ meant "Christ in us" for Calvin, and while he does not provide us the key to understanding our being "in Christ," he does give us genuine guidance in our present discussion. If not always perfectly clear, he is whole, of a piece, and does justice to the Pauline mystery.

As we saw much earlier, the problem for us, in our time, is how the benefits of what Christ did a long time ago can become our own. Calvin did not solve the problem but only restated it in the famous remark that sets the stage for his entire soteriology: ". . . as long as Christ remains outside of us, and we are separated from him, all that he has suffered and done for the salvation of the human race remains useless and of no value for us."[30] The problem is this: how does Christ overcome His separation from us and become the Christ "in us"?

Two things are nonnegotiable for Calvin. One of them is the limited, circumscribed status of Christ's humanity. Jesus is in a place where He, though glorified, is confined.[31] The other is the well-known Calvinist thesis that the divine and human do not mix; unity with Christ cannot be a blend of His divine and our

[30]*Institutes* iii. 1. 1.
[31]*Ibid*. iv. 17. 32.

human natures. Calvin is adamant here. And his stubbornness
sets up the peculiar character of his problem.[32]

Jesus in His humanity is "out there" apart from us. In His
divinity, He is with us. The Calvinist answer to the question of
how Jesus could be with us even though ascended is this: He is
with us in His divinity and Spirit.[33] But it is the *humanity* that we
need. Everything rests on the possibility of our sharing His humanity.[34]

After all, the benefits of His active obedience are not stored in
some benefit bank; they are not kept to His account in a spiritual
treasury somewhere. The benefits are Himself. They are His
righteousness, holiness, and wisdom—qualities of His own character. So, it is absurd to suppose that we, as genuine persons,
could receive His benefits without having Him.[35]

It is just as true, however, that we cannot isolate the humanity
of Jesus from His divinity. Jesus Christ is one, and if we have Him
we have Him whole. So in spite of his protests against Osiander's
notion of a unity with the divinity of Christ, Calvin seems at times
to talk Osiander's own language: ". . . God did not want to have
life hidden and as it were buried within Himself, and therefore He
transfused it into His Son that it might flow to us."[36] Like the
sacramentalist, Calvin talks as though the divine life is filtered

[32]This comes out in his fascinating argument with the Lutheran, Osiander.
That God's life and ours could be mixed was, as Wendel says, a notion
that "everything in Calvin's theology was bound to revolt against" (Wendel,
Calvin [Paris, 1950], p. 236). Yet, this did not seem to be the main thing
Calvin had against Osiander. If Osiander had only claimed that "the
essence of the divine nature is poured into us" he would have dwelt "on
these delights with less harm" (*Institutes* iii. 11.6). The real harm that
Osiander did was to rest the case for grace on the new and improved
character that we gain from this transfusion. In short, the issue was the
freedom of God in *grace,* more than the mixture of divinity and humanity.

[33]See Chapter Two, A, 2.

[34]Our future is dim and our prospects nil unless Christ "having been
made ours, makes us sharers with him in the gifts with which he has been
endowed" (*Institutes* iii.11.10). See R. S. Wallace, *Calvin's Doctrine of
the Christian Life* (Grand Rapids, 1959), p. 15. "God has made the
human nature of Jesus . . . the residing-place of all the graces of the Spirit
which are required to transform men into new creatures. . . ."

[35]*Institutes* iii.11.8; iii.16.1. Herman Bavinck thought that Calvin obscured his doctrine of union with Christ when he insisted on this. "Calvin
never succeeded in making clear the difference between communion with
the person of Christ and participation in his benefits" (*Kennis en Leven*
[Kampen, 1922], p. 176).

[36]*Commentary on John* 5:26.

through Christ's humanity to us: ". . . the flesh of Christ is like a rich and inexhaustible fountain that pours into us the life springing forth from the Godhead into itself."[37]

Calvin also talks as though there is a stuff called life which is ours by transfusion. There is no other life, he says, "than that which is breathed into us by Christ: so that we begin to live only when we are ingrafted into him, and enjoy the same life with himself."[38] He talks about a "sacred partaking of his flesh and blood, by which Christ pours his life into us."[39] On occasion, he is even willing to say that we share the "substance" of Christ's life.[40] When we read things like this in Calvin, however, we must remember that he was willing to use any language at all, as long as it functioned to get the point across: his point in these instances is to demonstrate that Christ is really in us, that our union with Him is not fictional nor merely moral, but real and personal.[41]

Well then, what does Calvin mean? We have already seen, in our discussion of the Spirit's relationship to Christ, that the Holy Spirit is the creative action of Christ in the new dispensation. In this sense, a change occurred at the time of the resurrection and ascension. God has *always* been everywhere as Spirit. But since the resurrection and ascension, He has been present in a particular way as the power and virtue of Christ. Christ is "present to those who believe in Him in the greater energy of his Spirit; He lives in them and dwells in their midst and even within them."[42] The Spirit, as Calvin often says, is the mysterious bond between the Lord "out there" and His earthbound disciples. And if Christ had not been provided with this power, "he would have come to us in vain."[43] The Spirit is the power of Christ to overcome the "ugly broad ditch" between Him and us.

We now come to the essence of Calvin's point. We must take seriously all that he says about a real communication, an inner

[37]*Institutes* iv.17.9.

[38]*Commentary on Ephesians* 2:4.

[39]*Institutes* iv.11.19.

[40]Calvin mentions the "substance" of Christ's life in the following places, and perhaps others: the *Institutes* iv.17.3; the *Commentary on Ephesians* 5:29; the *Commentary on II Corinthians* 11:24; the sermons on Deuteronomy 1:19-21, Matthew 28:1-10, and Galatians 3:26-29.

[41]Terms like "substance" are not a mere inadvertency on Calvin's part (as Wendel suggests, *op. cit.*, p. 237), but neither are they technical.

[42]*Commentary on II Corinthians* 5:6.

[43]*Institutes* iii.1.2.

assimilation of Christ's life, if we are to keep what now follows in perspective. When Christ comes, as Spirit, He does not deposit some stuff called "life." The situation is for Calvin far more dynamic than this. For instance, he explains what he means by having the life of God when he comments on Ephesians 4:18: ". . . the regeneration of believers is here called, *par excellence,* the life of God, because then does God properly live in us, and we enjoy His life, when He governs us by His Spirit."[44] And in his comment on Galatians 2:20, he says the same thing: "Christ lives in us in two ways. The one consists in His governing us by His Spirit and directing all our actions. The other is what He grants us by participation in His righteousness, that, since we can do nothing of ourselves, we are accepted in Him by God."[45]

The Spirit "governs" us and "directs" our actions. This is quite another thing than giving us a transfusion. We are on the right track, I think, if we keep in mind that the Spirit does come within us and that the Spirit is, in fact, Christ within us. Spirit speaks to spirit. And so Christ is truly within. But He honors who and what *we* are, persons who find their true and genuine selfhood in obedience to Christ. The Spirit does not displace us. He does not destroy our integrity as real persons. Nor does He somehow keep a still, silent vigil *alongside* our ego. Nor does He elevate our souls to a new metaphysical level. He brings us Christ to enable us to live the Christ life—to live in a way that is wise, holy, and righteous. Christ within us brings us back to the image of God—a life of action in obedience to God.[46]

The two nonnegotiable premises are kept intact. The Christ who is within us is the Christ "out there." He is a discrete man, in all the limitations that a man has even in heaven. The Christ who

[44]*Commentary on Ephesians* 4:18.

[45]*Commentary on Galatians* 2:20.

[46]Alfred Göhler says that Calvin's doctrine of union with Christ led him to a denial of the world, to asceticism, even to a desire for death (*Calvin's Lehre von der Heiligung* [München, 1934], p. 40). It is true that Calvin spends more time on mortification of the flesh than on vivification of the Spirit. It is also true that he made statements that suggest a pessimistic distaste for life. But he balances these by summoning Christians to love life, to be thankful for it, to hate only what is sinful in it, and to go into the world and make it a better world than it is (*Institutes* iii.9.4). The whole of Calvin's own life demonstrates his true perspective. Flight from the world is a different thing from discontent with the world. Discontent leads one into the world, not to enjoy it as it is, but to change it so that both man and God can enjoy it.

is within us is not an infusion of Christ's divinity. Still, the *whole* Christ is indeed within us. This is not made possible by theological sleight of hand.[47] Christ's significance is the quality of His life which, in turn, is concentrated in His act of obedience, His life of true humanity under God. And this is brought to us by the Spirit. Unless we see that the presence of the Spirit is the actual presence of Christ, the point will be lost.

Of course, faith is very much involved here. And we shall have to talk about that in the next chapter. But it is clear that Calvin would not agree that having faith is the same as having Christ within. Something deeper is going on between the risen Lord and believers than an act of faith. Something happens within us because Christ is there, working in and changing our lives at the center. My guess is that Calvin would feel more at home in some of the language used by sacramentalists than with that of Brunner —if only to agree with them that there is a real participation in the life of Christ at the depths of our own.

But he did not wish to say that our souls, as things apart, are substantially elevated or changed by Christ within. He did wish to say that our whole lives, in all their dynamic relationships, are basically reoriented and redirected. He keeps a personalism intact, but does not let his personalism get in his way of respecting the mystery of the Christ within us. The Holy Spirit is personal, always free, ever independent of our souls; yet He is at work within as the Christ in action on earth. The Christ within can be ignored, spurned, and offended. He can also be obeyed, loved, and longed for. Not the substance of life as a metaphysical property, but the moral dynamics of life are Calvin's interest.

Was Calvin a mystic? Is there room in this theologian of the free Lord for anything like mysticism? This question is asked by almost all interpreters of Calvin. It has no simple answer, because no two definitions of mysticism are the same. If mysticism means that man experiences something he cannot explain, Calvin was a mystic. If Christian experience is mystical when it cannot be categorized in a psychology textbook, Calvin was a mystic. If

---

[47]Bavinck, too, says that for Calvin "the mystical union is . . . a union with the person of Christ, with His divine and human nature, with His soul and body, with His flesh and blood and thereafter a communion in His treasures and gifts" (*Kennis en Leven,* p. 174). Calvin does use a scholastic distinction to explain this. The whole Christ is present, he says, even though every part of Christ is not present (*Institutes* iv.17.30). The *impact* of the living Christ is there as fully as if He were present *en toto.*

Rudolph Otto is right when he says that anyone who talks Spirit talks mysticism, Calvin was a mystic. But if mysticism involves a concentration on pious feelings, if mysticism involves any loss in man's individual identity, and, in particular, if mysticism implies an identity between God and man—even for the moment of mystical ecstasy—then Calvin was not a mystical theologian. Several convictions stopped Calvin short of mysticism: the conviction (1) that Christ within provides no insight or vision not included in the *word* of the gospel; (2) that Christ within provides the believer with no basis for claiming, even for a moment's experience, that his soul is perfectly cleansed, let alone deified; (3) that Christ within is not the privilege of the spiritually elite, but the basic requisite for the beginning of Christian existence for every man; (4) that Christ within does not offer material for a theology of the pious or deified man; an accurate theology is and remains a theology of Christ and His work; (5) that Christ within does not offer ecstatic escape from the world, but compels men to go into the world to do the will of God there.[48]

C. THE PAULINE PATTERN: THE SPIRIT AND THE POWER

"Christ lives in me." We can be sure that Paul does not let a thought like this drop unconnected, detached from the rest of

---

[48]Kolfhaus overstates the case when he says, "Everything typical of the mystic is absent in Calvin" (*Christus Gemeinschaft*, p. 129). But the point is well made. K. Reuter is clearly exaggerating when he writes, "The concept of piety, as Calvin develops it, forecloses on all mystical tendency and tends only toward a proper discipline" (*Das Grundverständnis der Theologie Calvins* [Neukirchen, 1963], p. 99). In fact, Reuter's book strangely ignores the significance for Calvin of union with Christ. Reuter construes Calvin as a Christian of pure intellect and cold obedience. Paul Wernle wrestles with the tension between Calvin's mystical language and his concept of authority and the dynamic of the will: "Amazing at first sight, this language of mystical passivity in the mouth of the most tremendously *willed* person of the century." Wernle concludes that Calvin, after a pass at mysticism, reverts in the end to a "law religion," to the centrality of authority, transcendence, and the dynamic movement of the will (*Der Evangelische Glaube*, III [Tübingen, 1918], pp. 31ff.; pp. 229ff.). This sort of talk rises, in my judgment, out of a common but one-sided view of Calvin's so-called "law religion." And equally out of a failure to take his so-called "mystical passivity" in the total context of his view of Jesus Christ and His living relationship to men. Calvin is neither mystically passive nor is he committed to "law religion." He is committed to a constant dependence on Jesus Christ, crucified in the past and alive and in action in the present.

his gospel. It is the port at the end of a long theological voyage, the kind of thought we arrive at intellectually and spiritually only after a great and decisive preface. We can really tell where we are with climactic thoughts like this only by taking stock of how we got there. If we try to grasp what this sentence means simply by examining it independently, we are likely to abort any real theological understanding; we shall probably either get lost in vague talk about Paul's mysticism or, in the face of the strangeness of it, deny the reality it points to. What we must do is look for a pattern in Paul's thought, a design in which the sentence "Christ lives in me" can fit and take on its meaning.

Can we find the pattern? I think we can. Indeed it lies at hand almost everywhere in Paul, not least in the immediate associations of the "Christ in us" passages. Basically, the pattern is this: the Spirit and the power. In more expansive shape, it is Christ working in effective power in the lives of people who have been brought within the new order established under His lordship.

The approach we shall take is this. First, we shall take a look at the most celebrated passages to see if the pattern emerges there. Then, we shall look beyond these to see whether the pattern is sustained in broader perspective.

Paul asks his Corinthian readers, "Do you not realize that Jesus Christ is in you—unless indeed you fail to meet the test" (II Cor. 13:5)? He asks it as though he assumed any ordinary Christian reader would know what he was asking. What bell did he expect to ring in the mind of his readers? What associations were his readers expected to make? What kind of test were they to pass? And what sort of personal experience was it that all of them were presumed to have had? That is, what is Paul working at in this passage?

The thought is much like that in II Corinthians 3, where we found the surprising statement that "the Lord is the Spirit." Paul is still bothered with aspersions people were casting on his apostolic authority—his apostolic power, his *exousia* (II Cor. 13:10; 10:8). He is forced to press his claim that Christ is really speaking through him (II Cor. 13:3). What is his proof? The proof lies with the experience of the people who came to Christian awareness under his ministry: Christ is *"powerful* in you" (13:3). His answer here is the one he gave in the third chapter, where he said: "You yourselves are our letter of recommendation, written . . . with the Spirit of the living God" (II Cor. 3:2, 3). The test of

Paul's credentials as an apostle of Christ is this: is Christ at work powerfully in the lives of people? Do they have the Spirit and the power?

The pragmatic dimension is possible because of the reality of Christ's own power. He lives in the power (the *dunamis*) of God (13:4). The christological pattern is familiar: crucified in weakness, raised in power, and stationed as Lord with the power of God at His disposal. Apparent impotence and real power. Christ is Lord, free and able to bring within present history the saving effects of His cross in the past. Therefore we share now, and we shall share more fully later on, in the power of His life. For we shall live with Him by the power of God (13:4).

The test of Paul's authority is the power of Christ in the moral and spiritual lives of people. What, then, is the test they must pass if they are to prove that Christ is within them? It is the very same: they must demonstrate the effective action of Christ in their lives. Comparing this with II Corinthians 3, we have the pattern once more: The Spirit and power—Jesus Christ the Lord in action.

In Ephesians 3:17, Paul says that he prays for the indwelling of Christ: "that Christ may dwell in your hearts through faith." What is the pattern here? We could, of course, examine the clause by itself: we could ask what Paul means by "in your hearts" and what he means by "through faith." And we must ask these questions later. But first we should look for the broader pattern.

We must look back to chapters one and two. There we find Paul's magnificent view of God's eternal purpose in Christ: "to unite all things in him, things in heaven and things on earth" (1:10) and to create a place for us in that reconciled world. Here again is the cosmic embrace of God's redemptive intent, accomplished in Jesus of Nazareth who is now the Lord Jesus in power. The Gentiles to whom he writes had heard the gospel—"the word of truth"—had believed it, had learned to live in the love that is the style of the new creation, and had been "sealed with the promised Holy Spirit" (1:13). And in this reality they had come to know "what is the immeasurable greatness of his power [*dunamis*] in those who believe (1:19).

What power is this? It is the power of the risen Lord—the *power* (*dunamis*) by which Christ was raised, was exalted, and now functions as the power (*exousia*) above the outmoded and defeated "powers" (1:20, 21). This is the power by which the

Gentiles were saved, made alive, and brought together with the
Jew as one temple for "a dwelling place of God in the Spirit"
(2:22). And so the pattern emerges again: Christ as Lord, and the
Spirit working in us as Christ in effective action.

This is the grand context for the prayer that Christ may dwell
in the hearts of believers. But the whole prayer is a commentary
on this petition. What comes first is this: that "he may grant you
to be strengthened with *power* through His Spirit in the inner man"
(3:6). Further, that by this power, with their lives rooted in
Christ's strong love, they may come to know the full scope of His
redemptive love (3:18, 19). And finally, there is the doxology:
"Now to him who by the *power* at work *within* us is able to *do*
far more abundantly than all that we can ask or think, to him be
glory in the church . . ." (3:20). Christ in us? Can this be different from the actions of Christ the Lord who works by the power
of God, the actions of the Lord who is the Spirit?

The pattern again: Christ Jesus is Lord, able to influence human
lives at their center because He works through His Spirit. The
Spirit and the power: this is the pattern in which we must see the
reality of Christ within.

The same pattern takes on slightly different detail in Galatians,
where we find the classic passage of Pauline mysticism: "I live,
yet not I, but Christ lives in me" (Gal. 2:20). Once again we
could stress the clause that follows—the one about faith: "The
life I live in the flesh I live by faith in the Son of God." We could
do this, and must do it; but it is likely to get us stymied by the
polarities of faith vs. mysticism. This is what has often happened.
People who are convinced that Paul was a mystic manage to put
the "in me" in focus and leave the "by faith" fuzzy; others are
too quick to let the "by faith" tell them *everything* about the "in
me." And this leaves us with the dilemma posed by sacramental
and fideist theologies, a dilemma which leaves the Christ "pro
nobis" in tension with the Christ "in nobis." We will do well to
keep looking for the basic pattern first.

What is at stake in Galatians is the gospel that Paul preached,
and with it the genuineness of Paul's power (*exousia*) as an
apostle. The gospel of Christ is "the power [*dunamis*] of God unto
salvation" (Rom. 1:16). It is the power that liberates men. But
in Galatia, "another gospel" was being taught, the gospel of
religious achievement (Gal. 1:6, 7). This "gospel" is not a power
at all; it is weak and therefore destructive. It leaves men in bond-

age. This is the contrast: the power of God versus the weakness of human effort. Or what comes to the same thing, faith versus works or grace versus law (Gal. 2:4). Small wonder, with so much involved, that Paul says, "If any one is preaching . . . a gospel contrary to that which you received, let him be accursed."

The gospel is power, but the power is experienced through the Spirit. "Does he who supplies the Spirit to you and works miracles among you do so by works of the law, or by hearing [the gospel] with faith" (3:5)? The power to live a new life, oriented around Jesus Christ, carried on within the new order of the Lord—this is the power of the Spirit at work. The epistle to the Galatians is full of this. God has put His "Spirit into our hearts" (Gal. 4:6) to move and lead us into the new life. By the Spirit, we have real hope for gaining personal righteousness (5:5). Led by the Spirit, we are liberated from the law's indictment against us (5:18). By the work of the Spirit we begin to demonstrate as our own the very characteristics of Jesus (5:22) and so "fulfill the law of Christ" (6:2). Living by the Spirit, we live forever (6:7), for Christ has become the life-giving Spirit. Once again, the Spirit is here, working in power to effect within us the style of the new order in Christ. Christ the Lord works in the present time as the Spirit. For this reason, "for me to live is Christ"; that is, Christ becomes my life (Phil. 1:21). But this, in turn, means that nothing else really matters as long as "I may know him and the power [*dunamis*] of his resurrection" (Phil. 3:10). "For me to live is Christ" means the same thing as "Christ lives in me": both mean that I know by experience "the *power* of his resurrection."

The pattern is clear. It is the pattern of God's redemptive movement within human history. The statement "Christ lives in me" crystallizes the personal experience of the reality of the new order that Christ Jesus established when He became Lord through the cross and resurrection. As the concrete individual named Jesus, He is "out there," away from us in time and in the mode of His present existence. But as Lord, He is at work in the present time through His Spirit. He is at work bringing into the reality of life here and now the new reality of His salvation. "The kingdom comes, not in words, but in power" (I Cor. 4:19). The power of the kingdom is the power of Christ as He works effectively through His Spirit. This is the big context that defines all the "Christ in me" passages.

To make the picture complete, we must refine our view still

more. As we do, it becomes clear that the pattern throughout is the same—Christ's ability to communicate power through His Spirit. We can make three observations.

First, the gospel is the power of God unto salvation (I Cor. 1:18; II Cor. 1:24; Rom. 1:16). What does this mean? The gospel is a story, a set of words that say something urgent about the event of the cross and resurrection. These words, spoken by the apostles, are the power of God because they introduce men to the reality established by Christ at the cross. Christ overcame the debilitating powers of evil there; the cross of weakness is a powerful victory. As men hear the news, believe it, submit themselves to the order of life under Christ the Lord, they experience the "power of his resurrection" (Phil. 3:10). That is, they are identified by God as members of the new order and share all its benefits and, at once, experience within the life-changing power of Christ. And this, in turn, is the work of Christ's Spirit: none calls Jesus Lord—none hears, believes, and lives according to the gospel— except the Spirit enables him (I Cor. 12:3). The gospel, then, is able to bring the reality of salvation into human lives, not through the ordinary function of the symbols we call words, but in a "demonstration of the Spirit and the power" (I Cor. 2:4). The Spirit is married to the Word, not merely in that the Spirit guides the intellect to a proper understanding of the words and sentences of the Scriptures, but in that He brings the reality of Christ's power into human lives as they hear and identify themselves with the word about the cross. This is why the apostle, whose task it is to proclaim the good news, stakes his authenticity on the fact that the Spirit is at work in power within the lives of those who believe as well as on his agreement with the tradition or the word about Jesus.

The second thing we can notice is that the Christian community shares the resurrection of Jesus Christ through the Spirit and the power. There is no clear-cut distinction between these two, Spirit and power; they are the same reality. This is clear from Romans 8:11 and I Corinthians 1:14:

> If the Spirit of him who raised Jesus from the dead dwells in you, he who raised Christ Jesus from the dead will give life to your mortal bodies also through his Spirit which dwells in you (Rom. 8:11).
> And God raised the Lord and will also raise us up by his power (I Cor. 1:14).

Here, the Spirit of God and the power of God are one. Having the Spirit of power within us, we are assured that we live forever. But in the new order, since the resurrection, the Spirit and power of God are invested in the Lord. "The Lord is the Spirit" and, we may add, "the power." Paul does not de-personalize the Spirit by using "power" as a synonym. He personalizes the power of God by showing that it is the direct action of the Spirit.

The point I am trying to make is this: the Christian community shares the life of Christ because the Spirit—that is, the power—of God is at work in it. Indwelt by the Spirit, the community knows and shall know by experience "what is the immeasurable greatness of his power in us who believe" (Eph. 1:19). What could it mean, then, to say that Christ is in us except that the Spirit is powerfully at work in us, bringing us the ability to live the risen life with Christ.

Finally, we should notice that the effect of the Spirit and the power is the conformation of our lives to the ethical order of Christ's lordship. In the new creation, it is possible, says Paul, to expect "that our God may make you worthy of his call, and may fulfill every good resolve and work of faith by his power" (II Thess. 1:11, 12). The work of faith is after the style of Christ's own life, the life of power through His unconditional acceptance of weakness. He "was crucified in weakness, but lives by the power of God" (II Cor. 13:4). At this time, prior to the *parousia* and the final resurrection, our own experience of His power is in the form of earthen vessels. The power is never obvious; we never get a self-evident reason for pretensions. We can glory only in the cross. This was Paul's painful, but powerful discovery. He hated his weakness, and had to discover that Christ's power is "made perfect in weakness" (II Cor. 12:9). Our career as people in whom Christ is present in *power* is to "complete what is lacking in the sufferings [weakness] of Christ" (Col. 1:24).

Within this paradoxical form, we are empowered by the Spirit to live in love, to be men for others as Christ was. Paul's imperatives follow from the presence of the Spirit and the power, and their direction is always deeply humane. This is not the place to elaborate on all the ethical dimensions of the life of Christ within. They are summed up in Galatians 5:22, in Paul's list of the Spirit's fruits. They are epitomized again in the summary of the law of love in Romans 13:8-10. Deissmann, for whom Paul was first and centrally a mystic, called Paul's mysticism a "reacting mysticism"; he meant that it was a mysticism that had its proper effect in the moral life. This much is unavoidably clear: for Paul the net effect of Christ within us is moral, dynamic, active; faith exhibits itself in works of love. The "law of Christ" is the style of life in the new creation, a law written in our hearts by the Spirit; and this means that Christ reaches out by His Spirit and enables us to live His kind of life. We are not supernaturalized; we are naturalized. That is, we are restored to true humanity. For to be man is to be related to others in self-giving love and to God in the obedience of faith and the response of gratitude.

We have managed, I think, to gain a perspective on the Pauline pattern. "Christ within us" is a reality of the new creation. Jesus Christ is Lord. The Lord is the Spirit. The Spirit is Christ in effective action within the present time, leading, enlightening, calling, and pulling us from within, shaping our lives to the pattern of Christ and His way. The power, or the Spirit, is at work within us and on us, in our inner man, in our hearts, "on our spirits." This is Christ within us.

The question of Christ's location in the believer disappears within the perspective we have gained. Paul says he prays that Christ may dwell in our hearts (Eph. 1:17). But obviously Paul is not talking anatomy, nor even psychology in the strict sense. The "heart" is a metaphor for the "inner man" (Eph. 3:16), for the spirit of man (Rom. 8:16). Calvin, discussing the "heart" in Ephesians 3:17, enjoys noting that Paul is thinking of something deeper than the intellect. But it is deeper too than the emotions. The heart is man himself, at the very center of his existence, man where the crucial issues of life are settled and the largest perspectives gained. A man's heart *is* man, the whole man, at the center where he is always available to God. After tracing a large number of references to the heart, Behm concludes: "Thus the heart is supremely the one centre in man to which God turns, and which determines moral conduct."[49] The heart is man as vulnerable to Christ. When we speak of Christ in the heart, we should not ask where He is, but what He is doing. The important thing is not location, but action. Christ is not in confinement at an address labelled "my heart." He is operative, freely, as Spirit in my life where it really counts.

[49]In Kittel, *Theological Dictionary of the New Testament,* III (Grand Rapids, 1965), p. 612. Cf. Berkouwer: "The term 'heart' deals with the total orientation, direction, concentration of man, his depth dimension, from which his full human existence is directed and formed" (*Man: The Image of God* [Grand Rapids, 1962], p. 203).

Having said all this, we should add that to think of the indwelling Christ as an infusion of something called "life" into something called our substantial souls only tends to reduce *Christ* to an abstraction, and to reduce the reality of Christ *within* to an *effect* on our souls of that abstraction. Still, I should think, we have kept the motives of sacramentalism intact: we can hold that there is a very real presence of the Christ within us as long as we think, with Paul, of the Spirit as the Christ in lordly action, and we can hold that there is a very real effect on our lives as a result—that we share the indestructibility of Christ's life and that the lives we carry on here and now are conditioned at their centers by Christ directly at work upon us.

It also seems a mistake to reduce the reality of Christ within to a lively faith in the Christ "out there." To believe, to identify ourselves with the judgment of God on sin at the cross and to identify ourselves with God's affirmation of man at the resurrection, is indeed indispensable to and inseparable from the reality of Christ within; but this conscious and volitional and total response on our part is the *effect* of Christ within and not the same thing as Christ within. Still we have in our discussion honored the motives of men like Barth and Brunner. We have held that we are always dealing with an objective Christ, that our egos are not absorbed in a universal spirit whom we honor with the moral characteristics of Christ.

The Christ within is the Lord Jesus. He is at work in all His lordly freedom, at work in our lives at the center. As the Christ at work, He is the Spirit active in power. This, in brief, is Paul's answer to the question we raised at the very beginning of this book: how can a person of long ago radically affect our lives in the present?

The Christ *for us* and the Christ *in us* are not two poles destined to exist in unresolved theological tension. They are two facets of the same ongoing, eschatological program of Jesus Christ. We cannot be *in Christ* without Christ being *in us*. (This, by the way, is also why there can be no justification without sanctification.) The possibilities this offers to life are unlimited. Outside of Christ, we are doomed to frustration. In Christ, we are changing "into his likeness from one degree of glory to another; for this comes from the Lord who is the Spirit" (II Cor. 3:18). History is being made. It is the history of the Christ who in His powerful action as Spirit sweeps us along into it.

We cannot claim to have defined and described the mystery of "Christ within." What we have tried to do is get it within a *pattern,*

Paul's perspective of how Christ the Lord is at work in human lives. What we ought to do now is build some intellectual fences to get some boundaries for any further effort to define and describe our union with Christ.

D. BUILDING FENCES

Loving and being loved is far more important and interesting than trying to understand what love is. Communication between real people is far more important than the science of linguistics. And living out the actual life of "Christ within" is infinitely more important than trying to forge a respectable theology of it. But we ought to know something about it, and we ought to try to say something, if only to better respect the mystery of it and to honor the Christ who graciously elects so modest a dwelling as ourselves.

The best we can do is to build some fences. But we must understand what fences are for. Theological fences are not meant to corral God's truth, to keep it under control and within our sight. Fences are built to keep our own thoughts in check. Fences theologians build must be for themselves, lest they try to capture too much within their systems, lest they make no allowance for God's mystery. Here are a few such fences:

(1) Any theology that reduces the reality of "Christ within" to an experience of one's own morality, one's own faith, one's own free decision, or one's own deepest feelings is inadequate.

(2) Any theology that diminishes the person of "Christ within" in favor of a supernatural infusion of deity is inadequate.

(3) Any theology that diminishes the realism of the word "in," even though that theology may respect the whole personality of Jesus Christ, is inadequate.

(4) Any theology that diminishes the genuine personality of the indwelt person, even though that theology may respect the personality of the Jesus Christ "out there" and the reality of His presence within, is inadequate.

These are high fences, and they seem to close every avenue of exploration. They prevent us from diminishing the reality of Jesus Christ as an independent person, from diminishing the reality of Christ's indwelling, from diminishing the integrity of the believing person, and from explaining the whole mystery by saying that it is only an exaggerated way of talking about ourselves. This leaves us with the task of elaborating on some of the specifics, with the clear concession that we shall end up admiring a mystery.

1. The Christ Within Is Jesus

There is, it is safe to say, no hint that when Paul says "Christ lives in me," he has anyone or anything else in mind than the very person of Jesus Christ. He means Jesus who died and rose again and is coming to establish His kingdom. He means the Jesus who is nothing if not an authentic and concrete person. He is the Christ who calls us into service through His Word and Spirit. He is the whole Christ, and always the personal being whose name is Jesus. Büchsel is right, I think, when he writes:

> Christ who is present in Paul is not merely a power or some kind of principle; he is the historical person with his individual character and his own experiences. When Paul says that Christ is in him he means that this individual person is present in him.[50]

2. The Christ Within Is the Lord Jesus

While Christ is always, for Paul, the concrete individual, He is never merely a concrete individual; He is now the Lord, the representative person who dominates the new order. History moves on in redemption. The specific person of Calvary becomes the specific Lord of heaven and earth. And His *modus operandi* changes, not to fit the changing epoch, but to create the new epoch. He is now the Lord who operates effectively through the Spirit. This is not merely a change in title; it is not only an elevation in status. It is a shift in the kind of work He does and in the manner in which He does it. Being the Lord Jesus within us, He is *at work* within us in the freedom of His lordly power.

3. The Christ Within Is the Spirit

At first sight, we may seem to be taking away with our left hand what we have just claimed with our right. But we have to say it because this is how Paul says it. We have already seen what theologians have sometimes done with the person of Jesus Christ in the name of Spirit. We must, however, let the person of Christ

---

[50]*Der Geist Gottes im Neuen Testament* (Gütersloh, 1926), p. 294. Wikenhauser says the same thing: Paul "always thinks of Christ as a Person, and when he says that Christ dwells in him, he is thinking of the Christ who died on the cross, and now sits at the right hand of the Father interceding for us" (*op. cit.,* p. 74).

qualify what we think of the Spirit. The Spirit is not a vague, impersonal power. He is not the immanent psychic stream of the universe, in Jung's sense. He is not any longer even merely the active presence of God. He is the functioning Christ.

We have no idea of what it means within the inner relationships of God, but the fact is that God's actions on earth shift in step with the changing historical situation that God Himself brings about. There is a real *history* of redemption; and in history things really do change. This is the era of the victorious lordship of Jesus Christ. And in this era, the Spirit is indistinguishable from Christ the Lord. Christ at work in this time is the Spirit at work. As surely as the Spirit of God was God in creative power, so now, in our experience, the Spirit of Christ is Christ in effective action. He is Christ within.

This is bound to tell us something about *how* Christ is within. The Spirit is free; after all, it is the Lord who is the Spirit. As Jesus said, you cannot tame the wind. The Spirit is not contained in a soul. He is not wrapped up in a package. We cannot put Him in confinement. When He indwells us, He does this in keeping with who and what He is—and, more than anything else, He is free.

4.   Christ Is Actually Within

I am tempted to say that Christ is "literally within." But this would not help us much. *How* one is in something depends on the kind of thing he is in. A man is in a suit of clothes. The same man may be in the government. And the government may be in a lot of trouble. What "in" means can be talked about only if we know what one is in. Christ is within *persons*. And this tells us something.

The bare fact of inwardness is not decisive. Christ's indwelling could mean a kind of static, metaphysical imprint deep in our souls. It could also mean that an inner partnership is created, with two egos side by side—His and ours. A thoroughly mystical interpretation could involve the absorption and loss of our personalities into His. But when Christ is within us, His presence is of a kind that suits what we are—real persons.

5.   Christ Within Respects Our Personality

The person in whom Christ dwells remains his own self. He is not more than a man; he is not less than a man. He is not a crea-

ture with a supernatural addition built on. He is not drowned by
a tidal wave of divine Spirit. When Paul says "I live, yet not I," he
wants us to take the first clause seriously. He does live—he, Paul,
the Christian Jew, with his unique character, living with his whole
psycho-somatic-social being as an apostle of Christ. He is not replaced; nor is he sublimated. He does not have less of the individual Paul nor something besides. The Christ-indwelt person is a
real person. He is united with Christ, not swallowed by Him.

This is surely obvious in Paul's case. Who is more of a genuine
individual than Paul with all the idiosyncrasies of his character?
He wanted to be captive to Christ. But this captivity meant freedom, freedom to be the strong-willed, somewhat intolerant man
that he was. He was an authentic man. He was authentic as a
person because at heart, where the issues were settled, what
mattered to him were people and their personal destinies in Christ.
The apostle demonstrates that the work of Christ within is a work
that enhances the integrity of a person.

The presence of Christ in His Spirit leaves the Spirit free, but it
also leaves us free. Christ does not "take over." The Spirit can be
quenched, offended, and ignored—though only at great cost to ourselves. He communicates to our spirits that we are the sons of
God (Rom. 8:16). Spirit to spirit—the identities are intact.

He moves and awakens our moribund hearts to conform themselves to the mind of Christ. He stimulates us to righteousness and
holiness (Eph. 4:24), to knowledge (Col. 3:10) and understanding (Rom. 12:2). He stimulates us to a renewed style of living
(Rom. 7:4), He helps us mature into the form of Christ (Gal.
4:19). These are all dynamic effects; they are subject to growth
and lapse, increase and decrease, affirmation and denial; they are
the kind of things that stress *our* action as persons. They demand
a personal response. This is why Paul tells us to "keep putting on
Christ" (Col. 3:10).

Christ is within us in a way that fits His own Self and our own
selves. How a Spirit communicates to a spirit is mysterious in
itself. But in this mystery, the other one is honored—the mystery
of the human person in deliberate and responsible action. Christ
communicates Himself in a way that changes us without diminishing us, transforms us without deifying us, Christianizes us without making us Christs. In all the validity, freedom, and responsibility of our human being as God's image, we are "transformed
from within" by the presence of Christ.

There are dimensions to Christ's gracious presence in Christian people that the intellect cannot so much as guess are present. All we have done is build a few fences for our thought. We have said that He who "lives in" us is none but Jesus Christ. We have said that in coming to us, He does not destroy us, but lets us be our true selves, freely responsible to Him and His Spirit. And we have said that His indwelling is important not so much for the fact of His proximity, as for the significance of His work.

6. *Christ Within Is a Temptation*

Every great spiritual reality men come to experience offers unique temptations. The reality of Christ within is the most meaningful fact of our personal histories. But to the person who knows this comes one of the most subtle of all temptations. He is tempted to equate himself, his thoughts, and his actions with Christ. The spiritual arrogance of the person who presumes on Christ's presence in him can be intolerably offensive. Whenever a person justifies his acts and claims validity for them on the basis of the indwelling Christ, he has monstrously distorted that precious reality. What sins of pride have been committed in the name of the indwelling Christ only God knows. But the history of Christendom suggests that they have been many.

To say "Christ in me" is to say that I give up all pretensions before God and man of any final morality or understanding. To say that Christ is in us means precisely that we spurn pretensions and throw ourselves fully on the Christ who, though *in* us, is first of all the Christ "out there" in His exclusive righteousness and holiness. Aware of our penchant for pretension, Paul insisted that we seek our salvation—and our spirituality—outside of ourselves and in Christ alone, even while he insisted that Christ had to be *in* us if we were to be saved.

Brunner was right in warning against a "theology of glory." This led him to minimize the reality of Christ within us. But the thing he feared was indeed a thing to be feared. Christ in us does not mean, and Paul nowhere gives us reason to think it means, an equation of ourselves and the Christ.

There is an irony in equating one's own moral insights with the mind of Christ. For in doing so one can appear humble: "This is not what *I* say, it is what Christ says," or, "This is not *my* claim, it is the claim of Christ." But the disclaimer is, of course, false. For the voice and the claim are always the voice and claim of a man. And the imputation of one's own thoughts, of one's own moral judgment, to Christ is simply a subtle way of claiming absoluteness for one's self.

The presence of Christ within is not a basis for saying, at any time or under any circumstances, as individuals or as institutions, that the distinction between us and Christ has been overcome.

The life we live "in the flesh" is still the life of the proud and ignorant, the compromising and ambiguous, the devious and lustful self; this is why the life lived "in the flesh" must be a life of "faith in the Son of God." Though "Christ liveth in me" is a reality, it is not a complete and total actuality. It offers a promise, but it does not provide an absolute victory over the inner and outer contradictions of life. When, instead of a basis for responsibility and hope, it is made a claim of "secure possession," it becomes an occasion for the very sin of pride from which it is intended to liberate us.

This brings us to the subject of the next chapter. The reality of Christ within is not a self-evident reality at all. It is known only in faith. This is one reason why we cannot make any claims for ourselves on the basis of it. The reality of Christ within cannot be measured like one's IQ, or counted like one's basal metabolism, or used as a credential like one's passport. It is experienced in faith alone; and here, too, faith is the "substance of things hoped for, the evidence of things not seen." So we must talk about our faith and the reality of our union with Christ.

Chapter Six

Believing and Being

When St. Paul urges his readers to review their hold on faith, he adds this question: "Do you not realize that Christ is in you" (II Cor. 13:5)? With this, he lets it be known that believing and being are married. He does not say that faith and union with Christ are the same thing; but he does want us to think about faith in the awareness that Christ indwells the man who believes. Nowhere is the merger of believing and being clearer than in Galatians 2:20: "It is no longer I who live, but Christ who lives in me; and the life I now live in the flesh, I live by faith in the Son of God, who loved me and gave himself for me."

The question is *how* being is related to faith. What is the connection between "faith in the Son of God who . . . gave himself for me" in the past and the Son's living "in me" in the present? I cannot recall that Paul ever directs faith to Christ's indwelling; we are summoned to believe the Christ of past time, the Christ of the cross and resurrection. Faith, consciously practiced, is a response to the message the apostles preached about a certain person in the past and the events surrounding Him: if you "believe in your heart that God raised him from the dead, you will be saved" (Rom. 10:9). But the person in whom that Christ dwells is the person who believes. Or, with a shift of emphasis, the person who believes *the facts about Jesus Christ* is the person in whom Christ dwells. What is the connection?[1] We want, of course, to shun the unbiblical nonsense that faith is merely a willingness to affirm certain propositions and that faith is a substitute for a new being. If we were to suppose that a holy God accepted our faith

---

[1] A half-century ago, Charles Gore called theology's failure to unite the "Christ for us" with the "Christ in us" a scandal (*Belief in Christ* [London, 1921], p. 299).

instead of moral excellence, we would make God out to be a second-rate moral bargainer. And if we suppose that being is joined to believing as a reward for our assenting to certain propositions in the absence of proof, we would only be attributing a kind of merit to faith. Faith in the Christ of past history may not be a substitute for reality. Nor may reality be thought of as a reward for our belief in the resurrection.

Earlier we asked how the Christ of the past is related to the Christ of the present. Now we must ask how our *faith* in the Christ of the past is related to our *experience* of Christ in the present. We must ask how "faith in the Son of God who . . . died for me" is related to our experience of the "Christ who lives in me?" To get at this, we must ask what sort of thing faith in past events is. And we must ask how one does live out the reality of Christ within. So in this chapter we have two questions: (1) How is faith related to the Christ of the past? (2) How is faith related to the Christ of the present?

A. OUR FAITH AND THE JESUS OF HISTORY

Paul obviously thought that the past event of Jesus' resurrection was the inexpendable basis for the faith that changes a person. This is the clear implication of I Corinthians 15. His kerygma, Paul insisted, was in line with what the Church believed from the beginning and wanted passed on. This is why he attaches such importance to the many witnesses who had seen the risen Christ —not to prove that the resurrection did indeed occur, but to prove that his kerygma was what the Christian community from the beginning held as the *sine qua non* of faith.[2] Faith was tied to this piece of past history—the resurrection of Jesus of Nazareth. If Christ be not risen, Paul says, "your faith is empty" (I Cor. 15:14).

The proclamation of the gospel, therefore, summons men to affirm the past events of the cross and resurrection. The kerygma included an assertion about them—that they happened—and it

[2]Bultmann thinks that Paul is trying to prove the fact of the resurrection but that he is utterly unconvincing (*Theology of the New Testament* [New York, 1951], p. 295). Barth, however, insists that Paul was showing that his message was the one that had been preached from the beginning, and was of a piece with the convictions of the whole Church (*Church Dogmatics,* IV/1, pp. 331ff.). Ridderbos adds that Paul is stressing the *trustworthiness* of the Church's tradition (*Paulus* [Kampen, 1966], pp. 265f.).

would make no sense if the kerygma did not require men to affirm this assertion. The factuality of the resurrection, as well as of the cross, is the point of orientation for faith. But it would be a terrible misconception of both kerygma and faith to suppose that the kerygma was merely a historical report about these two events and demanded only that listeners assent to its accuracy.

The kerygma demands a special kind of affirmation because it makes a special kind of assertion about a special kind of past event. The Church felt a compulsion stronger than life itself to keep the kerygma alive, because it knew the profound significance of those past events for human life. The past events were proclaimed because they were known and affirmed as *saving* events. The kerygma does not merely assert that Jesus "died and rose again," but that He died "for our sins" and rose again "for our justification." The apostolic tradition, expressed in preaching, was not interested merely in keeping facts straight; it was concerned with the facts because they were of crucial significance for human history and human experience. Accordingly, the affirmation the kerygma calls for is always an affirmation of the *significance* of these events for men.

The kerygma calls for an affirmation of the facts. But it calls for an affirmation of the facts in their significance for us. And this kind of affirmation involves the whole person. It is not merely a stubbornly held intellectual assertion that the resurrection is true in the face of many arguments against its possibility. It is a decision to bring my whole being within the new reality that the past events of the cross and resurrection created. The response that the proclamation of Christ demands is an affirmation *in action*. To affirm the events is to enter into the reality that they created, the reality of the new creation in Christ.

What I have just said is open to gross misunderstanding. It could be taken to mean that the cross and resurrection are significant for my life *because I affirm them in a way that changes my life*. Thus it would not be the events of the gospel that change my life; it would be my creative faith that does so. This could be understood in two related but different ways. It could mean (1) that what is important about the early Christian community is that it *believed* that the life of Jesus changed their lives. It was their belief, and not the events of the gospel, that brought them into a life of new meaning and new hope; their belief changed their world. And if this faith was this powerful, it does not really matter whether what they believed about Jesus was historically true or

not—that is, whether it happened "out there" and before they believed. In fact, with such a powerful faith, it may be that the believers *created* the myth of the resurrection to explain their new
lives. Hence, we in the present can share the lively power of their
faith even though we know the resurrection could not have happened. This is the way many readers of the New Testament have
accommodated their inability to square the historical facts of the
Gospels with science to their desire to share the reality of Christian
faith.[3] To say that we are affected by Christ only *as we believe*
could also mean (2) that the past events—the cross and resurrection—did in fact occur in history, but that their *significance for us*
becomes a reality only because and when we believe them. At its
crudest, this becomes a legalistic orthodoxy that says: *because* we
hold that Jesus did in fact arise from the dead, God endows us with
a new life. At a more subtle level, this becomes a pietism
that says: *because* we believe that the resurrection was meant *for
us,* its effects are given to us. In either case, the resurrection would
not itself be the saving event in history; the "for us" would not be
true at the cross and resurrection, but would be true because we
made it true for us. Believing would make it so.

We must, it seems, affirm with Paul that Christ "arose for our
justification" back there in history. The "for us" lies in the victorious event itself. We ought to steer clear of the subjectivistic
impasse. But we ought to avoid as well the objectivistic trap. Saving faith is not merely an agreement that such and such about
the resurrection of Jesus is true, not even that it was true "for
me" back then. There must be a correlation between fact (back
there) and faith, a correlation that transcends both subjectivism
and objectivism.[4]

---

[3]The problem of relating the dynamics of faith to the historical objectivity
of Jesus Christ is enormous, to be sure. It is true, in a sense, that, as
John Knox says, "The present reality [the Church's new life] does not
exist because the past event is affirmed; rather the past event is affirmed
because the present reality exists" (*The Church and the Reality of Christ*
[New York, 1962], p. 66). But what *is* that present reality? The apostles
were convinced that the present reality existed only because the past event
really did occur.

[4]"The Gospel does not come coolly to inform men of a new objective
state of affairs. It involves men's lives as a call to belief and conversion,
to love and obedience. It is so pointedly directed to the concrete existence
of men that we can speak of an essential correlation between faith and
salvation" (G. C. Berkouwer, *Faith and Justification* [Grand Rapids, 1954],
pp. 33ff.).

The saving events are not savingly affirmed unless the believer is personally involved in and radically affected by them. The events of Christ crucified and raised are proclaimed because they have saving significance; they are proclaimed and heard *in* their significance. But their significance is precisely that they have saving power (I Cor. 1:21). They have significance *in* saving people, and *as* they save people. How then can they be affirmed by people other than as events that have in fact saved *them*? Affirmation of the past facts is a Christian affirmation when it is at the same time an affirmation that one has entered into their significance. When I genuinely affirm in faith that Christ died and arose again, I am also affirming (equally by faith) that *I* died and rose again too. This is the affirmation that the kerygma demands.

Bultmann is quite right when he contends that we affirm something about ourselves when we affirm Jesus Christ risen. When I assent to the fact that Christ dies for me, I am saying that I am the kind of person who needs dying for, and was in fact died for. When I affirm that Christ rose again "for my justification," I am concurring with God's assessment of my self and His liberation of my sinful self from judgment. I do indeed "reckon *myself* dead to sin and alive to God in Jesus Christ." And only as I affirm this in free decision and with my whole attitude and action, am I also affirming the real truth about the events that happened in past history. This is the kind of affirmation that is demanded because this is the way in which the facts of Christ's history are proclaimed by His witnesses.

If my affirmation of the facts of Jesus' death and resurrection is not one that sweeps my whole existence into its power, I am not making an affirmation of faith in the biblical sense. The statement that "Jesus died and arose again" is not in itself a statement of faith. One does not even necessarily make a statement of faith when he says, "Jesus died *for me*." Both of these become statements of faith when they verbalize the reality of my entrance into the new order of life that was created when He died and arose again. Believing does not make the cross and resurrection saving events for me; but the truth is genuinely affirmed only within the circle of my personal involvement.[5] It should now be repeated that

[5]We must remember this truth when we speak to others of Christ's death for them. In the biblical sense, it is untrue to affirm as a purely rational matter of fact that Christ died for them. That is, it is untrue to the kind of witness the New Testament gives of Christ's death. The fact always carries

this does not leave open the question of whether the proclamation of the past event is true in the historical sense. The historical factuality of the past event is the ground and assumption of the very possibility of a genuine affirmation of faith.

But we must also ask *how* a past event can be affirmed in such a way that it radically alters the core of my existence. How does the past event reach out into my life today? How does it reach me and touch me at the center of my life? How does it affect me in a way that turns my affirmation of it as a fact into an affirmation involving my deepest being? This question brings us back to what this book is all about.

Much of modern theology simply denies that the past history of Jesus Christ can in fact reach out and radically affect my life here and now. My existence here and now is determined by *my* momentary decision; I am created as a real person in the fits and starts of my decision to be a genuine human being. And nothing, not even the most remarkable events of the past, can create my personal existence for me. Faith has its own power; and its power is the power of each personal decision. "To believe in the cross of Christ," says Bultmann, "does not mean to concern ourselves with a mythical process wrought outside of us and our world, or with an objective event turned by God to our advantage, but rather to make the cross of Christ our own, to undergo crucifixion with him."[6] This, of course, is to cast faith on its own, as *the* creative event in human history. The crucial event in human history is our decision to "make the cross of Christ our own."

For all that he has written to illuminate the dynamics of human faith, Paul Tillich too weakens the biblical relationship between past history and present faith. For him, anything historical, any individual or event in history, is severely limited in its capacity to help the believing person. At best, everything historical can be a symbol of ultimate reality; as a symbol, *everything* shares in ultimate reality, but nothing can *be* it. What is historical can only point away from itself to the really real. This is as true of Jesus

---

in its bosom a demand for involvement. The indicative mood of the kerygma about Jesus always implies an imperative: "Accept Him as Lord." The truth of the indicative is not whole until the imperative is obeyed. The language of the gospel reports the fact in the faith that the Spirit will use the telling of it to bring the listener, as a whole person, into a living obedience to the fact. "Christ died for you" is true—in its peculiar sense— only within the convergence of objective fact and subjective response.

[6]In Bartsch, *Kerygma and Myth* [London, 1953], p. 36.

and His life and death as it is of every other historical person
or event. Jesus may point more clearly to ultimate reality than do
most other symbols; but He thereby points only the more clearly
away from Himself as an object of faith. Faith, therefore, cannot
be dependent on Him or on stories about Him. His death and
resurrection, as historical events of the past, surely could not be
the creative source of our new life even if they were true. Our new
life is created when we have the courage to trust ourselves ulti-
mately in Being Itself, to trust its basic friendliness in the face of
history's many threats and existence's many contradictions. The
"new being" is created by my courage. Faith is on its own.[7]

But, it should be noted, John Calvin too held that simply as
an event in past history what Jesus Christ did cannot touch us in
the present. If we are to be involved, if we are to be grasped at the
center of life, if we are to receive salvation, we must not be left
with a sheer historical event. Something of the reality of Jesus
Christ Himself must be in our present, here and now, if "all that
He suffered and accomplished" for us is to save us. This, however,
is *not* to say that the past events cannot save us. It is to say that
they can save us only because *they do not remain mere past events.*
And for this very reason the past event of the resurrection is
necessary to faith—not simply in the sense that God demands that
it be assented to, but in the sense that it opens the way to the living
reality of Christ here and now. Without a risen and therefore living
Christ, there is no point of contact between past event and present
faith. More, unless the risen and living Christ enters our own lives,
grasps us at the center of our existence, and is affirmed in our own
decision of faith, His past remains—as far as we are concerned
—the dead past.

This is a way of saying that faith in the historical Christ is significant for us only within the reality of our union with the risen
Lord. What the Bible calls faith is our total response to the
presence of Christ within us, a response that takes the form of a
total commitment to the way of life in the new creation. We have
called it our personal openness to the Christ whose actions in the
past created a new situation of which He is Lord and therefore
ready and able to enter meaningfully into union with us. The past
events do not reach out and grasp us simply because they hap-

[7]*Systematic Theology,* II (London, 1957), pp. 108 and 131. A reading of
Tillich's "The Truth of Faith" (*The Dynamics of Faith* [New York, 1957])
will bear out the remarks in the paragraph above.

pened. And for this reason, faith—in its biblical sense—cannot be a mere conviction that they happened back there, as the New Testament records them. The effect of the saving event in all its universal grandness reaches out to us from the past because Christ continues as Lord above and His Spirit continues His action on earth. Our faith is our personal, and therefore total, obedience to and concurrence with Him. And this is why, in turn, faith *includes* an affirmation that the past event actually happened.

We must now examine this personal openness to the living Christ as He comes to us and unites us to Himself. Since faith is a personal openness at the center, it has dimensions that touch all sides of our psychological experience. All of these dimensions are aspects of the one thing called faith. They are dimensions of faith because faith is the response of a person at the center (or heart) of life—where Christ is—and they are expressed in all the various dimensions of the human personality in action. We distinguish them, but we cannot separate them. All together, they form the whole believing response of the believing person to Christ; it is a response that is made *within* the reality of union with Him.

B. FAITH AND OUR UNION WITH CHRIST

The relationship between the reality that we experience and our experience of that reality is hard to keep clear. In a dynamic, personal reality, we are especially hard put to draw precise pictures. After all, we are not talking about a relationship between abstract ideas. Nor are we dealing with static realities. We are trying to understand our active, personal role within the reality of the union that Jesus Christ initiates and sustains with us. What we need here are helpful pointers; the more precise we are, the more likely we are to exclude some dimension of the relationship that will show up later on to betray the inadequacy of our analysis. We do not want definitions that will last forever; we will be satisfied with signs that we can move about as our view of this complex reality changes. As long as they point in the right direction, they will serve.

The reality is union with Christ; our way of experiencing that reality is called faith. The two should be neither confused nor separated. We ought not make our faith the whole of the reality. This is the temptation that we observed and criticized in Brunner and others; for them, faith tends to be everything and "Christ in us" only a rather loose and exaggerated way of expressing the reality of our faith in the Christ "out there." But we must not separate them either. This is the temptation of Catholic orthodoxy, and sometimes of sacramentalists in general; for them, faith tends to be a preliminary assent to revealed truths with the result that a person can have faith without being united to Christ. We need a formula something like the classical christological definition: the human and divine natures united, but neither confused nor separated. In our union with Christ, faith is one thing and the fact of union with Him another. Faith is indispensable to union, but is not a description of it. Yet, they are interrelated in a dynamic, inseparable, and often indistinguishable way.

Faith is the *how*. Union with Christ is the *what*. Together, they form the broad reality of Christian experience and existence. They are so thoroughly interdependent that we can—and Paul does— use either of the terms to point to the whole relationship. "Faith" is a word that covers the whole life in Christ as we experience it, affirm it, live in obedience to it, and speak to it. Faith is our way of living in Christ and with Christ, and of demonstrating the power of His living in us.

St. Paul has a way of mixing his references to our life of faith and our life in Christ. When we discussed his doctrine of "in Christ," we saw how his whole life was lived in Christ. Paul speaks "in Christ," he relates to others "in Christ," he walks and hopes "in Christ." But it is with the same accents that he talks about living in faith. We "walk in faith" (II Cor. 5:7); we are told to "stand firm in [our] faith" (I Cor. 16:13; see too Phil. 4:1); his readers are congratulated because they do "stand firm in faith" (II Cor. 1:24). Moreover, we can stand firm "only through faith" (Rom. 11:20). In each case, the apostle could have substituted "Christ" for "faith." Living in Christ and living in faith come to the same thing, but only because "faith" is the multi-dimensional word for our whole experience of Christ.

Our faith, therefore, is the human correlative of our existence in Christ, of our identification with Christ in His death and resurrection, and of His presence in us.

Our purpose in talking about faith is to show *how* we experience the reality of union with Christ. Our discussion, I dare hope, will also show something of the nature of faith. But we will not try to examine the whole subject of faith and its dynamics. We shall only distinguish a few broad dimensions of the reality of faith as a human act, hoping that they in turn will suggest how the whole of it —if pursued exhaustively—should be construed.

1. Faith Is the Authentic Response of the Whole Person

Faith is an experience *within* the reality of union with Christ. This is the conviction of Paul and, following him, of the Reformers. Only by the Spirit at work within us are we able to believe and therefore to say that Jesus is Lord (I Cor. 12:3). This settles the matter of priority. Our faith rests on "the power and the Spirit" (I Cor. 2:4, 5). Christ is not only the content, but the stimulus of faith. Christ within, as Spirit, creates faith.

But if anyone suspects that faith is a kind of involuntary reflex to the Spirit, Paul would be quick to disabuse him of that notion. More, Paul allows no one to suspect that faith is really not decisive in the establishment of union with Christ. We receive the Spirit by "hearing [the gospel] with faith" (Gal. 3:2). Christ dwells in our hearts "by faith" (Eph. 3:17). In Christ Jesus we are the sons of God "by faith" (Gal. 3:26), and *because* we are sons of God, "God has sent the Spirit of his Son into . . . [our] hearts" (Gal. 4:6). No one can listen seriously to St. Paul's expression "by faith," or "through faith," without observing that for him faith is an authentic personal action which contributes to the reality of union with Christ.

It is not surprising that theologians have always been at a loss for a definition of the relationship between our faith and Christ's work within us. We usually have to be content with metaphors, and even they tell us more about what the relationship is not than about what it is.

Protestant theologians used to call faith an *instrument* by which a man appropriated Jesus Christ.[8] This metaphor functioned at the time to show that the Spirit was the initiator of regeneration. But it hardly demonstrated the personal and dynamic function of man in believing. In our time, alert as it is to the existentialist categories of human decision, that metaphor is hardly useful. Calvin worked hard to find a metaphor that could point to the role of faith. Once he called faith an empty vessel, to show that Christ Himself takes the initiative in entering our lives.[9] Another time he called faith our "warm embrace of Christ."[10] The

---

[8]Faith was called the *instrumentum justificationis*. See H. Heppe, *Reformed Dogmatics* (London, 1950), pp. 554ff., for several citations from 17th and 18th-century theologians. The Belgic Confession (Art. 22) says that faith is "merely an instrument"; its intention was to confess that faith is not a human act by which salvation is earned or caused.

[9]*Institutes* iii.11.7.

[10]*Commentary on Ephesians* 3:17.

two metaphors complement each other. Together, they point to two dimensions of our union with Christ, neither of which is expendable—the initiative of the Spirit and the authenticity of our action. What is just as illuminating in Calvin is his apparent willingness to say that the union we have with Christ is created by the Spirit and to say that it is begun by faith, with no effort to make a clear distinction between the two statements.[11]   Calvin is the first to ascribe the totality of salvation to God. But he is equally at ease ascribing our new life to the dynamics of faith. Faith is man's very real assent to Christ's initiative.

Berkouwer likes the metaphor "way" to suggest our experience of salvation. The marvelous fact, he writes, is "that the way of salvation is the way of faith just because it is only in faith that the exclusiveness of divine grace is recognized and honored."[12] Ridderbos speaks in the same vein when he interprets Paul as teaching that faith is our "mode of existence" in the Spirit.[13] The Roman Catholic scholar W. Grossouw describes Paul's understanding of faith as "the surrender of the entire man—his reason, his emotions, his capacity for acting and suffering—to Christ."[14] Faith is a human act, sweeping our whole life into its power, a human act that affirms in will, word, and work that Christ begins in us.

Faith is decisive. And it is total. This is why St. Paul can say that our life is Christ and that it is a life of faith, and mean the same thing by both. He does not reduce the reality of Christ within us to our action of faith; he does suggest that our entire experience of His union with us can be set under the one word "faith." While we admit in faith that Christ initiates, we are also aware that faith is an authentic human action without which there is no union with Christ.

Our faith is our total response to Christ's initiative. Christ is Lord. He is the representative person of the new reality; therefore, we are in Him when we are part of the new reality. Faith is our desire to be identified with Him; it is our identification of ourselves with His death and resurrection, and our trust that God makes

---

[11]In the *Institutes* iii.1.3 and iii.11.5 Calvin says we are united to Christ by the Spirit. In the *Institutes* iii.2.30 and in his commentaries on Luke 23:42 and Matthew 22:30 he says that we are united to Christ by faith.

[12]*Faith and Justification,* p. 188.

[13]*Paulus* (Kampen, 1966), p. 253.

[14]*In Christ* (Westminster, 1952), p. 74.

the same identification; it is our commitment to the style and order of life within the new reality; it is our obedience within the partnership He offers us.

2. Faith Is Obedience

The content of faith is Christ the Lord. This is why faith is tied to the Word of the gospel. We are called into union with the Christ who lived and died and rose as Lord "according to the Scriptures." The Word protects faith against the construction of other images of Jesus Christ than He who is in fact the Lord. The content of faith can in fact be caught in one sentence: Jesus is Lord (I Cor. 12:3). And the goal of faith is "to live a life worthy of the Lord" (Eph. 4:1). Therefore, to say in faith that "Jesus is Lord" is also to commit one's self to obedience. To believe the fact is to obey the summons implicit in the fact; and only in obedience is the fact truly acknowledged.[15]

This is why Paul tells us that we are *called* into union with Christ. "God is faithful, by whom you were called into the fellowship of his Son, Jesus Christ our Lord" (I Cor. 1:9). Faith is our answer to the call; but it is obedient faith. Moreover, we are *constantly* called into union with Christ, and we are expected to keep on hearing and believing (I Cor. 1:2). We are called from nonbeing—'life' outside of Christ—into being—life in Christ (Rom. 4:17; 9:11, 25). Hearing and believing is itself an act of obedience; it is an act of will, a decision to be identified with Christ in His new order and to submit to the rule of the Lord and the Spirit within the new order. This is why Paul speaks of the "obedience of faith" (Rom. 16:26).

For Paul obedience is the same as faith, just as disobedience is the same as no faith. In Romans 16:19, he tells his readers that their "obedience is known to all," just as in Romans 1:8 he says that their faith is known to all. The parallel between disobedience and the absence of faith is also present. In Ephesians, Paul talks about the "sons of disobedience" who are willfully committed to the order of life outside of Christ (Eph. 2:2; 5:6), and in Romans

---

[15]I think Berkouwer is saying this when he writes: "Faith is not one modal manifestation of a basic concept called obedience. . . . Faith is the basic concept which is further described and characterized by the expression 'obedience of faith'. . . . To hear the gospel is to obey it. . . . The obedience of faith, then, is really just faith—the total response to the gospel" (*Faith and Justification*, pp. 195ff.).

he refers to them as those who "do not obey the truth" (Rom. 2:8), which means those who disbelieve the truth.

The dynamic reality of union with Christ is, then, a reality to which we must respond as obedient partners. This is why the kerygma has to be repeated again and again. The kerygma does not merely assert the truth about the events of redemption; it is not repeated merely to help us remember or analyze the meaning of the words of Scripture intellectually. The kerygma is repeated because the fact which it asserts carries a renewed summons to obedience with it.

Faith as obedience, then, illuminates the nature of our union with Christ. The Christ with whom we are united is the Christ proclaimed in the gospel as the crucified and risen Lord. The response we give to Him is the response of our total selves to the style of life within His new order, a style that has uncounted dimensions, the most important being love. We are moved and enabled to live in Christ by the "Spirit and the power"—which is to say, by the Christ within us. I cannot recall that we are ever called to obey the Christ within; rather, the Christ to whom we are united in the obedience of faith is the Christ of the gospel, the Christ "out there," while the power by which we respond in the obedience of faith is the power of Christ within.

We are called to faith, we have said, within our union with Christ. But we are also called *to* union with Christ. Union with Christ is the *goal* of obedience as well as the context of obedience. No one whom Christ has not stirred at the depths is moved to obey; therefore, union has already been initiated when we call Jesus Lord. But we are summoned to union with Him in active partnership, union in the ministry of reconciliation, union with Him in the ongoing service of love to the world. Faith gets its power through Christ's coming to us. And faith is obedience to the Lord's summons to act in union with Him.[16]

In this context, the obedience of faith is not a new form of legalism. The Christian does not first believe as a fact that Christ

[16]Whatever criticism may be justly made of Barth's doctrine of reconciliation as a whole, he has forcefully reminded us of this. Union with Christ is not a slumbering reality that lies vaguely in the background of our life with Christ; it is an active partnership to which we are constantly called, called into action with Christ. Its climax is not a mystical "vision of God" but the "common action of the Lord and His servant." Hence, union is both the beginning assumption and the goal to which we are summoned (*Church Dogmatics*, IV/3/2, p. 651).

is Lord, that the new creation is real, and then, that having been
taken care of, check into its laws. Faith is never done with; it is
the act of response that is renewed every morning, like God's
mercy. Faith is never done with because it is a renewed act of
obedience in every new situation of life.[17] It is obedience to a new
Lord, within a new life situation, by a new power. Of course, the
Lord we obey and the situation to which we adapt are known only
through the gospel. The power is the Spirit of that Lord and no
other. But we have no more calling to make a code book of the
gospel and the epistles than the scribes had to make a code book
of the old covenant law.

Finally, the fact that faith takes the form of obedience demonstrates the integrity of our own persons within union with Christ.
Paul does not give us any reason to suppose that Christ displaces
our free and responsible selves in any sense. Otherwise, the calling
and cajoling of the gospel would be sham. The Spirit is at work
within us, silently pushing and pulling, goading and guiding, con-
vincing and convicting us. He moves us to recognize that the Jesus
of the Scriptures is the Lord of our lives. But we are still responsible; and we must be responsive. There is always a perverse possibility that we may not be responsive. We may choose to live
as though we were not in Christ. Our commitment to the new
order in Christ and our response to the Spirit within are not taken
for granted.

Christ's presence within is the assurance that our faith will not
be futile; the reality of His power within our lives is the assurance
of final fidelity.[18] But Christ's presence is not an escape from
doubt, nor from the very real threats that still come from the
defeated "principalities and powers." Union with Christ is sustained only within our actions of free obedience. The dynamic
interplay between our obedience and His Spirit and power will always elude our efforts to catch them in a still-life portrait. But
we do know this: we can trust His intention and His power to
keep us in Him, even as we are called in freedom to live in union
with Him.

[17]On this, Bultmann translates Paul correctly. "Faith," he writes, "is the
acceptance of the kerygma, not as a mere cognizance of it and agreement
with it, but as that genuine obedience to it which includes a new understanding of one's self. Therefore, it cannot be an act that takes place once
and then becomes a thing of the past" (*Theology of the New Testament,* I,
p. 324).
[18]This Calvin saw. See *Institutes* iii.2.24.

3. Faith Is Hope

Hope is faith turned toward the future. It is faith fastened in courage to the new creation which is yet to be. When in faith the Christian says, "But we anticipate a new heaven and a new earth wherein dwelleth righteousness," he is expressing faith in the form of hope. Only when faith is understood as a belief that certain things happened in the past is it something other than hope. Calvin rightly discerned that when "hope is taken away, however eloquently or elegantly we discourse concerning faith, we are convicted of having none."[19] This must be true, for Christian faith is life's openness to Jesus as Lord, whose Spirit is the down payment of the new creation still to come.

In the same moment that it summons us to faith, the kerygma of the cross summons us to hope. While it calls us to involvement in and commitment to the new creation that was established at the cross and resurrection and is present now, it also calls us, in the same act, to the firm hope that the new creation will be fulfilled and visible in the future. Past, present, and future converge in the decision of faith.

Union with Christ takes the form of hope in two ways. One has reference to the eschatological reality of the new creation. The other has reference to the personal reality of Christ within us. Both converge in the faith that Jesus is Lord, the Lord who "is the Spirit."

We must speak first about the new creation. Where is the "new order" that was created by Christ? Where in the present time—the time since Christ's resurrection—is the situation in which the "old things" have definitely passed away and "all things" have become new? Where is the new creation?

We must face up to the question that was raised in the third chapter: is there really a new creation? On the broad plains of history, the principalities and powers of darkness loom very large. In every phase of history, the state has been on the verge of capitulating to the demonic. The arrogance of national pride and power that Isaiah condemned in Assyria and Babylon besets every nation, not excluding the "Christian" nations of Western history. Where is the lordship of Jesus Christ? Where was His lordship when six million Jews cried to heaven from the gas chambers of modern Europe? Where was His lordship while powers that denied His very existence established their control over half the world's population in our time? Where is His lordship in the compromise and weakness of the United Nations? Where is His lordship in Viet Nam? Where is His lordship while the richest nation in the world's history, saturated with words about the power of Christ, is unable to cope creatively with its own crises of poverty and racism? Where is the evidence that Christ is Lord and the kingdom of God is come in power and the Spirit?

What was asked about human history must also be asked of the individual. Where is the person in whom Christ is the center from which his whole personal existence creatively emerges? Where is the individual in whom Christ is "all and all?" Where is the man in whom Christ is obviously present? Where is the person whose life-style is clearly fashioned by the power of the new creation in Christ? Is it not true that a hundred vices rear their heads for every genuine claim we can make on Christian virtue? And is this not why, in the sphere of his inmost life, the Christian's hold on the new creation is at the point of hope? And is this not why Paul adds to his broad imperatives for the totally renewed life the promise of achievement when Christ returns (Titus 2:11f.)? Hope is the Christian answer to the ambiguities and frustrations of the present reality both within man's general history and within his personal life.

What the Christian hopes for is the full realization of his present union with Christ, not only as a personal experience, but as part of the universal complex of Christ's lordship. He hopes for the complete transformation of history by Christ, for the fulfillment of the new creation in Him. He hopes for the completion of his own conformation to the life of Christ by the power and the Spirit. He hopes for his assimilation wholly into the new order of life established at the resurrection and initiated into history by the Spirit as the down payment of things to come.

Hope is a necessary ingredient of faith because the new creation is yet unfulfilled. Hope is the answer to the problem of the present time in Christian experience. But the reality of union with Christ in the present time prohibits us from making hope the be all and end all of faith. In this regard, Jurgen Moltmann's profound effort to make hope the center of theology for our day is open to criticism. Moltmann's *Theology of Hope*[20] is a desperately overdue antidote

[20] I am sorry that the manuscript for this book was at the publisher when I first set hands on Moltmann's book.

to that existentialist theology which swallows up the futurist dimensions of Christian reality in the act of personal decision. Existentialist theology tends to be so consistently pessimistic about the possibilities of ordinary human history that it can tolerate no hopes for it at all; indeed, the redemptive event is understood as a means of escape from the limits of ordinary history rather than as a transformation of history. The best that existentialism offers is the possibility for a human being to accept whatever a basically hopeless future may bring. And, as in Bultmann's case, when existentialism is married to radical demythologizing, it jettisons all Christian hope for an actual realization of the new creation in the future just as it abandons all faith in an actual victory by Christ in the past. As a constructive reaction to existentialism's eternalizing the present in the form of a radically individualistic personal decision, Moltmann's work is to be gratefully acknowledged and will, I expect, be widely accepted. The weakness of Moltmann's theology of hope, however, is that it is an overreaction.

To Moltmann, the problem of the future is "the only one real problem in Christian theology."[21] But is the future the real problem for theology? In my judgment, *the* problem is not the future; rather, it is that of the *present* in the light of the future. Moltmann interprets the resurrection almost wholly in terms of the future of Jesus Christ; the resurrection is our assurance that Jesus does indeed have a future of lordship over history. But what of the Christ of the present time, the Christ who is Spirit extending His lordship in effective power here and now? Moltmann reads the coming of Christ as an exclusively futuristic event. "The parousia of Christ . . . is conceived in the New Testament only in categories of expectation, so that it means not *praesentia Christi,* but *adventus Christi. . . .*"[22] He so consistently reads the influence of Jesus Christ in futuristic categories that he even wants us to understand God essentially in terms of promise; along with E. Bloch he tends to see "future as His essential nature." But this must be judged one-sided, and to that extent misleading. Moltmann is forced to ignore a great deal of New Testament witness to the present reality of man's union with Christ, the present reality of the Christ within us, the present reality of the Spirit as Christ's presence within history, and the present reality of the Church, not only as the Church of the Exodus, but as the locale of the new creation itself in the form of the body of Christ.

[21]*Theology of Hope* (New York, 1967), p. 16.
[22]*Ibid.,* p. 31.

We should not compel hope to prove its power by emptying the present of Christ's reality. It is true, as Moltmann often insists, that we are in conflict between hope and experience, between promise and present reality. But this conflict is not between hope and the absence of experience, nor between promise and the emptiness of present reality. It is a conflict between hope and incomplete experience, between promise and an unfulfilled present. As we have said earlier, creation groans in anticipation of its redemption because it has already tasted the power of it in the Spirit. The reality of the Spirit is, in fact, the most serious omission in Moltmann's study. Where the Spirit is taken in earnest, God will not be defined as essentially future nor will Christ be understood only in terms of His future.

Hope, we have insisted, is necessary because our union with Christ is yet unfulfilled. The problem is with the present. In the next chapter we shall look at the body of Christ as the theological answer to that problem.

4. Faith Is Knowledge

When we speak of faith as a form of knowing, we usually point to the object or content of our knowledge. Now faith knowledge is a knowledge of something that is known in a special way. *What* we know determines the way by which and in which we know. What we know, in short, is this: Jesus is Lord. And the nature of this truth conditions from beginning to end the nature of our knowing it.

Jesus is Lord. That is, by His resurrection He established a new pattern of life and a new order of history that is under His rule of love and grace. This we know in faith. Further, we know God's will as it is demonstrated in Christ's kind of lordship. Paul says that he has "all wisdom and understanding by which the mystery of his *will* is made known" (Eph. 1:8, 9). That revealed mystery is, of course, God's purpose to reunite a divided, fractured world to Himself and to reconcile men to each other within it (Eph. 1:10). His will is to save men, including the Gentiles, who until Christ had been strangers to His commonwealth. This is the mystery that is known now. To know this, is to know the power of the resurrection of Christ (Eph. 1:17-20).

How do we come to know the real force of the future in this world? How do we come to know that the last word in human history is Christ's lordship over history? Paul is sure that nothing in history itself, nothing in the accumulated wisdom of mankind, will suggest it to us. It is known through the "power and the Spirit" that works through the "preaching" of Christ crucified. In short, the reality of Christ is known in the convergence of the gospel preached and heard by us and the Spirit at work within us (I Cor. 2:1-4). The reality of Christ's new order, and the firmness of our place within it, are known only as we are united to Christ Himself.

But knowledge in faith has a deeply personal thrust. With beautiful insight, John Calvin not only speaks of faith as a form of knowledge, but goes on to demonstrate how knowledge of faith cuts into the heart of our personal relationship with Christ. Knowledge in faith, he says, is not an intellectual comprehension, but a personal persuasion of God's benevolence, and that not in general, but towards me personally.[23] To know in faith is not to be theologically literate; those who know have a "spirit of wisdom and revelation in the knowledge of him, having . . . [their] *hearts* enlightened" (Eph. 1:17). That is, to know in faith is to know a *person* with the knowledge of the *heart*. We are talking about something, not less than intellectual, but certainly more primitive and deeper than an intellectual grasp of things.

To know in faith is to know the love of Christ which is beyond the grasp of intellection. And this requires the Spirit and the power, the presence of Christ within our hearts (Eph. 3:17, 18). Obviously, Paul is not telling us that faith provides a built-in theory of divine love. He is saying rather that it provides the knowledge that comes through the experience of personal love. When I come to know the love of Christ in faith, I am amazed not at love in the *abstract*, but at the *concrete* fact that I could be so freely and deeply loved.

Faith knowledge within our union with Christ results not in a Hegelian vision of a divine order, but in the personal persuasion that the powers Christ defeated cannot separate me from His love (Rom. 8:39). It is a knowledge that gives not a superior theory, but a power to live fruitfully. Paul prays that we may be "filled with the knowledge of his will in spiritual wisdom and understanding to lead a life worthy of the Lord, fully pleasing to him, bearing fruit in every good work, and increasing in the knowledge of God" (Col. 1:9, 10). This is the kind of knowledge

[23]*Institutes* iii.2.2-5.

which faith provides in a person whose life is consciously committed to the new reality of Christ and subconsciously drawn into
union with Christ by the indwelling of His Spirit.

When we say that faith knowledge is practical and personal
rather than theoretical, we are not saying that it is anti-intellectual
or nonintellectual. To say that faith is not merely an assent to
truth is not to say that faith does not involve truth. To make the
knowledge of faith anti-intellectual would be to remove it from
the arena of factuality in the objective world. It is a fact that
Christ is Lord; it is false to say that He is not. And the lordship
of Christ is a fact affirmed by the intellect. But we must distinguish
between the believing function of the intellect and the technical
and theoretical function. The knowledge of faith is not technical or
theoretical, but it does involve the intellect as much as it involves
the volition and the feelings.

Faith knowledge does involve the will: we choose to believe and
hence to know. It also involves the emotions: we are firmly persuaded that God's love is real in Christ and are profoundly moved
by it. When a person says that he "knows Christ," he is affirming
a truth by an act of the will that is emotionally involved.

We know the Christ of the gospel because the Christ within
opens our minds to Him. That is, the Christ within stimulates us to
faith. But how do we know that it is the *Christ* within—and not
some other stimulus—who opens our minds to the gospel's Christ?
We know this by faith also. And, in turn, we believe this, too, in
response to what is said by the gospel about the Christ within.
This is the circle of faith. We admit that it is a circle, not reluc-
tantly, but as the only way of keeping the right relationship between the act of believing and the reality believed.

5.   Faith Is Love

The life in union with Christ is a life of love. And love is a
dimension of faith. We do not believe certain facts and *thereupon*
proceed from faith to love. Nor do we obey the law of Christ, and
then add love besides. Love itself is obedience; we are commanded
at the heart of the gospel to love. And yet love is impossible
except in man's total openness to the Christ of love, which means
openness in faith. Love is the primary form that obedience of faith
assumes.

Paul says that faith works by love (Gal. 5:6). He does not mean

that love is an additive that enriches faith; he means that belief
takes the form of love. Love *is* faith turned outward in action. But
Paul also says that love is a fruit of the Spirit within (Gal. 5:22).
This means that the acts of Christian love are impelled by the
indwelling of Christ. More, the upshot of the indwelling of Christ is
that love becomes the ground of our lives (Eph. 3:17, 18). Faith
and love are intertwined, and there is no way to separate them.
Where love is gone, faith has failed. To say "I believe" and fail to
practice the "works of love" is a grotesque contradiction.

How could it be otherwise? The new creation begun at the resurrection means the reunion of men, the creation of "one new man"
reconciled in Christ. The reunion of men is the meaning and goal
of love. The fulfillment of the new creation is the embodiment of
love in life on earth. This is another way of saying that in the new
creation, Christ shall be all and in all. For He is the divine incarnation and the divine work of love. In faith a man responds with
his whole self to the order and style of Christ, to His summons,
to His presence. What then can he do in faith but love as he has
been loved?

The life in Christ, lived by faith, is the union of erotic and agapic
love. Greek life was founded on erotic love; its fatal weakness was
that one properly loved only what was *obviously* lovable. This is
why the Greek was obligated to love only the beautiful; it was
why his gods could love only gods, and men could give love fully
only to the ideal of love—there were so few obviously lovable
creatures. The life in Christ is a life of erotic love, too. It is a mistake to say, as Nygren does, that Christian love is only agapic.
But the Christian has to love *by faith;* and his erotic love is based
on faith, not on the obvious. He has to *believe* in the worthiness
of men to be loved.

This is why he offers his erotic love—the love for the lovable—to *all* men. He knows, in faith, that the cross of Christ
demonstrates the worthiness of men to be loved. To say this may
sound foreign to the depths of men's need for the cross. But we
must remember that the cross tells us not only that men needed
dying for, but that they were worth dying for. God died for His
creation—the creation He made and found good, and kept pursu-
ing after it fell. And so, in Christ, we are called to make the mind
of Christ our own in this respect as well as others.

When I see a hoodlum looting a store, I am called to believe
that he is worth loving. When I see an Eichmann, callous to the
end about his demonic obedience to Hitler, I am called to believe

that even he is worth loving. And when I look at the ugly man within my own soul, I am called to believe that I am worth loving. But it is Jesus Christ and His cross who call me to believe in the worthiness of men. It is the Christ within me who gives me the power to believe that they are worthy of love. My point is this: love as the outgoing dimension of faith is an erotic love. And erotic love within Christian perspective is *believing* love.

But eros is united with agape. For agapic love accepts the other person in spite of everything in him that obstructs reconciliation. Agapic love accepts him in spite of what he is. Agapic love is the constraint from within to seek him and accept him, as he is, in spite of the distortions of his created worthiness. Both erotic and agapic love are rooted in faith. We should not speak of the erotic as natural love and the agapic as Christian love. For the Christian, loving and living in faith, *everything* is rooted in his union with Christ.

It should also be said that suffering is a permanent characteristic of the love born of faith. The Church, the body of Christ, is the ministering servant of Jesus Christ, the ongoing body of reconciliation. Within the community, the believers reciprocate both erotic and agapic love, and so form the model of the coming redeemed society. This involves suffering for one another as a form of the life of Christ within. Only in this light can we understand Paul's statement about his own suffering, a statement that to this day remains a problem for many who are committed to the notion of a once-for-all redemption through the "completed work" of Christ. Paul says: "Now I rejoice in my sufferings for your sake, and in my flesh I complete what remains of Christ's afflictions for the sake of his body, that is the church" (Col. 1:24). Paul is talking about himself as the minister, and the body of Christ as continuation of the reconciling ministry of Christ. The body of Christ, as we shall speak of it in the next chapter, is the earthly means of Christ's continuing action. The Lord identified Himself with the Church that Paul was persecuting; it is not strange, then, that Paul should identify the sufferings of that Church with Christ's sufferings. What the Church suffers in its ministry of reconciliation are the sufferings of Christ. Christ must suffer throughout history.

The agapic life comes to concrete embodiment in suffering. This is a statement of faith. For Paul and we must *believe* that the Church is Christ's body. We must believe that our own sufferings "on behalf of the gospel" are the afflictions of Christ because they are endured in pursuit of His purpose. Paul spoke of his sufferings as a man in union with Christ.[24] But this was faith's interpretation of them. Suffering, we may say, is an inescapable part of union with the suffering Servant; suffering is a corollary to the work of healing in our world. But to suffer in this perspective is to act in faith.

6. The Life of Faith Is Our Own

We have been discussing the life of faith as our conscious experience of union with Christ. All that we have said about the several dimensions of faith precludes any suggestion that the indwelling of Christ diminishes our own personal identity. Christ does not overpower us; certainly He does not supplant us. Nor does He add Himself to our ego, as though union with Him makes us sanctified schizoids. My life in Christ is my own life. The life of Christ within is also my own life. Here, as everywhere, grace does not destroy but restores creation. To have Christ formed in us (Gal. 4:19) is to have our individuality shaped in action to the character of Christ.

Paul's own life is a living testimony to the quickening of his own personality through the indwelling of Christ. His whole career stamps him as a man of action, not as a man of merely pious feeling or of mystic absorption. He is not a man eager to lose his identity, but rather a man eager to go to the ends of the world to proclaim the advent of a new reality in history and a new possibility for man. He looks forward not to an elevation into divinity, but to a coming age of history. He disciplines himself not to escape the flesh for the "cloud of unknowing," but to fight the battles of life in the rigors of bondservice to Christ. He downgrades ecstatic experiences in which people "get outside" of themselves, and calls for the authentically personal practice of faith, hope, and love. He never describes his experiences with Christ in the favorite mystic vocabulary of sweetness and light, he never talks of losing himself as a drop in an ocean of infinity. When he experiences Christ, he senses himself as a sent person. And in all of his actions in union with Christ, it is Paul himself, the over-

[24]It is not clear whether Paul says that he is suffering instead of the body of Christ or in service to it. He could mean that he is suffering what the body would suffer were it with Paul in his "afflictions, hardships, calamities, beatings, imprisonments, tumults, labors, watching, hunger" (II Cor. 6:4, 5). Or he could mean that his sacrifices are on behalf of the existing churches.

sensitive, driving, demanding, vigorous personality in all its Pauline idiosyncracy, whose life is indwelt by Christ.

Bonhoeffer takes the Pauline injunction to conform to Christ as the key to Christian ethics, and is quite right in doing so. He shows that conformity to Christ is not a new legalism, but a personal response to the grace of God by which man becomes a true man again. Conformity is not a moral ideal which we strive for on our own in trying to be like Jesus. This kind of Jesus idealism breeds only a new Pharisaism. Rather, "Christ remains the only giver of forms. It is not Christian men who shape the world with their ideas, but it is Christ who shapes men in conformity with Himself."[25] Christ is the source and the power. But, as the whole of Bonhoeffer's ethics of personal responsibility shows, we are responding persons in all our individuality. The same Bonhoeffer who makes conformity to Christ the key to Christian ethics wrote in the *Letters from Prison* those profoundly true remarks about Christian respect for the individuality of a person.

To be conformed to Christ, in union with Him, means to be restored and recalled to the genuine humanity of God's image. Union with Christ is the God-given secret of true humanism. For conformation to Christ is the restoration of the whole man, in all of his relationships, to the image of God in its social totality. In a deep sense, the goal of union with Christ can be summed up in one command: Be a real man.

C. SUMMARY

"Faith" is a word that signals a man's total response to the new order of life in Christ. It can be distorted to mean simply a man's willingness to affirm as true certain facts about Jesus. It can also be distorted to mean simply a man's dynamic commitment to a way of life, with no real reference to the facts about Jesus. But the personal and total response that is called faith both depends on the reality of Christ as Lord and demands in response to that reality a commitment to a new way of life.

"Faith" is a word that points to our conscious and willed life within the union that Christ enters with us. There is no union without faith. There is no faith except in union with Christ. In a sense there is no reality to Christ as Lord—"out there" and "within us" —except along with faith. Without persons who respond in faith,

[25]Bonhoeffer, *Ethics* (New York, 1965), p. 18.

without persons who live in union with Christ, any talk about Christ as Lord would be meaningless. Christ as Lord *means* the Christ who created a new situation of which He is the representative and ruling Head, a situation so identified with Him that when we are part of His situation we can be said to be "in Him." Therefore, Christ is not Lord except along with those who, in faith, are committed citizens of His new creation.

But there is also no reality to faith, in the Christian sense, unless Jesus actually is Lord. Faith is the subjective side in the convergence of Christ and us. The reality of faith and the reality of Christ join in the creation of our union with Him. Faith is not the same as union; it is our living affirmation, in thought, in word, and, above all, in deed, of His union with us. This is why the broad reality of faith can be called by so many names: knowledge, love, hope, and obedience, and others. These are words taken from ordinary relationships between persons; but within the Christian life, they all are defined as dimensions of faith—the total response of persons at the center to Christ as Lord.

It is tempting to make faith—especially in view of its total and dynamic character—identical with the reality of Christ within us. This must be resisted. Faith is one thing. Christ within us is another. Yet, as far as our experience and our consciousness are concerned, we live in faith. Our faith reponse, moreover, is to the Christ "out there" as He comes to us in the Word and in the Spirit. But, we are let in on the secret that behind and beneath our faith response, Christ is within us through His Spirit as the creative source of our responding life.

In a sense, we are not aware of Christ within at all. We do not feel, or intuit, or sense His presence as something distinct from ourselves. To make the claim that Christ is directly sensed within us is to fall prey to spiritual temptation. We are not even summoned by the gospel to believe that He is there; we are summoned to faith in the Christ of the cross and resurrection. Nor are we urged to investigate our inner lives to discover Christ there; the test is in the effects of the Spirit and the power in our moral lives. We cannot make a boast of Christ within us; we can only witness to the Christ of Calvary.

His indwelling is His affair. It is a reality of the new creation. He summons us to obedience to the Spirit who speaks through the Word. But His indwelling is His business. We can thank Him for it; we can never press any claim on our neighbor on the basis of it. We can be compelled by the power of it; we can never be smug about the privilege of it. But when we have made a little progress in the life of faith, the reality of Christ within reminds us that even the "small beginning" that the Heidelberg Catechism speaks of is owed to His Spirit.

What I hope to have said in this chapter is that the Christian *experience* of union with Christ is the response of faith in all its ethical imperatives and ontological assurances. Faith, then, must never be equated with orthodox thought; it is as wide as life in union with the Lord. Nor must faith be equated with the dynamics of the moral life in isolation from Christ. Faith is man assenting with the whole of his life to the reality of the new creation "in Christ" and to the reality of the Spirit and the power within the new creation, the reality of Christ "in us."

Chapter Seven

The Body of Christ

God who created men to live in community reconciled them as a community. That His saving purpose should be of a piece with His creative purpose is not at all surprising. After all, Christ is the Creator. That God's will is for all things to be gathered together in Christ (Eph. 1:10), for all walls between men to be broken down and one new man created in Christ (Eph. 2:14f.), is only consistent with the song of creation. But that the apostle calls the new community in Christ the *body* of Christ should astonish us. The only reason we fail to be amazed at this strange turn of language is our habit of letting familiarity dull the sharp edges of biblical realism. But the more we think about the Church being Christ's very real body, the less sure we are of what the apostle had in mind. But one thing is certain about it: Paul could not have found words more compelling than these to say that we have union with Christ together, commonly, and in no other way. Union with Christ is a corporation.

A. WHAT IS CHRIST'S BODY?

1. *Paul's Vocabulary*

a. *The Community Is Like a Body and It Is a Body*

The simplest thing Paul says is that the Church is like a body. Christians function—or ought to function—the way parts of a human body function together. The Corinthians obviously were not living and working together as a body; they were divided into several private enterprises competing against each other for the Spirit. So Paul, in I Corinthians 12:14-26, says they should take a lesson from the way a human body is put together and functions: each member needs the other and respects the other.

217

The apostle speaks as though eyes, ears, and limbs have personalities; each defers to the other and none counts any other expendable. Thus the human body is an example of how the community of Christians *ought* to act. The analogy lies in the area of *function*.

He also says that Jesus Christ is like a body. As one reads I Corinthians 12, he expects Paul to stay with his analogy of the *Church* to the body. But, awkwardly, in the middle of his talk about the diversities within the unity of the fellowship, he injects a new ingredient: "For just as the body is one and has many members, and all the members of the body, though many, are one body, so it is with Christ" (12:12). Surely, he should have said: "so it is with the *Church*." But he catches us off guard. The New English Bible makes it plainer: "Christ is like a single body with its many limbs and organs. . . ." What sense can we make of this?

After saying that Christ is like a human body, Paul simply goes on to tell the community to begin acting like a body. And after elaborating on how a human body works, he says, "Now you *are* the body of Christ and individually members of it" (12:27). Here, Christ *has* a body—the community of Christians. A strange kind of body indeed; but a body. And this body is like an ordinary physical organism which we call a man's body.

So we have two comparisons. On the one hand, Christ is like a human body and the community is like a human body; on the other, the community *is* Christ's body. Thus when Paul says that Christ is like a human body, he evidently means that Christ and His community together form a body of sorts which functions like the physical organism we call a body.

Christ and His community are a body. He is a self-determining, transcendent person. But He has a body, as I have a body. And He and His body form the whole Christ. The whole Christ—He and His body—are, then, *like* a physical organism. There is a similarity between the whole Christ and a physical body. Now this simile is not strange. What is strange is that Christ and the community should *be* a body.

Paul's statement in I Corinthians 12 comes down to this: Since you *are* a body, Christ's body, you ought to function as a body; let a physical organism tell you how.

Other passages play variations on the same theme. In Romans 12:5 Paul says that we are "one body *in* Christ." It is a slight shift from "the body *of* Christ," and the difference should be noted. Here he does not say that the community and Christ are related as an ego is related to its physical organism; he says that the secret of the community's existence as a body is its life in Christ. But, in Ephesians 1:23, he falls back on the more striking image again: he speaks of the Church "which *is* his body." There is still another variant in I Corinthians 6:15 where Paul reminds individual Christians that their physical "bodies are members of Christ." Every individual, whole and entire, including his body, is a limb of Christ's body.

b. *Jesus Christ Is the Head of the Body*

In Ephesians and Colossians one discovers another nuance in the imagery. Here, Christ is the *head* of the body:

"He is the head of the body, the church" (Col. 1:18).
"For the husband is the head of the wife as Christ is the head of the church, his body, and is himself its Savior" (Eph. 5:23).

Perhaps we should not press the image too hard. But the suggestion is that Christ and the community are distinct parts of what we would call the whole body. He is the head, and the community is the trunk and limbs. Paul says that we tend to be spiritual individualists because we fail to keep a firm hold on the head who keeps the body in organic harmony (Col. 2:19). Whatever special meaning Paul gives to the Church by calling Jesus Christ its head, it is clear that no image could be more suggestive of intimate and mysterious unity than this one.

c. *Christ Lives in the Body*

Paul does not say in so many words that Jesus Christ indwells the Church as His body. But the implications are strong. He once reminded the community that Christ's presence among them was their firm ground for hope (Col. 1:27). And if we put together all that has been said about the Spirit's being Jesus Christ at work, we must assume that the Spirit's continuous activity within the Church is a creative source of the Church's existence as Christ's body. At any rate, the Spirit's restless prodding and gracious giving is the source of the community's ability to *act* like a body. (Cf. I Corinthians 12:13.)

So much for Paul's vocabulary. We have seen that his imagery of the body has a variety of forms. Later we must examine some of these pictures more closely to discover what they tell us of that union with Christ that the community is privileged to have.

There are temptations we should avoid at this point. One of them is to isolate the image of the body from its broad context

within Paul's whole gospel and then to draw wonderful conclusions from the image itself. We must let Paul's whole message
illuminate his imagery. Robinson is quite right in insisting that
Paul's doctrine of the Church is determined by his Christology.[1]
The other temptation is the scholarly ambition to go too far afield
behind Paul himself in search for light on his strange metaphor.
Scholars have spent prodigious effort to prove that Paul learned
his imagery from the Stoics, from gnostic mythology, or from
Judaism.[2]

2.   What Is a Body?

What did Paul think when he said body? One clue comes from
his certainty about the resurrection. The thought of an immortal
soul living by itself, without a body, made no sense at all to Paul.
There were people in Corinth who supposed that the human soul
drove a body about this earth much as an angel would drive an
automobile; when the body wore out, the soul was free to go its
own way, better off on its own. This is why they could ridicule the
resurrection and still have hopes for a life after death. But for Paul,
a soul without a body was a naked and half-real thing. He did
not suppose, of course, that we need an exact duplicate of the particular bundle of flesh and bones we have now; indeed, he
was convinced that we shall have a new construction, and that we
shall be much better off for it. But the idea of being without a body
at all was fantastic. A man, after all, is a body (I Cor. 15:35-54).

The body, for Paul, is not a piece of fleshly baggage that can be
dropped to allow the soul to float aloft in freedom. Man is not a
soul wrapped in a fleshly package. He has two dimensions—an
inward and outward. The body is the one person turned outward.

This is why the things we do with our bodies matter spiritually.
Some people in Corinth supposed that what one did with his
body did not count for much in the long run. He could, for instance, sleep with a prostitute with moral impunity. After all, he
could reason, it only involved his body. This was horrible nonsense
to Paul. What a person does with his body touches the heart of
morality; it is a sign of whether he is spiritually united with Christ.
One cannot have sexual relations with a whore and keep his soul
clean. For the body is the soul in action.

Everyone knew that when a man sleeps with a woman he be-

[1]J. A. T. Robinson, *The Body, A Study in Pauline Theology* (London,
1952), p. 49.
[2]See Additional Note 6, pp. 264-265.

comes one flesh with her. But what Paul wanted his readers to know was that he also became one spirit with her. For the flesh is only doing outwardly what the spirit is doing. Anyone who, claiming to be one spirit with Christ, sleeps with a prostitute, is divorced from Christ. The reason is clear. We cannot be one spirit with Christ without being one body with Him. We cannot be one flesh with a whore without being one spirit with her. Union with a prostitute breaks up the union with Christ (I Cor. 6:15-20).

That the body is the person turned outward comes out in many of Paul's challenges to live the spiritual life. His word about offering our body as a living sacrifice is a case in point (Rom. 12:1). Our spiritual service is body service. Paul is simply saying, "Turn your inner life outward in service to God." The death and life of Jesus are to be represented in our bodies; we are, he says, "always carrying in the body the death of Jesus, so that the life of Jesus may also be manifest in our bodies" (II Cor. 4:10). He means, obviously, that we as personalities represent the death and life of Christ; the only way we can do this is as bodies. We are also meant to glorify God in our "mortal bodies" (I Cor. 6:20). When a person renounces his destiny to live bodily for God, he becomes, Paul says, a "body of sin" (Rom. 6:6). Or a "body of death" (Rom. 7:24). Or a "body of dishonor" (I Cor. 15:43). Paul is not saying something about the physical life alone. The body is the outward dimension of the person.

When Paul talked this way of the body, he was revealing the mind of a Hebrew in words that are Greek. The Hebrew, we are told, had no specific word for body because he did not think of the body as a thing in its own right, distinct from the soul. The Hebrew thought of a man as God-animated flesh.[3] Man *was* flesh, weak and withering, kept alive by God. Man was flesh, but with a spiritual dimension; he was a *responsible* creature of flesh. He was flesh, like all other creatures, but with a special window open to his God. He could respond to God in gratitude or ingratitude, obedience or disobedience, service or rebellion; but he always responded *as flesh*. He was not invited ever to contemplate a life of the soul; he was called to service in the flesh. The religious question that faced him was not whether his soul was immortal, but whether his flesh-life was a response of obedient gratitude.

---

[3] "The Hebrew idea of the personality is an animated body, and not an incarnated soul" (W. H. Robinson, *The People and the Book* [Oxford, 1925], p. 362). See my discussion of "flesh" in Chapter III, B. 1.

This is why God's salvation was for the Hebrew a *history*. The Hebrew did not look to God for an escape from flesh; nor could he look to God for an escape from history. Nor could history be looked at as an endless cycle from which the only refuge was final release from the flesh. If man *is* flesh, salvation must come *into* history and *as* history; for flesh can be real only as it is historical. The end of history would arrive, therefore, not when we had laid aside flesh for spirit, but when God's Spirit took on all flesh (Joel 2:28f.). For men of flesh, salvation comes in the form of a covenant in history.

So when Paul talks about the body, he is carrying the Hebrew idea of man into the New Testament community. He makes no capitulation to the Greek dichotomy between body and soul. He does use the Greek word *soma,* which means body. But he attributes to it a Hebrew meaning. He means by it *man*—man turned outward in action.

What Paul says about the body in general is of a piece with his language about the body of Jesus. Paul was obviously not interested in Jesus' body as a thing; he does not seem, for instance, to have had the slightest curiosity about what it looked like. But if he was not interested in Jesus' body as a thing, he was enormously interested in Jesus as a person and what He did bodily. Everything focuses on the person of Jesus turned outward in action as body.

God was in a body reconciling the world to Himself (Col. 1:22). Christ gave His body for us (I Cor. 11:24). We "died to the law through the body of Christ . . ." (Rom. 7:4). Jew and Gentile were reconciled to one another and to God "in one body through the cross" (Eph. 2:16). When Paul thought of Jesus as a body, he always zeroed in on one moment, one event—the cross and the resurrection. And when he spoke of the body here, he obviously meant the *person* called Jesus, the whole man in sacrificial action for us; the "body" is shorthand for all that Jesus the person *did* for us. The body of Jesus is Jesus in action for the world's salvation.

3. What Makes the Community Christ's Body?

a. The Origin of the Community

The Christian community was created by what Jesus Christ *did* with His body. The event of the cross and the resurrection is the dividing line between chaos and community, between the old race in Adam and the new community in Christ. Everything else that is said about the community as Christ's body has its point of orientation here, at that time and place in history at which Jesus died and came alive again.

The cross creates the new community because it was there that the law came to an end (Rom. 10:4) and the righteousness of God in all its surprising dimensions was revealed apart from the law (Rom. 3:25). Men become God's free partners once more because the curse was removed from mankind at the cross, and the blessings of Abraham, God's first covenant partner, came to the Gentiles (Gal. 3:13). More, the spiritual powers lurking behind and fostering man's alienation were defeated (Eph. 2:1). Those men who were strangers to God's partnership are, therefore, now part of the community (Eph. 2:11ff.). Both Jew and Gentile were reconciled "in one body through the cross" (Eph. 2:16). The cross brought peace, reuniting humanity into one redeemed reality, as one new man (Eph. 2:17, Col. 1:20). The turning point for the God-willed community is the same as the turning point for history—the cross and resurrection of the Son of God incarnate.

The cross, it must be noted, brought in a new community to replace the old disunity; it did not destroy the old covenant. The "ordinances that were written against us" in the law were abolished, but the covenant community that began with Abraham was not abolished. After all, what happened at the cross was exactly the means of gaining what God's partnership with Abraham was all about. God "preached the gospel to Abraham" (Gal. 3:8), a gospel the law could hardly have annulled (Gal. 3:17). He who died was the "seed" of Abraham promised from the beginning as a blessing for all; and when He died, He managed to bring "the blessings of Abraham" to the Gentiles (Gal. 3:14). And all who believe in Him are the "sons of Abraham" (Gal. 3:7). No, the cross did not divide the new community from the covenant partnership God entered with Abraham. It created the new community from the chaos created by Adam. The cross draws a line between community and loss of community, and rescues humanity as communion.[4]

[4]This, of course, does not mean that everything else Jesus did and said was unimportant to salvation. A baseball game that is won with a home run in the ninth inning has been preceded by eight full innings of crucial play that were necessary to set the stage for the game-winning run. Had any inning been different, the home run might not be a climax at all. In this sense, the incarnation and the entire life of Jesus Christ were *the* eschatological event.

The point I have made in this section is elementary in a sense, but important. The body of Christ as a community was established by what Jesus did at Calvary and at Joseph's tomb. And what He did there, Paul summarizes as His *body* for us (I Cor. 11:24). The body of Christ was founded by the body of Jesus; that is, it was established by Jesus *in action*.

b.   The Spirit in the Body

Probably the first intellectual reflex to hearing the Church referred to as Christ's body is to think of the indwelling of the Spirit.[5] And this is a sound response. But much depends on how His presence is conceived. There is a long tradition of interpretation which has it that the Spirit's presence within the Church provides the body with its soul. The Spirit brings Christ, and the Church indwelt by Christ becomes the living body whose soul is Jesus Christ. Theologians within this tradition think of the Church, therefore, as an extension of the incarnation. Now undoubtedly, the community is Christ's body only as the Spirit is within it. But what interests Paul is what the Spirit *does* for and within the community.

The unity of the Church is credited by Paul to the Spirit (I Cor. 12). But the focus is on the Spirit in action. The Spirit gives gifts to the individual members for the common good (12:7). These gifts are roughly parallel to the various offices that are assigned for the work of the community. Sometimes they are gifts of power to heal, sometimes to speak, and sometimes to exercise unusual faith. There is work to be done within the community—the work of love. And there is work to be done outside the community—the work of love in witness.

The new life of Christ is germinated, nourished, and exercised by Christ Himself in His Spirit. Christ incorporates new members within the body of baptism (I Cor. 12:13). He awakens members to the knowledge of salvation (Rom. 5:5). He instills the optimistic perspective of hope, as the down payment on the new creation (Gal. 5:5; Rom. 15:13). He opens the members to joy (Rom. 14:17; I Thess. 1:6). He gives confidence of their personal sonship (Gal. 4:6). He opens the new perspective on suffering, providing not only a hope of overcoming it, but the ability to

---

[5]Traugott Schmidt says that "the body of Christ language is an application of the thought that Christ is in us, as individuals, to the collective personality of the church" (*Der Leib Christi* [Leipzig, 1919], p. 142). This is probably true.

seize on suffering as a partnership with Christ (Rom. 8:18). The picture is always a moving picture; the Spirit is within, but at work governing, building, enlightening, provoking the members to be the body of Christ in reality.

When we speak of the Spirit within the community, making it Christ's body, we are reminded again that the Spirit is Christ in lordly action.[6] This underscores His free and sovereign power. It also tells us that the Spirit's aim is to make the lordship of Christ effective in the body—to move the community into the service of reconciliation.

The Spirit represents Christ on earth, at work in the power and purpose. of His lordship. He baptizes individuals into the body where Christ is remembered and expected, into the community established by the action of Christ at the cross (I Cor. 12:11). He awakens and reawakens the community to Christ through the recollection of the saving events in preaching and the sacraments. He is the down payment on the future and the catalyst in the present. He works on earth within the new community to make effective the new thing realized in Christ's resurrection. And he brings the community out into the open as the body of Christ in visible action.

It warrants saying, I think, that the Spirit is not the exclusive property of the Church. He is always free. Nor does He quietly run an assembly line where He pours into members a substance-like stuff called life. Moreover, there is the possibility that He may be ignored, denied, and offended. His presence does not offer a unilateral guarantee. He works and the members must work; He acts and they must react. And where the human side of the dynamic equation is lacking, the body is dormant at best, dead at worst.

---

[6]Thomas Torrance stressed the Spirit's work in the Church as the work of witness. He is right in doing so. But the work is much more than this; Paul is talking in I Cor. 12, for instance, not so much about witnessing to the world as about the service of love within the community. The point Torrance makes is, however, relevant to this discussion. He correctly emphasizes that Christ in His Spirit is not the captive of the Church, but the the Lord who graciously uses the Church. The Church does not replace Christ during His absence; but the Church "is chosen to be the locus of his presence among men and . . . he himself, the risen Lord, is at work in and through it, yet transcended it in the freedom and power of his Spirit, for in spite of the constant failure and inadequacy of the church Christ fulfills through it his own ministry as prophet, priest, and king, on earth as in heaven" (*Theology in Reconstruction* [London, 1966], p. 254).

c.   The Head of the Body

Paul's images move about, and it is hard to keep up with them. As Christ's body, the Church is whole—head and trunk. But Christ is also the head of the body:

> "He is the head of the body, the church . . ." (Col. 1:18).
> ". . . we are to grow up in every way into him who is the head, into Christ" (Eph. 4:15).
> "For Christ is the head of the church, his body, and is himself its savior" (Eph. 5:23).

The image of the head has two suggestions. One is of a master, governor, or leader. This is the aspect most readily convertible into the currency of common metaphor: we speak of heads of corporations and heads of state when we mean the chief or governing directors. But when Paul talks of the head of the body, he could also be stressing the closeness of head to body and the dependence of the body on the head. The first image stresses the distance between head and body. The second stresses their intimate connection. Paul seems to want the image to function both ways.

(1)   The Superior Christ

When Paul calls Christ the head of the Church, he means that Christ is its Lord. He is head of the universe, too (Col. 2:10), but there is a difference between this and His lordship over the Church. In Ephesians 1:21f., Christ is praised as the effective Lord over the powers and authorities that once pretended to be lords of the world. But now God "has put all things under his [Christ's] feet and has made him the head over all things for the church." That Christ is head over the universe is a fact subordinate to His concern for the Church.

But he is head of both; He rules in triumphant lordship everywhere. The new situation is world-wide. It embraces every dimension. Not all men everywhere know Him as Lord and head, but He is head of all nevertheless. This means that as the body of Christ, the Church has the whole world as its concern and ministry. It means that the Church should not presume that it alone is subject to Jesus Christ. A fundamental optimism about the world around us is a Christian possibility.

Obviously, the fact that Christ is head means that He rules. It also points to the superiority of His status. Christ is the head of every man as a husband is head of his wife. The husband is head of the wife (Eph. 5:23) because the male in general has a status superior to that of the female (I Cor. 11:3). Paul's view that women are of lower status than men may be quite unpalatable to modern society; but it must be remembered that Paul is talking not about quality or character, but about a distinction in status.

Paul is not always this direct. Take, for instance, Colossians 1:18: "He is the head of the body, the church; he is the *beginning*, the *first-born* from the dead, that in everything he might be preeminent." Leading up to this, Paul has been reciting—perhaps from a liturgy which is now lost—a song of Christ's preeminence in creation. Christ alone images the invisible God. He is the first-born of all creation. He created all things, even the "gods." He holds all things together. He is the purpose for which all things exist. He is the source, the sustainer, and the end. He is, in short, the preeminent one. Having said this, Paul adds his word about Christ as head of the Church.

He tells us what it means to be head of the body by saying that Christ is the "beginning" and the "first-born." The word "beginning" is probably as good as any to translate the Greek word *arché*. This word has a wide range of meanings. The Stoics used it to indicate a primeval principle that surged through all things, a universal force that kept the cosmos together. Maybe Paul saw possibilities in the Stoic vocabulary and appropriated it for his own use, although he did hold that the force of the universe was personal. Christ, then, is the creative force, behind all other energies, that sustains the Church as well as the universe. As head He is the *imminent* creative power; but He is that as a free person, preeminent over the body in power as well as in authority. The word "beginning" (*arché*), then, indicates superiority in a context of imminence or closeness.[7]

The word "first-born" has Hebraic overtones. The first-born was the heir designate, the figure of authority in the clan. He was, of course, also the first of the brothers to have been born; but the importance is his superior status. Certainly Paul is not telling us that Jesus was the first in history to have been raised from the dead. Not only would this be contrary to biblical history, but it is not the important issue. Christ is the first-born in the sense that among all who share His life, He is the most prestigious and authoritative. He is the "first-born" so that "He might be preeminent."

[7]See G. Delling, in Kittel, *Theological Dictionary of the New Testament,* I, p. 482.

All this adds content to the image of Christ as head of the Church;
as head, He is *superior*.

We have been leading up to this conclusion: the first and most
obvious meaning of Christ as head of the body is that Christ is
superior in status and governing function.

(2) The Christ with Us

Paul also indicates that Christ is intimately and vitally united
with the body because He is its head. But the language he uses is
grotesque, even "violent" as Robinson says. We are told, for
example, that "we are to grow up in every way *into him* who is
the head" (Eph. 4:15). Possibly he is drawing on some strange
biological notion no longer familiar to us, although experts tell
us that ancient literature has nothing that parallels Paul's figure
here. That Paul has a physiological image in mind seems, however,
clear from what follows; he talks about the "whole body, joined
and knit together by every joint with which it is supplied" (Eph.
4:16). He is apparently saying something about the body's
dependence on the head for growth and life.

But how does he want us to transfer this image to the Church
and its dependence on Christ? We can readily understand why
some readers think Paul is talking about a stream of life flowing
from the Lord into the sacramental life of the Church. But what
is he talking about in the context? Ephesians 4 begins by affirming
the lordship of Christ. As Lord, Christ gives the gifts and offices
by which the Church is served (4:11f.). We are all summoned
into our vocations, there to serve one another in love, so that the
unity of the Spirit may be kept. Together, then, we may achieve
"unity of faith" and unity of "knowledge," growing up as one
into perfect manhood (4:13f.). The picture is a most dynamic
one: we hear about a summons to obedience, about the practice
of love, about the attainment of faith and knowledge, and about
the service offered to all of us by the special offices of the Church.
These things form the setting in which the figure of "growing up
into the head" must get its sense.

Obviously the figure of the "head" of the body suggests an organic relationship between Christ and His Church. We cannot
think of Christ as the head without thinking of how inseparable,
how wholly one He and His community are. Paul's talk about the
presence of the *Spirit* in action within the community accomplishes
this as well. The question is what purpose Paul had in mind in
extending the figure of the body of Christ to the distinction

between the body and the head. We have seen, I think, that while the figure of the *body* of Christ emphasizes the oneness of Christ and the community, the figure of Christ as *head* re-introduces the fact of distinction between them. But, of course, it is a distinction between two who are as much of a unity as I and my body are.[8]

Before leaving this section, we ought to ponder a moment over one more thing that Paul says about the head and the body. The body, he says, is the "fulness of him who fills all in all" (Eph. 1:23). The Church, Paul seems to say, holds within itself the whole of Christ. What does this mean?

This kind of passage is interpreted, usually, not by an exegesis of the words, but in terms of the whole tenor of Paul's message. Sacramentalists interpret the passage by way of their whole view of the significance of Jesus Christ as the incarnate resource for the deification of man. So they speak of Christ's divine-human life overflowing into the Church. Christ is full of the elevated life, and from Him there is a "distribution within the body of the fullness that is continually fed into it."[9] The Church, then, is the repository of a kind of life-stuff, and can in turn dispense it through the sacraments. The sacramentalist pushes the head-body figure to its limits; the body is connected to the head, from which a life-substance is poured to the community.

Now it is true, of course, that the head gives life to the body. Christ gives life to the Church; He is the life-giving Spirit, creative and powerful within the Church. The Spirit does come from the head and fill the body. But alternatively there are also many ways in which the body fulfills Christ. The Church must complete Christ's suffering; it must carry on the ministry of Christ's suffer-

---

[8]The same biological image is found in Colossians 2:19. In this chapter, Paul is warning the Colossians against ways of salvation and systems of religious teaching and discipline that compete against the lordship of Jesus Christ. Christians, in the body of Christ, have been liberated from the condemnation implied in the law (2:14) and from the demonic forces that used the law to condemn us (2:15). Now the only reason that people in this situation could be lured into some degrading religious discipline and cult is their failure to hold on to Christ, the head of the body. Just as in some way the physical body gets its life from its head, so the Christian community will fail if it cuts itself off from Christ.

[9]J. A. T. Robinson, *op. cit.*, p. 70. Austin Farrer speaks of the "overflow of His glorious body" in the Church (*The Parish Communion*, ed. A. G. Hebert [London, 1937], p. 80). Almost all Anglo-Catholic theologians speak this way.

ing for the world (Col. 1:24). It must become the locale where the "one new man" in Christ is visible and real. Those who are elect in Christ must be brought into the community and so fulfill the comprehensive Christ. The body of Christ *completes* Christ as it is "filled" with Him. When reconciliation is attained, when men are at peace with God and themselves, when the whole new race is subject to Jesus Christ as Lord, when He is in every way preeminent, and when the whole creation is His new creation, the body of Christ will have been filled by Christ, and Christ will be complete.

This is all a challenge as much as it is a fact. "You have come to fullness of life in him" (Col. 2:9f.), writes Paul. But he also prays that "you *may* be filled with all the fullness of God" (Eph. 3:19). The body *is* the fullness of Him (Eph. 1:23), but still has to *grow up* into Him (Eph. 4:15). The indicative carries with it the imperative. There is a call for prayer, for effort, for decision. The fullness does not come by way of sacramental infusion or mystical biology. If the body is to be filled with Christ, the body must listen to its Lord and obey Him.

In sum, the image of Christ as head of the body points to Him as superior in status and authority to the Church, but conveys as well the fact that He is the powerful source of the Church's existence; in both cases, His function and status is qualified by His close identification with the Church as His body.

d. The Work of the Body

The body of Jesus Christ was established at the cross and the resurrection; there, at a place in concrete history, the walls were broken down so that men once alienated could be united as "one new man." The body is sustained and augmented by the Spirit who is Christ in action within the new age begun at the cross. When we ask what the body of Christ is, we must remember that it is the community committed to the ongoing service of reconciliation in the power of the cross. Within the community, faith is directed to the cross. The word that the community speaks to the world is the word of the cross. The life the community lives is the life styled by the cross—the sacrificial life of loving service. The cross stands at the center of the reality of the body.

On the cross Jesus acted in sacrifice as a body. It is what Christ did with His body for the world that is celebrated by the community. Jesus' body was Jesus Christ at work, fulfilling His own sacrificial mission to the world. *That* body is gone; *that* Jesus is in heaven. But His work goes on; His suffering must be completed (Col. 1:24). His ministry of reconciliation is now committed to the community. In that sense, Jesus is still at work—in His body.

The Spirit is Christ at work; but the Spirit does not work by Himself. He works behind, and in, and by means of the community. He forms and shapes the community, equipping it to be Christ's body in action. He makes it a minister of reconciliation by speaking the word of the cross through it and by leading it into sacrificial action for the world. The body of Christ refers to the ongoing action of Christ in and through the community established by His act at the cross and resurrection.

The body has, of course, a receptive function. It receives the effects of Christ's redemptive action. But the body is not essentially passive. It is active. It listens as it is spoken to. It obeys as it is summoned. Sometimes it refuses to listen and refuses to obey. When this happens, and to the extent that it happens, it fails to be the body. Only insofar as it is the organism by which Jesus Christ fulfills His service on earth is the Church His body.

Christ and the Church are a genuine identity. The identity is of the kind that Paul is always most interested in—not one of substance, but one of function. Just as the apostle sees the Spirit identified with Jesus Christ in function, he sees the body identified with Christ in function. It is true that the body of Christ does not do over again what Jesus did in His body at Calvary—not even in the most subtle sense. This decisive moment does not need repetition. But we are called to appropriate and keep alive its effects. What Jesus began with His body at Calvary goes on in the ministry of reconciliation through His body in history.

What, then, is the body of Christ? It is the community which the Christ, in action as Spirit, forms and equips to continue His work of reconciling men in every city, village, and town of our time, reconciling them to God and one another.

e. Summary

I should like to summarize what I have said so far in this chapter. The concept of the body of Christ has several complementary meanings or nuances. The root meaning is that of *action*: a body is a person as he faces outward in action. When Paul calls the community of Christ His body, what must be foremost in our minds is the function of the body. The background to the reality of the Church as Christ's body is the total redemptive event of the cross and resurrection: the community as a body was created when the new humanity was called into being at Calvary. The action of the body is twofold: (1) bringing into actuality the new humanity established at the cross and (2) continuing the ministry of reconciliation to the world. It is in this sense that a real identity exists between Jesus Christ Himself and His body the Church. The identity is one of *function*: as Jesus in His body created the new humanity at the cross, He continues the ministry or service of reconciliation through His body the Church.

Christ as the head of the body is the superior in status, in authority, and in power. Christ as head of the body is also the Lord who freely and graciously calls the Church into partnership with Him in the service of reconciliation. The Church is summoned by its head to reflect in its own life the catholic nature of the life that Christ created by breaking down the wall of hostility between men. It is called by its head to work with Him and to sacrifice itself for others who are not in the body, to sacrifice itself in the total ministry of the prophet who speaks, the priest who serves, and the king who restores and unifies life. Where it does not act as Christ in outward going action, it is either dead or dormant. And a dead body is not a body, but a corpse.

So the Lord chooses to have a body on earth. The community is called to be part of Christ's mission, and so become His body. There is union between Christ and His body, even though it is a union of unequal partners. Christ the head is always the Lord. The Church, the body, is always the servant. And where there is no obedience, where there is no reconciling action for the sake of the world, there is no body. For a body is the person in action.

The body of Christ, then, is the community of Christ in which His new creation has begun to take effect.

B.   WHERE IS CHRIST'S BODY?

But where is the body? This is one of the hard questions of our time. Can we locate the body in a specific place? Can we say for certain where the body is not? Can we give it a name? Is it any particular organization? Is it at the corner of Main and Maple streets? Is it a particular denomination of churches? Or is the body of Christ an invisible community existing behind and perhaps hidden by the institutional Church?

Two things are, I think, clear in Paul's mind. The first is that the body of Christ is the *visible* fellowship in the action of worship and service. The second is that the body is *local*. "Now *you* are the body of Christ and individually members of it," says the apostle

(I Cor. 12:27). It is as though he is pointing to a group of Christians gathered in the living room of a Corinthian home. That group—with its name, its officers, its liturgy, and its visible actions —was Christ's body. When we say that it is local, we do not mean that it is *limited* to the corner of Main and Maple. We mean that it is the type of reality that can be located on a thousand such corners, that it is the kind of thing that must be located somewhere on some corner. The body of Christ can be photographed.

Does this mean that wherever certain components of organization and structure are found, we have the body of Christ? And that whenever these components are absent, the body does not exist? The traditional Roman Catholic answer is Yes. The logic is simple enough. The necessary components rest with one institution: the chief component is the authority of Peter as the primate of the institution. The body of Christ exists only where men and women live and worship under the authority of the successor to St. Peter; the *ministry,* especially the governing and teaching ministry, is the visible trademark of the body.

The clear equation of Rome with the body of Christ was made by Pope Pius XII in his encyclical *Mystici Corporis* in 1943. He made it again in his *Humani Generis* in 1950. The Roman Church, as a social structure one can locate and point to, is the body of Christ. And there is no other place where the body of Christ can be found.

But the reality of Protestants who demonstrate the life of the Spirit has made it steadily harder for Roman theologians to maintain the equation. The growth and authentic Christian dynamic of the evangelical churches, giving clear witness to the Christ of the Church, keeps thrusting itself against the Roman pretension. And while the Roman Church has not abandoned the dogma that the body of Christ can be pinpointed in the visible establishment headed by the bishop of Rome, it has struggled to make some kind of doctrinal concession to what the facts seem to shout. The *Constitution on the Church,* published at Vatican II, says that the body of Christ *subsists* in the Catholic Church. The body and the visible Church, it claims, are two dimensions or phases of the one complex reality of Christ's community; the mystical phase—the body—extends beyond its visible structure.[10] In this way, a church-*like* dimension can be allowed to non-Roman groups; the body overlaps Roman boundaries.

[10]*Constitution,* Chapter I, Sect. 8.

It would be unrealistic to expect the Roman Church to do an official about face in a single generation. And while many Protestants may be unsatisfied with the concessions made, these concessions are straws in the wind. The Council, at the least, refused simply to identify Christ's body with the Catholic Church.

Protestant evangelicals, on the other hand, are seriously mistaken in their tendency to locate the body in the *invisible* fellowship of Christians. For many evangelicals, the institution at best serves to foster the invisible fellowship and at worst obscures and hinders it. The word "body," as tangible and concrete as its meaning would seem to be, is allowed to refer rather to a kind of amorphous, indefinite, unorganized kinship in faith and feeling. This view of Christ's body allows the evangelical the luxury of indifference to the Church's divisions and sometimes the license to cause them.

For both the Catholic sacramentalist and the Protestant evangelical the body of Christ is created fundamentally by the Spirit's indwelling. But while for the sacramentalist the Spirit brings to the Church a reservoir of grace and life which the individual then receives through the sacrament; for the evangelical, the Spirit brings new life to the individual, who then recognizes the same reality in other individuals and, by entering into some sort of common action and fellowship, creates the body of Christ. For the sacramentalist, the Spirit is in the body and individuals enter the body by a transfusion of the Spirit's life; for the evangelical, the Spirit is in individuals and they create the body. One subjectifies the Spirit individually; the other subjectifies the Spirit institutionally.

If, with Paul, we assume that the body of Christ is visible and local, we cannot take refuge in a phantom body. On the other hand, if we accept the thesis that being the body of Christ is a dynamic reality, with the possibility of losing the privilege, we cannot share Rome's belief that a particular visible institution unconditionally is guaranteed the status of Christ's body forever. We must face the fact that the institutions of ministry and sacraments do not guarantee the perpetuation and life of the body. The body exists only as long as it responds to the dynamic action of the Lord in the Spirit.

This means that the visible and local community is the body of Christ, but that it is the body truly only as it acts as the body. The body of a man is the man in outward action. The community is called the body of Christ because it is Christ in action here and now. And the community can claim to be the body, therefore, only as it does indeed act for Christ. When it is constantly pointing the world to the cross and resurrection of Christ as its creative ground, when it is constantly active as our Lord's reconciling community, when it does the work of Christ as healing priest, conquering king, and witnessing prophet—then it is His body.

C. HOW MANY BODIES?

There is only one Lord Jesus Christ. Has He only one body to do His work on earth? Or have we really created many bodies of Jesus Christ? When Paul asked in horrified disbelief, "Is Christ divided?" he was recoiling at an accomplished fact. But it was also his way of saying that, given the Church's identity, division of it boggled the mind, was incredible, unthinkable, unnatural.

Division of the body is a grotesque contradiction of the new creation. The very unnaturalness of it, however, forms the basis for warning against it. Paul asked another question, like the one about division: "How shall we that are dead to sin live any longer therein? (Rom. 6:2). The question is not a basis for smug confidence; it is a danger sign pointing to a very real possibility. Sin does not belong in the new creature; it is unthinkable and has an air of monstrous unreality about it. But it is as big as life. So with Paul's disbelief that the body could be divided: a divided body is unthinkable, contradictory, inconceivable—yet too real. He is not saying: "It can't happen here." He is saying: "This horrible situation violates nature."

One could claim that the body cannot be divided, that people can only separate themselves *from* the body. This has been the pretension of Rome, a pretension that is more of an embarrassment than a conviction these days. One could also claim that the body is the invisible bond of fellowship between the "true believers" around the world, and thus while institutions split and increase, the *real* thing, the body, is untouched. But if what we concluded in the previous section is true, both of these theological solutions are only paths of escape from the problem. What is a better solution?

St. Paul's immediate concern is for the unity of the *local* community. When he speaks of the body of Christ, he points to a very specific community of men and women and children who have been baptized into Christ's death and regularly proclaim His death by their eucharistic meal. The unity being broken by the

brutish treatment of the poor at the church suppers was the unity
of the congregation in one place. Conflicting internal alliances
were breaking the body in one concrete instance. Paul's first concern about the unity of the body of Christ is the community at
Main and Maple in Crosstown, U.S.A.

One is reminded of the words that Jesus used in His prayer
for the unity of His body: "that the world may believe that thou
hast sent me." The unity of the body is part of the visible proclamation of the power of His resurrection. But where does the world
see the unity or disunity of Christ's new mankind? Does not the
world of real people see the unity of the body in the local community, at least first of all? Is it not at Main and Maple that the
world can recognize where individuals of various races, or different social backgrounds, professional identities, and worldly
accomplishments are forged into a single body of service and
worship in the powerful agapic love of Jesus Christ? And is it not
here, on the local level, that the claims of oneness in Christ are in
wildest disagreement with the actual situation? Is not the first and
primary tragedy of separation the fact of individualism and faction-
alism within the local church? And is it not here where the offense
to the world is most apparent and therefore most harmful?

If in one community—in Corinth or in Crosstown—there are
several bodies, with several tables in isolation from or even conflict with one another, we have in our sin achieved the horrible
impossibility. Christ *is* divided. And it is here that the most imperative and most difficult process of healing must be worked at
and prayed for.

The concern for unity cannot, of course, be limited to the
local community. The body of Christ does exist in a larger sense.
St. Paul speaks of the lordship of Christ over the whole church
which is His body (Eph. 1:22f.; Col. 1:18). Not that local communities are merely limbs of a larger body; the whole body is
present wherever the local community is in action as Christ's
servant. But the several local bodies, and the several regional
denominations, are together the reality of Christ on earth in the
ministry of reconciliation. Separated by miles, each recognizes
the other, is open to the other, serves the other, and prays for the
other.

In Paul's day it was assumed that each local body was a complete expression of the one body. The body in Antioch worshiped
and worked in its place. But it was meant to be open to the others,
to sacrifice for them, to pray for them, to suffer for them, and to

recognize them as *the* body of Christ. For there was one Spirit, one Lord, one faith, one baptism—one new reality in Christ.

If our study of Paul's doctrine of the Spirit and the body is at all accurate, the present situation of the body of Christ must be deplored and declared intolerable. It is least tolerable on the local level where competing, exclusive, embittered, and pretentiously separate communities all claim to be the body of Christ. But what is patently true locally is becoming increasingly true across the boundaries of continents. Where denominations exclude one another's ministries, compete with one another's missions, are closed to one another's sacraments, and publicly accuse one another of abandoning Christ, we have arrived at Paul's impossible possibility.

We cannot make this general observation without saying something about the ecumenical movement of our time. Surely the gigantic effort of today to discover ways to reunite the body can be observed only in gratitude. But the effort is confronted with roadblocks of serious proportion. Not the least of the roadblocks is the reluctance of denominations to break the comfortable pattern of separatism, or to confess that they really do need the communion of other Christians—even if these Christians have strange traditions and disagreeable associations in the past.

The reason for much of the resistance to ecumenicity is doctrinal. At its worst, it rises from an unjustified theological fastidiousness and pretension. At its best, it rises from a desire to keep the body faithful to the Lord Christ and His redemption. Confessional churches are very hesitant to enter alliances that threaten their belief in the person and work of Christ, in the reality of His Spirit, and in the historical character of His salvation.

On the other hand, reluctant churches must remember that the Lord did create one body by rising from the dead and sending His Spirit. That body exists—sometimes sick and always sinful —but it does exist. And it exists where the Spirit is at work leading men and women to call Jesus Lord. And where the body of Christ exists, it is of one and the same reality as the body anywhere under any name and with any creed.

Confessional exclusivists and ecumenical inclusivists may well ponder John Calvin's word to the Catholic, Sadoleto:

> The Lord grant, Sadoleto, that you and all your party may at length perceive that the only true bond of ecclesiastical unity consists in this, that Christ the Lord, who has reconciled us to

God the Father, gather us out of our present dispersion into the
fellowship of his body, that so, through His one Word and Spirit,
we may join together with one heart and one soul.[11]

Perhaps confessionalists need to share more of the intense desire of Calvin's remark, the Christocentric heart of it, and the
hope of it. And perhaps the ecumenicists need to share the certainty that it is, after all, the Lord who must do the work and
that He does it by the *Word* and the Spirit.

D. THE BREAD AND THE BODY

In talking to a group of newly baptized people who are ready
to join the community in the holy supper of the crucified Lord,
St. Augustine says this:

'The body of Christ,' you are told, and you answer 'Amen.' Be
members then of the body of Christ that your Amen may be
true. Why is this mystery accomplished with bread? We shall
say nothing of our own about it, rather let us hear the Apostle,
who speaking of this sacrament says: 'We who being many are
one body, one bread.' Understand and rejoice. Unity, devotion,
charity. One bread: and what is this one bread? One body, made
up of many. Consider that the bread is not made of one grain
alone, but of many. . . . Now for the Chalice, my brethren,
remember how wine is made. Many grapes hang on the bunch,
but the liquid which runs out of them mingles together in unity.
So had the Lord willed that we should belong to him and he
has consecrated on his altar the mystery of our peace and
unity.[12]

The mystery of Christ's body is, as Augustine says, "accomplished with bread." Here is St. Paul's statement: "The bread
which we break, is it not a participation in the body of Christ?
Because there is one bread, we who are many are one body, for
we all partake of the one bread" (I Cor. 10:16f.). At the very
least, we see that union with Christ through the sacrament is not an
individual piety, but a communal reality. Taken in community,

[11]Calvin, *Theological Treatises,* Library of Christian Classics, XXII,
J. K. S. Reid, ed. (Philadelphia, 1954), p. 256.
[12]*Sermons* 272 and 234. *Patrologium Latina,* xxxviii, 1247 and 1116.
This citation is found in H. de Lubac, *Catholicism* (London, 1939), p. 40.

the bread is the wonderful occasion for communal participation in the very body of Jesus Christ. And communal participation in Him, in turn, binds the many who join the meal into a single body of their own. The experience of the bread does not summon individual minds to commune with their private thoughts of a passion just for them. We are not invited by the sacrament to a trembling imagination within insulated souls. We eat together; and as we eat the bread we are recreated anew in the *corporate* reality that Christ created by His death. We are, Paul says, one body because there is one bread which we all eat.

Before pressing a few questions about the meaning of these strange, exciting, obscure words, these words in which the whole of mankind's needs are answered and the whole of God's promises are concentrated, let us stand still for a moment only to admire them. The bread! Here in a simple staple of everyman's diet is the hope that man's tragedy will be overcome, his divisions healed, and the final peace and unity of mankind realized. The bread! It is Christ's magnificent gesture of confidence in His power to restore man to God and his fellows. A piece of bread, held in an ordinary sinner's hand and put in a forgiven man's mouth, holds the promise for the healing of mankind. Near the end of his own grand vision of the new creation, Augustine speaks of man's tragedy of brokenness and God's mercy of repair. He says, near the close of *The City of God*:

> Adam himself lies now scattered on the whole surface of the earth. Formerly concentrated in one place, he has fallen; having been broken to pieces, as it were, he has filled the universe with his debris. However, God's mercy has gathered together from everywhere his fragments and by fusing them in the fire of his charity, has reconstituted their broken unity.

Paul tells us that the brokenness is restored by bread—the bread which is Christ's body.

But now we must ask questions. We shall content ourselves with three: (1) What is the body in which we participate? (2) What is the body we become through participation in the first body? (3) How does eating the bread enable us to become Christ's body? The third question is implicit in the first two.

What is the body in which we participate? Enough has been said in this chapter to give away the direction we will be carried now. But we must let Paul himself take us. The best place to begin is the context in which Paul's statement is made. As the chapter

opens, Paul is again telling the story of Israel. First he says that
Israel was baptized into Moses—and we may recall our discussion
of this in Chapter Four. Then he recalls how Israel ate and drank
spiritual meat and spiritual water together. (The R.S.V. has "supernatural" drink and meat, but the difference is of no import to
us.) This is the first thing we may light on.

St. Paul is rehearsing a key moment in redemptive history. The
fathers "passed through the sea." This is the ground work; it is
the event of historical redemption that started Israel on its trek
through history as the servant of Jehovah. Having been created a
people to do God's work on earth for the nations, they began their
journey to the *eschaton,* the occupation of the new earth in Canaan. And on their journey they ate and drank food and water
from God. The nourishment was supernaturally provided to keep
them alive and together during the time between the exodus (redemption) and the arrival in Canaan (the new earth). The food
and drink were, for Paul's purposes, sacraments of redemption
for the covenant community.

This is why the Rock from which Moses drew water is called
Jesus Christ. Paul knew that from the beginning the means and
end of the covenant enterprise were the Christ. Paul even makes
an obscure remark about the Rock following them through the
wilderness (10:4), an allusion perhaps to the Jewish tradition that
the Rock actually accompanied the Israelites on their journey.
The point to be made here is this: eating and drinking in the
wilderness provided an experience between the two *events,* the
event of creation (exodus) and the event of fulfillment (occupation
of the land). By eating and drinking, the Israelite was kept within
the reality of the community whose origin and meaning centered
on the mighty act of God at the borders of the Red Sea.

But alternatively, the Israelite could by eating and drinking at
a pagan sacrificial rite fail to live within the meaning and origin of
God's community. "Do not," says Paul to the Corinthians, "be
idolaters as some of them were; as it is written, 'The people sat
down to eat and drink and rose up to dance' "(10:7). Eating a
sacrificial meal involves one in the implications of the sacrifice.
"Are not they which eat of the sacrifices partakers of the altar?"
Paul asks (10:18). So, as eating and drinking from the Rock implicated the Israelite in the redemptive event of the Exodus, eating and drinking at the pagan sacrificial meal implicated him in the
event of the pagan sacrifice.

Now we must zero in on our question once more: what body

do we share when we share the bread? It is the body of Christ, of
course. But in what sense is the bread equivalent to His body?
Obviously the bread (as Christ's body) is distinct from the
Church (which is also Christ's body); we become part of the
Church as a result of eating the bread.[13] If not the Church, then
is it the actual physical body of Jesus—in the ordinary, discrete,
personal sense? Some interpreters think so, among them readers
of Paul[14] who are highly skilled. But after all that we have tried to
say earlier about the meaning of body in Paul, we need not go
into a lengthy discussion of this possibility. What we can do in
order to discover how the bread is the body is to let Paul speak
to us. Does he give us any hints?

The recital of Israel's history which opens the chapter is a good
hint. Eating and drinking of the supernatural "bread" in the wilderness was a commitment to partnership in the history that God initiated for the new community at the Red Sea. The notions of event
and history are crucial here. Furthermore, in the words imme-
diately surrounding the statement about the bread being equivalent to Christ's body (I Cor. 10:16f.), he points us again to
event and history.

We should recall that much of Paul's style here is liturgical;
some of his expressions are probably lifted from early liturgy.
And liturgies betray where the center of interest lies. For instance,
we note the following:

(a) He says, in his recital of the institution of the supper:
"This is my body which is *for you*" (11:24). The style is tele-
scopic, a cryptic abbreviation to anyone not initiated into the lit-
urgy. The "for you" refers to the death, the sacrificial death of the
Savior. He is saying, in less cryptic style: "This is the sacrifice that
I offered for you."

(b) He refers to the "night in which He was betrayed." Paul,
naturally, is not interested in dating an event. He is interested in
relating the meal to the event of history for the sins of the world.

(c) Speaking of the blood of Christ, which we also share, he
refers to it as "the cup" which is "the new testament in my blood."

---

[13]The distinction made here is not at all this sharp in some interpretations of this passage, as we shall see.

[14]For example, J. A. T. Robinson, *op. cit.*, p. 67; E. Percy, *Der Leib
Christi* (Leipzig, 1942), p. 44; Thornton, *The Common Life in the Body
of Christ* (Westminster, 1944), p. 343; and many others. Ridderbos calls
this a "monstrous error" and a "gross misreading of Paul" (*Paulus* [Kam-
pen, 1966], p. 417).

Here the words shade away from the suggestion of drinking real blood to the notion of participation in the new covenant partnership effected through the shedding of blood.[15] The interest again is in history, the new stage of redemptive history (11:25).

(d) He mentions the *anamnesis* twice, the dimension of recollection, and with this comes the notion of proclaiming the *Lord's death* until He comes again.

Taken together, these items provide a straw in the wind. They hint that the bread should wing our thoughts to a dark Friday afternoon and a bright Sunday morning when a new history began and a new community was born.

Keeping in mind the parallel with Old Testament redemptive history, recalling the various side references to the death of Christ in the words of institution, we may also now bring into play all that we have already said about the meaning of the word "body" in Paul's letters. The body that Paul is interested in is not the physical body of the man Jesus, except in the sense that all Jesus did in and to history occurred as a result of what He did bodily. What is recalled and proclaimed, both in Word and sacrament, includes the *significance* of what Jesus did bodily. Jesus is always Jesus in His *significance* for the community.[16] Without this, the community would not have bothered to recall His death or felt compelled to proclaim it. And the significance of what He did lies in the creation and growth of a new community within history which is the seedbed of a whole new historical order—indeed, of a whole new creation. Thus when Paul said "The bread which we break, is it not a participation in the body of Christ?" he meant to ask—rhetorically, since his readers had the answer—do we not in eating the bread have a part in the new history that Jesus Christ inaugurated at Calvary? "Body" is a liturgically telescoped refer-

---

[15]"The unusually complicated form found in Paul is probably due to his intention to avoid the misapprehension that real blood was consumed at the Eucharist" (J. Jeremias, *The Eucharistic Words of Jesus* [Oxford, 1955], p. 112).

[16]We should also notice Paul's word to those who were ready to defect from Christ's community by eating a sacrificial meal of pagan origin. Paul does not say that they took part in pagan sacrifices. Their mistake comes in eating the food from pagan sacrificial altars. In short, the meal was not a sacrifice, but it *was* a sacrificial meal. And eating it implicated the diners in the *significance* of the sacrifice: it made them partners to demons—just as the Israelites were implicated in partnership with demons when "they sat down to eat and drink and rose up to dance."

ence to all that Jesus accomplished in history and for history, all that had begun to take effect in Christ's community.[17]

Thus we have answered the first question. We can answer the second with dispatch. In fact, all that we have already said in this chapter answers it for us. The question, again, is this: what is the body Christians become as a result of their participation in Christ's "other" body? The answer is that they become what they already are—the community in which Christ Jesus is Lord, in and over which the Spirit dominates the way and style of life, the community which is the bud of God's new creation to come. It becomes what it is—the visible community in which the ministry of the redemptive work of Christ continues in history; it is the community by means of which Jesus Christ faces outward in sacrificial service as He did while on earth. It is, in this sense, identified with Jesus Christ: it is the ongoing, outward facing community engaged in the work of Jesus Christ as His partner. It is His body therefore. But it is the body of which He remains the head, the head in all the distinct authority and power and preeminence which the word suggests.

We come now to our third question: How does eating bread enable us to become Christ's body? We cannot really answer this. All we can do is repeat with Paul that we become the body of Christ *because* there is one bread which we all eat. We have seen enough to know that the bread contains no divine substance that is digested by the participants. We have seen nothing that convinces us that it involves a sacrifice offered for sin. But Paul does say enough to make us sure that something does happen in the sacramental meal. We *become* the body because we participate in the body. Without the participation, as far as we can tell, there is no body. The bread keeps the community of the new creation alive just as the manna and the water kept the Israelite community alive in the time between its times.

How does all this happen? How does the eucharistic event serve the community this creatively and profoundly? We must remember that Paul is using the concentrated language of the liturgy; he

[17]We have talked only about the bread; but everything is the same in reference to the blood of Christ. "The interest of the New Testament is not in the material blood of Christ, but in His shed blood as the life violently taken from him. Like the cross, the blood of Christ is simply another and even more graphic phrase for the death of Christ in its soteriological significance" (J. Behm, in Kittel, *Theological Dictionary of the New Testament*, I, p. 174).

does not develop a theory, but simply lets the intense, vivid, crystallized language of the liturgy do its own work. Bread does not stand for bread. Eating is not merely eating. Eating the bread stands for the entire eucharistic action. And the eucharistic action is two things, both specifically mentioned in the words of institution. It is recollection and proclamation. In the single event of the supper, the community both recalls and proclaims the death of its head. It sweeps the past into the present by means of recalling the past in its significance for the present. And as the community publicly and visibly *recalls* the saving event of the past—not merely as an event, but as an event with enormous meaning for the community then and there—it simultaneously *proclaims* the event in its full meaning.

To isolate the bread and to ask how eating a piece of bread recreates the body of Christ is to miss the dynamics of the sacramental event. Concentrating on the bread itself, in isolation, the Church in the past was frequently caught in truly fantastic controversies. It was this neglect of the total sacramental action that created the vocabulary of transubstantiation, consubstantiation, and all the other theological doctrines created to assure the real and effective presence of Christ in the sacramental bread. In fact, the bread is neither a mere symbol nor is it a container. It is the center of a community celebration in which the great event of all time is recalled into the present by the recollection of its significance. This is why the bread has got to be married to the words. Words do not merely validate the sacrament in a legal sense. Words and act together do the recalling and the proclaiming; and in this way the community is *doing* what the Lord told it to do until He comes again.

The total act is the event which recreates the community as the body of Christ. To say that the sacramental action is a recollection and a proclamation is not at all to minimize the effective power of the sacrament. For it is the recollection and the proclamation that recreates the body anew each time it is done. Christ is present in the action; His Spirit is at work in the community at that high moment, calling it back to itself and giving it the vitality to be what He calls it to be. And what He calls and enables it to be is Jesus Christ in action, visible action, during the time between the beginning and the end, the start and the fulfillment of the new creation.[18]

[18]Jeremias comments on the phrase "until He come," and shows that this futuristic expression is an "obvious allusion to the *maranatha* of the

This is the time of hope and faith. We are not able to see the new creation; it is still hid in the power of Christ. But at the sacramental moment, the past of Christ and the future of Christ converge on His body and make it the new creation on the basis of the past and in the promise of the future. This is the time of agony, the time when "creation groans" while it awaits its full redemption. But the moment when the past of Christ is recalled and the future of Christ is promised, this moment assures us that the new creation is real. How the sacrament, in certain Protestant circles, became a time of dreary introspection and dreadful self-accusation is a fascinating historical question. But the biblical sacrament is a delightful celebration of great joy and effervescent expectation.

The sacrament of the bread, then, is not meant to urge individuals to reflect in solitude on the dying Jesus. It is meant to create and recreate the community in union with Christ. And union with Christ at the sacrament is not a matter of individuals, here and there, now and then, enjoying or enduring pious sentiments about the tragic sufferings of Jesus. The sacrament of bread is for the *community*; and the community is summoned by it not to feel, but to *be*, not to mourn, but to *rejoice*. The action of the sacrament puts us in touch anew with the effects, the magnificent and exciting effects, of His *victory*. The sacrament is a means to make the body afresh what it already is—the body of Jesus Christ, and is therefore the assurance in the world of His ongoing ministry of reconciliation. We can truly say that the continued existence of Christ's body, and therefore of His future, is assured as long as the community gathers to celebrate His death in and with the bread of the sacrament.[19]

---

liturgy," in which the congregation prays for the Lord to come. "This means," he says, "that the Eucharist is an *anamnesis* of the Lord, not because it reminds the church of the event of the passion, but because it proclaims the beginning of the time of salvation and prays for the inception of the consummation" (*The Eucharistic Words of Jesus* [Oxford, 1955], p. 164).

[19]"Only in the eating of the body [properly understood] and in the drinking of the blood [properly understood] . . . is the community one. In this sense, the supper is the foundation and criterion of the unity of the Church as the new people of God" (H. Ridderbos, *Paulus*, p. 473). Stig Hanson says much the same thing: "On the basis of the Lord's Supper, where believers partake of the Body of Christ . . . Paul can argue for the unity of the Church and point out the ontological absurdity of the actual conditions with their divisions" (*The Unity of the Church* [Uppsala, 1946; reprinted in Lexington, 1963], p. 91).

Just as Christ's body is the body as long as it is active in the ministry of the Lord's ongoing historical action, just as the body is the avant-garde of the new creation, so it is utterly dependent always on the work of Christ at His supper. The life of the body is created ever anew and the ministry of the body insinuated ever anew into the world around it as it is called ever anew to the table where the bread is served. When the body gathers around the table to hear the event of redemption proclaimed and to receive its effects, it is kept alive by the bread it eats there. The enduring existence of the body, the vitality and vigor of the agapic life of the community, the outward facing service of Christ to the world depends on the family gathering at the eucharistic table. Is it more than Pauline to say that when the body stops eating, it dies?

A Theological Postscript to the Body and the Bread

In our day, we have arrived, I think, at a moment in theology when the subject of the sacrament can be discussed more fruitfully than at any other time since the Reformation. There are very high hurdles to overcome; we are still drawing caricatures of one another's position. But we are perhaps better equipped today to face one another biblically and with patience than our fathers were. The Catholic is still bound to confess that a miracle of transubstantiation takes place in the bread and wine, that in some sense the sacrifice of Christ is repeated there, and that the sacrament works *ex opere operato*.[20] This is indeed a high hurdle. But Protestants must also recognize that Catholic theologians are sincerely trying to find better and more meaningful ways, more biblical ways, of expressing the significance of the sacrament than the vocabulary of the sixteenth and seventeenth centuries allows. And Catholics must recognize that statements such as Louis Bouyer makes (in an otherwise admirable discussion of the sacrament) present an inaccurate picture of the Reformation viewpoint. He writes: "Accordingly, the efficacy of the sacrament as that of the Word preached was only to create and sustain our faith in a purely psychological way."[21] There is really no reason to say that

[20]Catholic theologians today often prefer to speak of the sacraments working *ex opere operantis*. The present tense—instead of the past, *operato*—is meant to put more stress on the entire celebration, including the communicants' action, rather than letting it lie wholly on the action of the priest.

[21]L. Bouyer, "Word and Sacrament," in *Sacraments, Gestures of Christ* (New York, 1965), p. 152.

the Reformers had so weak a notion of the sacrament. Calvin says that he is willing to use any language at all "to express the true and substantial partaking of the body and blood of the Lord, which is shown to believers under the sacred symbols of the Supper—and so to express it that they may be understood not to receive it solely by imagination or understanding of mind, but to enjoy the thing itself as nourishment of eternal life."[22] This hardly suggests that the sacrament sustains "our faith in a purely psychological way."

Within the Catholic tradition there is one sacramental school we ought to consider here. I refer to the Anglo-Catholic community, a community whose theologians are neglected in European discussions with regrettable consistency. This is especially unfortunate, since Anglo-Catholics have devoted great attention to sacramental theology and in many instances speak a language of intimate affinity· with many newer Roman Catholic theologians. I should like here, then, to add a brief note on what Anglo-Catholics are saying about the body and the bread.

Frankly, the Protestant is bound to be mystified by the Anglo-Catholic's apparently literal identification of the Church as Christ's body with the person (the body) of Jesus. The Anglo-Catholic keeps telling us that Jesus, the bread, and the Church are really the same. The bread and the Church are extensions of the incarnation into history. They are an overflow of the glorified Lord into time. There is only *one* body, they say, and it *appears* in different modes—the body of Jesus of Nazareth, the body called bread, and the body which is the Church. All are the same body, though in distinct modalities; this is sacramental modalism. What are we to make of this view? And what motivates Anglo-Catholic theologians to speak this way?[23]

In the first place, the Anglo-Catholic vocabulary is no stronger than Paul's. After all, it was Paul who said, in so many words, that when we eat the bread we participate in Christ's body. And we must credit anyone at all for taking biblical words in their fullest seriousness. But, granting this, it appears that the heart of Anglo-Catholic theology is its view of the incarnation. In the incarnation

[22]*Institutes* iv.17.19.

[23]I refer here only to a few supporters of the view I have briefly summarized: J. A. T. Robinson, *op. cit.,* p. 57; E. L. Mascall, *Christ, the Christian, and the Church* (London, 1946), p. 111; L. S. Thornton, *op. cit.,* pp. 256, 336, 343; A. Farrer, *op. cit.,* p. 80. See also L. Smedes, *The Incarnation* (Kampen, 1953), pp. 90ff.

a new life stream entered humanity. It was embodied in the total
life of sacrificial offering that Jesus made as a man. That same
life stream is present in the Church, and here too it is embodied
in a total life of sacrificial offering—for the world and for the
Church itself. The incarnation, therefore, brought to human kind
the divine life—which is sacrificial at its living heart—in order to
elevate man to his true destiny, which is to make of his own life
on earth an all-embracing offer to God. And it is in the loaf of
bread that the sacrificial life stream is given and the act of sacrifice
itself is sacramentally fulfilled to perfection. "By partaking of the
One Loaf they become what the eucharistic bread signifies, namely
the first fruits of earth offered in heaven, the true oblation of man
dedicated to the Creator of heaven and earth."[24]

The sacrament is a sacrifice, then. But it is the sacrifice of the
Church; the community offers itself in a special, sacramental way.
And this is a *perfect* expression of the life of sacrifice that it offers
imperfectly on earth outside of the sacrament. This means, however, that the sacrament is indeed also the sacrifice of Christ
Himself. Christ is not sacrificed by means of a transubstantiation
within the bread. Nor is Christ sacrificed in a repetition of the
crucifixion. Rather Christ is sacrificed when the Church sacrifices
itself; for the Church sacrifices itself through the share it has of
Christ's own life.

Here, as in our own discussion of the body and the bread, we
see an effort to avoid concentration on the bread itself as a
vehicle or package of the divine life. The "bread" is liturgical
shorthand for the entire eucharistic action.[25] The action at the
altar is a concentrate of the sacrificial life to which man is raised
by the incarnation. And as the community acts, it also *receives*
the divine life. Christ "pours divine life" into His body as "wine
is poured into a cup." The body of Jesus, in glory, which is the
divine-human life in outward expression, overflows its life into its
earthly manifestation.[26] In this way, the incarnation continues
through history.

There is a point of contact between Anglo- and Roman Catholic
theologians at this point. Almost every Anglican treatise on the
sacrament these days refers to such Roman theologians as Vonier,

[24]L. S. Thornton, *op. cit.*, p. 336.
[25]*Ibid.*, p. 328.
[26]*Ibid.*, p. 310. Farrer, *op. cit.*, p. 80. See also J. G. Davies who talks of
the Church as "a vessel into which the fulness of the risen Lord is poured"
(*The Spirit, The Church, and The Sacraments* [London, 1954], p. 62).

Masure, de la Taille, Mersch, and Rahner.[27] There is, thus, a certain Anglo-Roman community of thought on the sacrament that coincides with a community of thought on the significance of Jesus Christ Himself.

The word "sacrament" tends to be the inclusive term. Jesus Christ is the *Ursakrament* (Rahner's term). The Church, then, is the ever widening arc of the sacrament of Christ.[28] The eucharist is the middle sacrament, which connects the Church with Christ and concentrates the sacrificial life of the Church in a single, symbolic act. The difference between the Roman Catholic and the Anglican at this point is one of emphasis. The Catholic gives greater emphasis to the unique sacrifice of the cross. The Anglican tends to see the cross as a necessary *example* of the sacrificial life in general. Yet they share the broad sacramentalist platform: as a result of the incarnation, there is a plenitude of divine-human life for everyone who enters the sacramental community. One Catholic has concluded: "To say that we are offered, as Evangelicals are prepared to say, and that Christ is offered, as Catholics insist, need involve no contradiction, since what is offered is both Christ and the Christian, who are united by virtue of the mystical union that exists between the head and the members of the church."[29] It need involve no contradiction, but it does involve real tension as long as we are not of one mind on the meaning and effect of Christ's one act of sacrifice at Calvary.

No one who identifies himself with the Reformed community would object to Catholic sacramentalism on the flimsy grounds that it puts too much stress on the sacrament. He would not complain that the sacramentalist thinks the sacrament too important, or too effective, or too closely associated with Christ. "Too much" is never a valid objection to any view of how the Spirit works. We

[27]See the following: A. Vonier, *A Key to the Doctrine of the Eucharist* (London, 1925), pp. 40ff.; E. Masure, *The Christian Sacrifice* (London, 1943); M. de la Taille, *The Mystery of Faith and Human Opinion Contrasted and Defined* (London, 1930), pp. 13ff.; E. Mersch, *Le Corps Mystique du Christ* (Louvain, 1934); and K. Rahner, *The Church and the Sacraments* (London, 1963). I mention these because they, among others, represent Catholic theologians who have broken away from classic Catholic concepts and speak of the sacrifice of Christ in the sacrament as taking place in the Church's sacrifice of itself.

[28]Dennis O'Callaghan, "Christ, Sacrament of God" in *Sacraments, the Gesture of Christ* (New York, 1965), p. 43.

[29]Francis Clark, *Eucharistic Sacrifice and the Reformation* (London, 1960), p. 518.

need only recall Calvin's own theology of the sacraments to see
how un-Calvinistic the argument of "too much" is. How much
closer can you associate the bread with Jesus Christ than to say
as Calvin does that Christ is the "matter and substance" of the
sacrament?[30] How much more effective can one insist the sacrament is than to say: "to deny the true communication of Jesus
Christ to be offered to us in the supper is to render His holy
sacrament fruitless and useless"?[31] How much more important can
the supper be than when it gives us Jesus Christ as the "source
and substance of all good," and presents us with "the fruit and
efficacy of His death"?[32] No, one cannot say "too much" about
the sacrament.

The question is always *how* and *in what sense?* Calvin wrestled
with the how and was never satisfied with his answer; it was always
something he said he could better experience than explain. And
so it is for all of us. He was sure that when we talked of receiving
Jesus Christ through the sacrament, we had to talk about the
crucified Jesus Christ.[33] He was adamant on this point, and rightly
so. It was by His death that Christ established the new covenant,
and it is in giving us His crucified body that He recreates us as
members of the new covenant order. We have already seen that
Calvin mistakenly believed the virtues and effects of Christ to be
somehow *located* as "benefits" within His human nature, and that
this kept him from expressing the full historical or eschatological
meaning of the cross. But the historical element could not be
wholly missing in Calvin's thought; his grasp of the covenant was
far to strong. Christ, he says, "in some measure renews, or rather
continues, the covenant which he once for all ratified with his
blood . . . whenever he proffers that sacred blood for us to taste."[34]
That is, by the sacrament our Lord keeps the new order of history
on the move. What Christ gives is not merely stronger faith; He
gives Himself, as an effect of faith and following on faith.[35] But

[30]Calvin, *Treatise on the Lord's Supper,* in *Theological Treatises,* ed.
J. K. S. Reid, p. 146.

[31]*Ibid.*

[32]*Ibid.*

[33]"For we do not eat Christ duly and unto salvation unless He is
crucified, when in living experience we grasp the efficacy of his death."
Institutes iv.17.4.

[34]*Ibid.* iv.17.1.

[35]*Ibid.* iv.17.5. The question of whether Calvin considers the gift of
the sacrament unique or whether the sacrament gives only what the
Word gives as well is not relevant to whether the sacrament actually does

it is the Holy Spirit, as the effective agent and emissary of the risen Lord, who does the work with the sacrament. And the Spirit really does do it. So, it is never a question of *whether* or of *how much,* but only of *how.*

Our objection to the sacramentalist doctrine centers on the main theme of this book. It is a christological matter. The Anglo-Catholic sees this perfectly well. Both the Church and the sacrament are christologically defined. "What think ye of the Christ?" says Hoskyns, is the same question as "What think ye of the Church?"[36] Thus, we would here only invite the reader to consider the biblical evidence for the centrality of the cross, the pivotal significance of the resurrection, and the historical character of God's redemptive enterprise as the key to Christology. Redemption, I should suggest, is not achieved by the deification of humanity but by the decisive turn of events within cosmic history. It was begun, this reconciliation of all things, when Jesus Christ our Lord led captivity captive and put to flight the powers who in their delusion supposed they could frustrate this grand design of the Creator. It shall end when all creation is alive again with the presence and power of God's Spirit and all reconciled humanity is at one with its Lord and with itself. To live now in the style of that new creation and by the power of the Lord of history is to be in union with Christ.

---

give a share in Christ's sacrificial benefits. Krusche is trying too hard to rescue Calvin from mysticism when he stresses the sameness of the effect of Word and sacrament (Krusche, *op. cit.,* p. 202).

[36]E. C. Hoskyns, "The Christ of the Synoptic Gospels," in *Essays Catholic and Critical,* ed. E. G. Selwyn (London, 1950), p. 153.

ADDITIONAL NOTE 1

Paul's apparent disinterest in the amazing facts of Jesus' life has been noted often. He never mentions the virgin birth; he never quotes the parables; he never recalls the miracles. He does not retell the Gospel stories. Paul does not draw a picture of Jesus. This disinterest in the details of Jesus' earthly life seems to fit in with what he says in one place: "Even though we once regarded Christ from a human point of view, we regard him thus no longer" (II Cor. 5:16). In saying this, Paul left himself open to judgments that he was no longer interested in the Christ who was a man living out a life as one Jew among Jews. Add to this the stubborn claim that Paul was called to make concerning his apostolic office, his claim that he received his gospel directly through revelation and not from men (Gal. 1:12), and one has the major evidence for Paul's dissociation from the earthly Jesus.

Paul surely declared himself free of obligation to any man for his office as an apostle. But this is not the same as saying that, as an apostle, he was free from the Jesus preached by the other apostles. In his troubles with the Jewish church, he was criticized for branching out into unwarranted *implications* of the gospel by insisting on the inclusion of Gentiles within the church without circumcision. He had his well-known dispute with Peter. But in all the disputes that Paul had with other Christians who were closer than he to Jesus, Paul's portrayal of Jesus was never questioned. This is the more remarkable in the light of the intense interest that the early Church had in an accurate and complete portrayal of the words and works of the Savior.

The more we study the letters of Paul, the more we realize that he takes it for granted at all times that he and other Apostolic leaders are in essential accord in their faith in Jesus and their thought concerning him. As to the law, he may argue. But he gives no hint nor does any other New Testament writer, of a breach between himself and his fellow Apostles in essential Christology.[1]

[1]F. V. Filson, *The New Testament Against Its Environment* (London, 1950), pp. 38f.

In fact, there is considerable evidence to show rather explicitly that Paul's Christ was none other than the Jesus of history. Luke recalls how, shortly after his conversion, Paul was locked in debate with Jewish contemporaries of Jesus; *this* Jesus, argued Paul, was the Son of God (Acts 9:22). And, while he disclaimed interest in a judgment about Jesus made according to the standards of the flesh, he demonstrates over and over again that his Lord was the Savior who was born and lived in the flesh.

Emil Brunner makes a useful distinction between "after the flesh" and "in the flesh." He says that no one can come to faith in Christ and the forgiving love of God by essaying to measure Jesus "after the flesh." That is, no one can come to faith by means of strictly historical judgments about the accuracy of the story of Jesus. But, on the other hand, no one can believe in the Christian gospel without accepting the fact that Christ was "in the flesh" (*The Mediator*, p. 160). This is somewhat parallel to John's conviction that no spirit is of God who does not "confess that Jesus Christ has come in the flesh" (I John 4:2). On the other hand, it is John who, somewhat like Paul, is not required *for his purpose* to say a great deal about Jesus "after the flesh"; that is, John more obviously than the other evangelists speaks from the viewpoint of faith in the divine lordship of Jesus.

The Christ who saves us is He who was born of the seed of David, according to the flesh (Rom. 1:3). He was born "in the likeness of sinful flesh" (Rom. 8:3) and His true self was "revealed in the flesh" (I Tim. 3:16). It was "in the flesh" that He did away with the "law of commandments and ordinances, that he might create in himself one new man" (Eph. 2:15). He reunited those who were estranged, and did so "in his body of flesh" (Col. 1:22). We may safely say that if Paul did not appraise Jesus by fleshly standards, the Jesus he believed in by spiritual standards was the Jesus who lived and died in history.

The Christ Paul preached was the Christ whose birth and life fulfilled Jewish expectations of a Messiah. He was born of a woman under the law (Gal. 4:4) when the time was ripe. He was the seed of Abraham, the single offspring in whom all the promises are realized (Gal. 3:16). It was this Jesus, the Jew obligated to live under the law, whose death redeemed men from the law's ancient curse. And no other point of Jesus' ministry so absolutely defines Him as a specific, earthly individual than the event of His death.

The living Christ whom Paul preached as Lord of "all things" was *also* the Jesus who lived on earth. Paul knew that it took faith to believe in the resurrection; he knew that the resurrection involved more than the resuscitation of Jesus' corpse. But he was also sure that whatever happened when Jesus arose, happened to Jesus in such a way that the transformation restored *Jesus of Nazareth* alive. Faith in the resurrection involves at least this, that God raised the same Jesus "who was put to death for our trespass" (Rom. 4:25).

Finally, Paul never tolerated a suggestion that his gospel of Jesus Christ was at odds with anything in the oral tradition prized and guarded by the early believers. He made a point of asserting his dependence on the tradition. In his discussion of the eucharist, including a rather detailed account of the paschal meal that Jesus shared with His disciples before His death, he pointedly notes his reliance on the earliest traditions. The word used is a technical term that indicates a handing down of information to others for their safekeeping. "For I received from the Lord what I also delivered to you. . ." (I Cor. 11:23). He uses the same language in I Corinthians 15 when he sums up the high points of his message:

> For I delivered to you as of first importance what I also received, that Christ died for our sins in accordance with the Scriptures, that he was buried, that he was raised on the third day in accordance with the Scriptures (I Cor. 15:3, 4).

Whenever the tradition carries a direct word from Jesus, Paul affirms it. Whenever he adds to it, he insists that he too has the Spirit, and so also speaks as from the Lord. He never competes with tradition. At most, he supplements it.[2]

Paul's gospel was not born in a kerygmatic no man's land. He was not an innovator. Though his message may have gone further and deeper than others, it was tied to the historical events of the life and death of Jesus of Nazareth. If the implications of those events are as broad as the cosmos, Paul leads us to believe that they are only implications of the person and acts of an individual Jew who appeared on the world's stage at a time we can pinpoint on a calendar and at a place we can visit even today. He seems to be saying: whatever else you may hear me say about a new creation and about mysterious experiences of union with Him, "Remember Jesus Christ, risen from the dead, descended from David, as preached in my gospel" (II Tim. 2:8).

[2] See C. H. Dodd, *History and the Gospel* (London, 1938), p. 57.

ADDITIONAL NOTE 2

Sacramental Christologies are as old as theology, and I do not
mean to suggest that recent Anglo- and Roman Catholic theologians
invented it. Almost all of the Eastern Fathers worked within a sacramentalist framework. While they did not all develop this framework
in the same way, most of the leading teachers within the old Eastern
Church related it to God's method of redemption. I am not sure how
seriously we should take their doctrines of deification through the incarnation. I would suggest—although I am unable to substantiate this
—that the notion of deification grew out of a need to be relevant to
the age. That is, the doctrine of deification was an effort by theology
to show God's answer to the question that was paramount in Eastern
culture: how can I overcome the limits of my mortality and the tears
and frustrations that attend it? The answer was this: God has come
in Jesus Christ to give men eternal life. Who is immortal but God?
Therefore, to be saved, to *have* eternal life—to become immortal—is
to have a share in what belongs by nature to God.

Athanasius set the tone for Sacramental Christology by a sentence
that became almost a battle slogan in his heroic struggle for trinitarian
orthodoxy in the fourth century. "God became man in order to make
men gods." Over and over again, this sentence (with variations)
pointed to the necessity of the full divinity of Jesus Christ.[1] Of course,
Athanasius does not declare that men are deified by means of the
cross, nor does he say that the cross was really superfluous. There are
two levels in Athanasius' theology of redemption. Something happened
at the cross, to be sure. Atonement was made. But the issue of first
magnitude was whether man could be rescued from the mortality and
corruptibility that he sank into when he lapsed into mere nature as a
result of the first sin. And this issue was settled by the incarnation.
"None other could make a mortal being immortal, but He who is
life itself, our Lord Jesus Christ." The Word became flesh to make
a perfect sacrifice for sin. But first, that we "participating in His

---

[1]See, for example, *Ad Adelphos* 4; *De incarnatione* 54, and *Contra
Arianos* i.38. In *Orationes contra Arianos* the sentence appears repeatedly.

Spirit, might be deified."[2] This was Athanasius' practical argument for the necessity of the full divinity of our Lord Jesus Christ.

But Athanasius did not initiate Sacramental Christology. Irenaeus before him taught that the manhood of Jesus Christ recapitulated the whole of the human race since Adam. Recapitulation, summing up, including the whole in one living digest—this is the key to how redemption was accomplished. Irenaeus was the teacher of a very dramatic theory of the atonement. No one before him or after him spoke with greater vigor about the victorious event of Jesus' encounter with Satan. It is Irenaeus who is the source of the *Christus Victor* theme in the theologies of atonement that have tried to capture in a single motif the mystery of Christ's effective sacrifice for sin. One could even show, I think, that Irenaeus was the original *Heilsgeschichte* theologian. But the other side of Irenaeus reveals a Sacramental Christology of the first order. When God took humanity into Himself at the incarnation, He took not only a single instance of human nature, but all of manhood completely. The human race as a numerical whole was recapitulated in the manhood of Christ. No wonder that Irenaeus is claimed alike by such "event" theologians as Gustav Aulén and by those who hold to a Sacramental Christology.[3]

He who was the head of the whole creation because He was the creative Word spoken at the beginning and echoed all through time, became the head of the human race in a new way. "The Word of God is the Creator of the world," Irenaeus writes. "It is He, our Lord, who in these last days is made man, showing His presence in the world, He who by reason of His invisible reality contains all that has been done and is implanted in all creation, as Word of God, disposing and governing all things. And He has come visibly into His own, and He has been made flesh, and He has been hanged on the tree, so as to sum up all things in Himself."[4] Again, "He recapitulated in Himself the long series of mankind, and achieved salvation for us epitomized in His flesh."[5]

The Son of God sweeps all of the human race into His own humanity. Through His Spirit He extends the same elevating reality to the humanity to come. Thus He is the Head of all by taking all men, even all creation, into Himself. The manhood of Christ, as Daniélou points out, is the focal point on which all converges. With it, Jesus was a baby for babies, a boy for boys, a man for men, thus including all ages of men within Himself. From this inclusive humanity, there comes an order of life that supersedes any that has gone

---

[2]*De Decretis* 14.
[3]See G. Aulén, *Christus Victor* (London, 1951), pp. 32ff.; Mascall, *Christ, the Christian and the Church* (London, 1946), pp. 132, 167, 222ff.
[4]*Adversus haeresis* v.18.2.
[5]*Ibid.* iii.18.1.

before. Christ, having "recapitulated in Himself the long sequence of mankind," began a new race of deified men. There is no chance of reading a pure doctrine of sacramental redemption into Irenaeus; his teaching about the eventful history of Jesus Christ the victor is too clear for that. But the tendency to make the incarnation—the taking of humanity into the Word—the central fact of redemption is also very clear.

We can easily discover a sacramental core in the complex of ideas that form the seminal theology of Origen. Origen believed that the Son of God truly became incarnate. He saw the Incarnate not so much as He who rescued sinners by means of His flesh, but as He who led men out of the flesh into the Spirit by giving them a share in His own immortal manhood. True, we partake, according to Origen, not so much of Christ's manhood as of His divinity; but we share His divinity as it is channeled through His manhood. And partaking of His divinity incarnate, we ourselves are deified. "Everyone who participates in anything, is unquestionably of one essence and nature with him who is partaker of the same thing."[6] And so, as Jesus and His apostles taught, "that the human, by communion with the divine, might rise to be divine, not in Jesus alone, but in all those who not only believe, but enter upon the life which Jesus taught, and which elevates to friendship with God and communion with Him everyone who lives according to the precepts of Jesus."[7] Union with Jesus is achieved through faith and discipleship. But the point that is being made here is that for Origen the Word became flesh in order to share the divinity that was His with His own human nature and with the humanity of all others. The true end of man, a notch higher than temporal mortality, is achieved because the divine and human were united in Christ. With Origen, the result of deification is participation, not so much in immortality, but in the goodness of God. But the motif is still the same: salvation through experience of God's Being in our own being.

A touch of irony exists in the fact that orthodox Christology was so often defended to preserve a soteriology that is repugnant to those who today accept the Christology.

[6]*De principiis* iv.1.36.
[7]*Contra Celsus* iii.38.

ADDITIONAL NOTE 3

Spirit Christologies are very old, and seem to be a less complicated way of thinking about incarnation than the trinitarian. A passage in the Shepherd of Hermas (about 160 A.D.) puts it this way: "The holy, pre-existent Spirit, that created every creature, God made to dwell in flesh, which He chose. This flesh, accordingly, in which the Holy Spirit dwelt, was nobly subject to that Spirit, walking religiously and chastely, in no respect defiling the Spirit. . ." (*Similitude* V, Chapter 6). Such ideas of the incarnation of the Spirit lasted beyond the second century, but never took firm hold in the Church's mind. Echoes of it are still heard in Tertullian. "We declare however," he writes, "that the Son also, considered in Himself (as the Son) is invisible, in that He is God, and the Word and Spirit of God" (*Against Praxeas,* Chapter 14). But Tertullian is merely being reluctant to make a clear, ontological distinction between Word and Spirit. He recalls the angel's announcement to Mary that the "Spirit of God shall come upon thee" (Luke 1:35), and says that Luke implies that the Spirit Himself would be incarnate in her. "For both the Spirit is the substance of the Word, and the Word is the operation of the Spirit, and the Two are One (and the same)" (*ibid.,* Chapter 26). Obviously, Tertullian would not have been mystified at all by Paul's statement, "The Lord is the Spirit."

Father Kelly, in his study of early Christian theology, offers evidence that Spirit Christology persisted into the fourth century. He adds, by the way, that "it is also highly probable that the ancient clause of the Old Roman Creed, 'who was born from Holy Spirit and the Virgin Mary,' reflects the same idea that Jesus Christ, the historic Son of God, was the product of the union of divine spirit with human nature in the womb of the Blessed Virgin" (J. N. D. Kelly, *Early Christian Doctrines,* London, 1958, p. 144).

It is easy to see how Spirit Christology could have influenced the notion of our union with Christ. If one is united with Christ *through* the Spirit, he is united by the same Divine Spirit as was incarnate in Jesus. It is also easy to recognize the difference between the older Spirit Christology and those later ones that tended to evaporate the

ascended humanity of Jesus into pure Spirit. There is no hint that
the Spirit Christology of the Fathers led them into this idea. Spirit
Christology declined as the doctrine of the Trinity sharpened; as the
Logos was thought of as fully God, He replaced the Spirit as being
that of God which was in Christ, personally. Not everyone thinks
this decline is an unmixed good. Hendrikus Berkhof, in his fine book
on the Spirit, regrets it. "We must ask," he says, "whether a radical
return to a pneumatic christology would not do more justice to the
biblical message" (H. Berkhof, *The Doctrine of the Holy Spirit*,
Richmond, 1964, p. 21). Berkhof's motives are practical; he is concerned to develop a more biblical theology of regeneration. As we
have tried to put it, however, what is needed is a more Christocentric
pneumatology. I am not at all sure whether Dr. Berkhof would care
to quibble about the difference.

ADDITIONAL NOTE 4

Though it is not decisive to our concern, it may be of interest to explore the context somewhat further. Two things are involved: (a) freedom in the Spirit and (b) the glories of the two covenants. In the new covenant, there is *freedom* (II Cor. 3:17). Freedom exists where the Spirit works. The people who live in and under the rule of the Spirit live free from the judgmental and condemnatory code of the law. In the new covenant, we live in an atmosphere of righteousness (3:9). Paul is not saying that the people of the new covenant are righteous people ("Not that we are sufficient of ourselves to claim any thing as coming from us"—Paul means himself, but it is applicable to all): he is referring to the kind of administration the new covenant has. The new covenant introduces everyone to a new discovery of the essential nature of God's righteousness—a righteousness that is demonstrated in the justification of the *un*godly (see Rom. 3:21-24). This, too, recalls Jeremiah and his vision of the new order as one in which all men would know the Lord on the basis not of moral achievement but of forgiveness; in this time, says the Lord, "I will forgive their iniquity, and I will remember their sin no more" (Jer. 31:34). And this is freedom.

As to the "glories" of the two covenants (II Cor. 3:12-16), Paul does concede that the old covenant came with a certain splendor. But he grants a splendor to it only to show by contrast how very great the splendor of the new covenant is. That is, if the old was invested with a measure of splendor, we must assume—in view of the contrast between the Spirit and His life-giving power and the law and its death-dealing weakness—that the new is incomparably more resplendent.

The reason for the greater splendor of the new covenant is its disclosure of the essential righteousness of God, which grants life and freedom in the Spirit (3:9). Moreover, the old covenant's splendor was an evanescent thing; it soon passed (3:11). The splendor passed because the old covenant itself "faded away." But the Jews were not able to see the temporary character of God's

260

revelation at Sinai. Moses, says Paul, put a veil over his face to prevent them from seeing the splendor pass away (3:13).

I realize that I am accepting this interpretation against very good authority. The word *telos,* or "end," could possibly mean the summit or zenith of the glory that attended the giving of the law. If it meant that here, in verse 13, Paul would be saying that Moses kept the veil over his face to hide from Israel's view the peak of divine glory. The majority of commentators argue that this is the way the verse should be read. Even the law, temporary as it was, had a radiant glory—and Moses hid its glory with his veil. But Exodus 34 gives no hint that this is why Moses covered his face. And it seems to me that Paul's argument in the entire third chapter of II Corinthians rests on the notion that the law had only a passing function and is now obsolete.[1]

His point is that the veil still keeps Israel from recognizing the true meaning of Moses. The whereabouts of the veil shift; first it is over Moses' face (3:13), but then it is over the eyes of the Israelites (15), preventing them from seeing the real meaning of Moses. The "real meaning" could be the *passing nature* of the Mosaic covenant. If so, the veil would keep Israel from seeing that the old covenant was a temporary dispensation. Being veiled from the truth, Israel absolutizes what is passing, and turns what was meant to be a temporary expedient into God's ultimate and unchanging way of dealing with mankind. The "real meaning" is sometimes thought to be the hidden christological content of the law; this too would be kept from Israel by the same veil of unbelief. In either case, only as they turn to the Lord will the veil be removed and they be able to see the true glory of God (3:16).

[1]For H. Ridderbos's argument to the contrary, see *Paulus,* pp. 239-240. For an excellent summary of this argument and a complete list of authorities, I recommend Andrew Bandstra's detailed and lucid study of this whole matter in *The Law and the Elements of the World* (Kampen, 1964), pp. 79ff. But also see F. Neugebauer, *In Christus,* p. 80, and Oepke, in Kittel, *Theological Dictionary of the New Testament,* III, pp. 560ff., for an interpretation more favorable to the one I have suggested here.

ADDITIONAL NOTE 5

Just as we wondered whether modern sacramentalists really do mean as much as they seem to mean with their talk of deification, we may also wonder about the Eastern Fathers. To many of the Fathers, man's great need was immortality. But immortality is a peculiar trait of God. So if man is gifted with immortal life, he must share the life of God. Here too the Fathers used deification as an instrument of explanation; the only way they could account for man's immortality was by way of saying that man had been given something of God's own life, since God "alone hath immortality." According to Athanasius, man lost immortality when he forfeited the image of God. Mortality involved man in temporality, and temporality involved him in corruption and decay. Who could restore him to immortality, and so escape from corruption? "None other could make a mortal being immortal, but He who is life itself, our Lord Jesus Christ" (*De incarnatione* 11-16). This is why the Word became flesh. He came to offer a ransom to discharge the debt we incurred by guilt, but also "that we, participating in His Spirit might be deified" (*De Decretis* 14). To Clement, being deified meant being lifted above passion and appetite into true knowledge, and to be so lifted is to be brought into immortality. But to be immortal is to be divine. So, he writes, the Word "became man so that . . . [man] might learn from man how man may become God" (*Exhortation to the Heathen* 1). But what does it mean to "become God"? Answer: "To be imperishable is to share in Divinity" (*Stromata* v.10). Origen talked a great deal about coming out of darkness into the light of truth. God is the light and the truth, and He came down in the form of Jesus to display His truth. Taken up again into the presence of the Father, He makes it possible that all "might rise to be divine" who "enter upon the life which Jesus taught, and which elevates to friendship with God and communion with Him everyone who lives according to the precepts of Jesus" (*Contra Celsus* iii.38). Deification is for the Fathers so mixed up with knowledge, truth, light, immortality, and right teaching, that one is entitled to wonder whether they really meant to elevate Christian man so highly or whether they were only diagnosing his ills in terms relevant to the

262

problems of *their* time. D. Inge, it seems to me, comes close to the point I am trying to make. "If," he writes, "we try to analyze the concept of *Theos,* thus loosely and widely used, we find that the prominent idea was that exemption from the doom of death was the prerogative of a Divine Being, and that therefore the gift of immortality is itself a deification" (*Christian Mysticism* [London, 1899], p. 357).

ADDITIONAL NOTE 6

J. Weiss notes the Stoic penchant for thinking of the universe as a body, and cites some interesting references to demonstrate a similarity to Paul's vocabulary. For instance, Seneca: "All that you see, that which comprises both god and man, is one; we are parts of one great body" (*Epistles* 95:53). Then there is an interesting theory about the head being the source of the body's life: "It is from the head that comes the health of the body; it is through it that all the parts are lively and alert or languid and drooping as their animating spirit has life or withers" (Seneca, *De Clementatis,* ii, 2, 1). Weiss guesses that Paul is speculating about the Church with mystical notions purloined from the Stoics. But since Stoic pantheism was not native to Paul, he did not retain these speculations. Still, the idea that the Spirit formed believers into a living organism was a temptation for Paul, and forms a basically alien but influential thought within his otherwise unmystical message (see J. Weiss, *Earliest Christianity,* II [New York, 1937], pp. 621ff.). Another German scholar who more or less follows this line is Traugott Schmidt, in *Der Leib Christi* (Leipzig, 1919), though he thinks Paul is following the Greek notion of *society* as an *organism* patterned after a physical body. Ernst Käsemann concludes that Paul borrowed from quite a different source (*Leib und Leib Christi,* Tübingen, 1933). He is sure that the source of Paul's doctrine was the oriental myth of the heavenly redeemer who came to earth to defeat his enemy powers and open the way for man's freedom from them. This cosmic power, called *aeon* in the myths, is in Paul's thought Jesus Christ. The body of Christ is the new situation which people enter through certain ғites, a situation made possible when the evil aeons, or heavenly powers, were defeated (see especially pp. 65-94). Rudolf Bultmann rather agrees with Käsemann's theory (*Theology of the New Testament,* I [New York, 1951], pp. 310f.).

Each of these men has come to a conclusion as to the background of Paul's language, and this conclusion has led them in a certain direction for the meaning of that language. Weiss assumes that the body of Christ concept is defined by the imminent presence of the Spirit in the Church, a picture suggested by Stoic mysticism and pantheism. Käsemann assumes that the body of Christ concept is part of Paul's message about Christ's victory over the "principalities and powers," along with the inception of a new age. In any event, the background that each claims to have discovered for Paul's thought is of a piece with the interpretation that each gives to Paul.

I should also mention the study by Ernst Percy, *Der Leib Christi* (Lund, 1942). Percy is led by his examination of the Hebraic background of Paul's thought to say that the Stoic and the Gnostic world furnished no key to our understanding of Paul. The background is Hebraic, especially the Hebrew apocalyptic expectations. Albert Schweitzer takes the same view. To Schweitzer, looking for the key to Paul in Hellenism is overlooking the obvious in favor of the remote. What is utterly obvious is the influence of the Hebrew Old Testament and later Judaistic writings (*The Mysticism of Paul the Apostle* [New York, 1955], esp. pp. 101-140). Most recent expositors of Paul's concept of the body of Christ follow, with greater or lesser consistency, in the line of Albert Schweitzer and Percy (for example, E. Schweizer, *The Church as Body of Christ* [London, 1965] and P. P. Shedd, *Man in Community* [New York, 1958]).

Robinson suspects that Paul used "the language that lay to hand and does not seem to have been over-particular about where it came from" (*The Body, A Study in Pauline Theology*, p. 55). W. D. Davies adds this observation: ". . . it is wholly artificial to make too sharp a dichotomy between the Hebraic and the Hellenistic elements in Paul's thought . . . and any Hellenistic elements which may be found in his thought do not imply that he was therefore outside the main current of first-century Judaism" (*Paul and the Rabbinic Judaism* [London, 1948], p. 320).

I would add to this only that there is also a defense for simply letting Paul's thought speak to us on its own. Comparative studies have, no doubt, provided many interesting parallels and have, by way of showing contrasts or similarities, shed considerable light on Paul's vocabulary. Perhaps we can assume that Paul provides us with a context that is in itself clear enough to tell us where his images fit in. I should at least like to work on the following assumption: It is Paul's gospel of Jesus Christ, not the pagan world around him, that is the best guide to the purpose of his imagery.

Index of Subjects

Adam and Christ 60ff., 112ff., 115ff.

Aeon 35f., 264f.

Anglo-Catholicism 247ff.

Baptism:
  and faith 140, 149ff.
  and self-understanding 149ff.
  as infusion of divine life 139ff.
  into Christ's death 138ff.
  into the new order 147ff.

Body of Christ:
  as analogy of Christ 218
  as Christ-in-action 230
  as extension of the incarnation
    247f.
  as locus of the Spirit 224ff.
  location of 232ff.
  relation to Eucharist 238ff.
  source of the phrase 227ff., 264f.
  unity of 235ff.
  visibility of 232ff.

Christ:
  and Adam 60ff., 112ff., 115ff.
  and the historical Jesus 7f., 105
  as head of the body 219
  as Lord 34ff., 57f., 70, 226ff.
  benefits of 25f.
  identical with the Church 231
  obedience of 23ff.
  relation to the Spirit 43ff.

Christ-in-us:
  and faith 165f., 175, 198ff.
  and deification 170f.
  and self-identity 168, 187ff.,
    213ff.
  and the historical Jesus 158f.,
    168, 186
  as ontological reality 162f.
  as rule by the Spirit 173ff.
  as vocation 166ff.
  location of 183
  relation to Christ-for-us 184

Christology:
  Christus Victor 32f.
  Personal Transaction Christology
    23ff.
  Sacramental Christology 17ff.,
    255ff.
  Situational Christology 30ff.
  Spirit Christology 47f., 258f.

Covenant 54ff., 71ff., 120ff., 143ff.,
  260f.

Cult: Hellenistic and Christian
  45f., 141f.

Death with Christ 131, 134ff.,
  138ff., 151

Deification 18ff., 89, 139f., 160ff.,
  229, 255ff., 262f.

Ecumenical movement 235ff.

Election
  in Christ 117ff.
  of Christ 120ff.
  of Israel 120ff.

Eschatology 35ff., 40ff., 65ff.

Eucharist 238ff.

Faith:
  affirmation of facts 192ff.
  and baptism 140, 149ff.
  and mysticism 166, 179
  and self-understanding 187ff.,
    213ff.
  as hope 205ff.
  as knowledge 208ff.
  as love 210ff.
  as obedience 202ff.
  as union with Christ 175, 198ff.

Index of Authors

Index of Scripture References